FOREVERMORE
Nuclear Waste in America

Also by Donald L. Barlett and James B. Steele

*EMPIRE: The Life, Legend, and Madness of
Howard Hughes* (1979)

FOREVERMORE
Nuclear Waste in America

Donald L. Barlett and James B. Steele

W·W·Norton & Company

NEW YORK   LONDON

Published simultaneously in Canada by Stoddart, a subsidiary of General
Publishing Co. Ltd, Don Mills, Ontario.
Printed in the United States of America.

The text of this book is composed in Times Roman, with display type set
in Jana. Composition and manufacturing by The Haddon Craftsmen, Inc.
Book design by Jacques Chazaud

First Edition

Library of Congress Cataloging in Publication Data

Barlett, Donald L.
Forevermore, nuclear waste in America.

Includes index.
1. Radioactive pollution—United States.   2. Radioactive waste disposal—
Environmental aspects—United States.   I. Steele, James B.   II. Title.
TD196.R3B37   1985   363.7′28   84–22761

ISBN 0-393-01920-9

W. W. Norton & Company, Inc.
500 Fifth Avenue, New York, N. Y. 10110
W. W. Norton & Company Ltd.
37 Great Russell Street, London WC1B 3NU

1 2 3 4 5 6 7 8 9 0

For Allison and Matthew,

in hopes their generation
deals with the problem
more ably than ours

Contents

Preface

This book is an outgrowth of a series of articles that appeared in the *Philadelphia Inquirer* in November 1983. For eighteen months, we traveled some 20,000 miles, interviewing dozens of people and assembling more than 125,000 pages of documents. These included local, state, and federal government reports, state and federal court records, corporate files, congressional-hearing transcripts, scientific studies, and internal memoranda of public agencies and private businesses. The resulting newspaper series provoked a much broader reaction than we had anticipated. In response to requests for copies of the articles, more than 25,000 reprints were sent to individuals and organizations in more than forty states and several foreign countries.

Many of those who wrote urged us to expand the newspaper series into a book. In doing so, we updated the material and added new information, including sections on military waste, foreign reprocessing, and uranium mill tailings. We were tempted to delve into other areas, such as the design and construction of reactors and the economics of nuclear power. But we focused instead on waste—the amount produced, past efforts to manage it, the politics of its disposal, the state of current technology, and the outlook for the future. As it turned out, that was quite enough.

Our task was complicated not only by the complexity of the subject but also by the sharp division of opinion among the experts on such critical matters as how waste should be isolated and the amount of radiation the public should be permitted to receive. In addition, the subject is wrapped in strong feelings aroused by all things nuclear. Like abortion, gun control, and capital punishment, radioactive waste is an issue on which views are often solidly fixed. There are those who claim zealously that radiation is routinely causing cancer and genetic abnormalities. And there are those who claim with equal fervor that radiation is harmless, perhaps even healthful. Sorting out the extremists, as well as the vested interests in science, politics, industry, and the government bureaucracy, and the varied schools of thought in each on how to deal with waste, is an arduous process.

To complicate matters further, although statistics on nuclear waste abound, all are suspect. We go into this in some detail in the book. But a look at used fuel assemblies from nuclear reactors—which account for most of the nation's nuclear waste in terms of radioactivity—illustrates the problem. In December 1982, according to Nuclear Regulatory Commission records, 3,512 used fuel assemblies were stored at the Dresden, Illinois, nuclear generating station operated by the Commonwealth Edison Company of Chicago. Two months later, in February 1983, only 1,873 assemblies were at Dresden, by the NRC's count. Somewhere, somehow, 1,639 intensely radioactive fuel assemblies had disappeared. Not to worry. By March 1983, NRC records reported the number of assemblies had climbed back up to 2,880, still 632 short of the figure for the preceding December, but a marked improvement over the February total. But by May, the NRC records showed, the number of assemblies at Dresden had dropped off to 2,054.

This supply of seemingly elastic radioactive fuel assemblies, which expand and contract at a statistician's will, is a figment of the government's imagination. When the conflicting figures, issued in a series of monthly NRC reports, were called to the commission's attention, a spokesman said the NRC had no explanation. A representative of Commonwealth Edison was a bit more incredulous when the numbers were pointed out to him. "That's the most ridiculous thing I ever heard of," he said. "If you add everything together, [the number of used assemblies is] going to be constantly going up."

Not only must the number of used assemblies increase, but each has its own serial number so that utilities and the government can, at least in theory, maintain an accurate accounting of the most deadly waste ever accumulated. That the NRC's record-keeping system is out of balance is only one measure of the chaos that marks America's efforts to control radioactive waste. It also offers some perspective on the statistics on the pages that follow.

Because the federal government issues precise numbers on nuclear energy and waste production, we have used those figures. But they should be viewed, in every case, as nothing more than approximations. The story of the Dresden fuel assemblies attests to the need for caution—for that story is repeated not only at other nuclear plants but also in other phases of waste operations.

Acknowledgments

Many debts are incurred in the writing of a book. The following is not intended as an all-inclusive list, but merely an indication of the extent of our obligations and an expression of our gratitude to all who assisted.

We would first of all like to thank all of those we interviewed, who gave unselfishly of their time in helping us to unravel the complexities of this subject.

We would also like to express our appreciation to employees of local, state, and federal agencies and of state and federal courts in Washington and throughout the country who patiently assisted in the difficult task of locating records and documents.

As always, we are indebted to librarians at public, private, and university libraries across the country, including the National Archives and Records Service in Washington; state libraries in Illinois, Kansas, Kentucky, Louisiana, New York, South Carolina, and Washington; the staff of the government-publications room of the Free Library of Philadelphia; the University of Pennsylvania Libraries; the Samuel Paley Library of Temple University; and the Jenkins Memorial Law Library of the Philadelphia Bar Association.

Newspaper libraries proved invaluable at every stage, including those of the *Advocate and State Times,* Baton Rouge, Louisiana; *Barnwell* (South Carolina) *People-Sentinel; Bureau County* (Illinois) *Republican; Cooper* (Texas) *Review; Dallas Morning News; Hutchinson* (Kansas) *News; Kansas City Star and Times; Louisville Courier-Journal and Times; Lyons* (Kansas) *News; Prosser* (Washington) *Record-Bulletin; Salamanca* (New York) *Republican; Seattle Times;* the *State,* Columbia, South Carolina; and *Tri-City* (Washington) *Herald.* We owe a special thanks to the library staff of the *Philadelphia Inquirer* —M. J. Crowley, Gail McLaughlin, Jennifer Ewing, Joe Gradel, Frank Gradel, Mary Taffe, Gene Loielo, Ron Taylor, Frank Donahue, Teresa Banik, and Denise Boal.

We would also like to express our deepest appreciation to Ed Barber, our editor at W. W. Norton, for both his counsel and his confidence in us; to Hilary Hinzmann of Norton, for the energy and dedication he brought to the project; to Elizabeth Coady and Courtney Smith, whose diligent efforts as research assistants at the *Philadelphia Inquirer* helped fill in crucial areas of the subject; and to other *Inquirer* colleagues: Larry Williams, business editor; Susan Stranahan, a member of the editorial board; Johnstone Quinan, deputy design editor; Mike Jenner, former news editor, and Steve Lovelady, associate executive editor, for their valued assistance and judgement; and Gary Haynes, associate managing editor for graphics, and Nick Kelsh, photographer, for their superb photographic contributions. Finally, a special word of thanks to Gene Roberts, the executive editor of the *Philadelphia Inquirer,* who originally suggested nuclear waste as a subject to explore and then gave us the time to pursue it.

Calendar of Coming Nuclear-Waste Events

January 1985   The Department of Energy recommends three sites to the president as candidates for the nation's first high-level-nuclear-waste repository.

March 1985   The president acts on the Department of Energy recommendations.

April 1985   Excavation starts on exploratory shaft at the first of the three recommended sites.

June 1985   The Department of Energy proposes to Congress three to five locations for a monitored retrievable storage facility.

September 1985   The Department of Energy identifies possible sites for a second high-level-waste repository.

January 1986   All states must have low-level-radioactive-waste burial grounds or have joined a regional compact with such a facility. States that have failed to do this will be without a way to inter their low-level waste.

March 1987	The president submits to Congress a recommendation for the site of the first high-level-waste repository.
May 1988	The Department of Energy authorizes construction of a test and evaluation facility for high-level waste, if such a facility is deemed necessary.
January 1989	The Nuclear Regulatory Commission must approve or reject the federal government's application to construct the first repository.
July 1989	The Department of Energy recommends three additional sites as candidates for the second high-level repository.
March 1990	The president submits to Congress a recommendation for the site of the nation's second repository.
May 1990	Underground tests in the test and evaluation facility begin, if such a facility is built.
January 1992	The Nuclear Regulatory Commission must approve or reject the federal government's application to build the second repository.
January 1998	The Department of Energy plans to open the first underground repository for high-level waste.
January 1998	The Department of Energy takes title to all used fuel rods produced by electric utilities, whether or not a repository is in operation.
October 2004	The Department of Energy plans to open the second underground repository.

Sources: Nuclear Waste Policy Act of 1982 and the *Mission Plan for the Civilian Waste Management Program,* vol. 1 (Washington, D.C.: Department of Energy, April 1984).

FOREVERMORE
Nuclear Waste in America

Prologue

The Legacy

The turtles that creep along the banks of the Savannah River, near Aiken, South Carolina, are radioactive. So is the water in a well that serves the borough of Lodi, New Jersey. So, too, a drainage ditch that runs along a street in an industrial park in southeast Houston. The turtles, the water, and the soil were once free of radioactivity. They are now contaminated because of the ignorant and careless handling of radioactive materials. More important, they are a symptom of the inability of government and industry to control nuclear waste, a catchall phrase for scores of the most deadly and long-lived toxic substances ever manufactured.

The evidence of that failure, spanning more than forty years, can be found in hundreds of places where radioactive waste has been stored or dumped. It is in two tanker trucks buried in rural Barnwell, South Carolina; inside an inflatable nylon dome at Idaho Falls, Idaho; and in simmering liquids in an underground steel tank in a farm valley south of Buffalo, New York. It is found in calm pools of water in communities from Wiscasset, Maine, to Humboldt Bay, California; piled up in warehouses from Brooklyn, New York, to Newport Beach,

California; and dotted about an industrial park in Canonsburg, Pennsylvania. It is stacked up in a 165-foot-tall concrete silo in Lewiston, New York; sitting in barrels in Laurel, Maryland, and Bethel Park, Pennsylvania; mixed through the rubble of a razed factory building in West Chicago, Illinois; and loaded in trucks that crisscross the nation's highways.

No one knows how much there is. No one knows all the places where it is. And no one—despite all claims to the contrary—knows what to do with it. Not the government that encourages its production, not the industries that churn it out, not the scientists who created the processes that breed it. That is why radioactive waste in 1985 is held in "temporary" facilities, just as it was in 1945, just as it will be in 2005. Science, government, and industry have yet to devise the safe and permanent storage system they have promised for thirty years, one guaranteed to seal off the waste from people and the environment for as long as it will remain hazardous—forevermore.

You cannot see the radiation, or smell it, or taste it. But it is spreading across the American landscape. In 1950, waste from commercial use of the atom was counted in ounces. Today, it is counted in tons. Of far greater significance than weight is the curie content. The curie is used to measure radioactivity.* In 1950, the curie level of this garbage was counted

---

*A curie is the amount of a substance it takes to produce thirty-seven billion atomic disintegrations per second. There exist scores of radioactive substances, each with its own characteristics. Some pose a hazard for only a few hours, others for days. Some are dangerous for hundreds of years, others for thousands of years. Some are hazardous if exposure is external; others are more deadly if inhaled or swallowed. The effects of two materials illustrate the variations. A person who happened to stand next to one ounce of cobalt 60 immediately after it was produced would receive a lethal dose of radiation in less than one minute. Ten years later, that same ounce of cobalt would deliver a fatal radiation dose in about three minutes. By way of contrast, a person who happened to stand next to one ounce of yttrium 91 immediately after it was produced would receive a lethal radiation dose in less than one hour. But ten years later, a person could carry around that ounce of yttrium forever, and die of old age rather than from any radiation-induced disease. One curie, in some cases a minute fraction of one curie, may cause genetic abnormalities, cancer, or death, depending upon the length and circumstance of the exposure.

in the hundreds. Today, it is counted in the billions. At the end of 1984, waste kept in interim collection centers stood at 14.7 billion curies—enough to kill everyone in the United States.

The worst is yet to come. During the 1980s, businesses and institutions, but mostly electric utilities, will turn out twice as much waste—measured in terms of radioactivity—as they did in the three preceding decades combined. In December 1983, seventy-four reactors in twenty-five states generated a record 26.4 billion kilowatt hours of electricity, and with it a record 600 million curies of waste. That exceeded all the radioactivity in waste from the building of nuclear weapons during the first twenty-five years of the atomic age.

What's more, the curies will continue to accumulate even if not a single new nuclear power plant is proposed. Barring an unforeseen wholesale shutdown, waste will flow without interruption from the eighty-two reactors licensed to operate as of January 1984, and from the two dozen or so nearing completion and still expected to go on-line. By the year 2000, it is projected, waste stockpiles will top 42 billion curies—enough to kill everyone on the face of the earth.

It was not supposed to end this way. At the birth of the commercial nuclear industry, in the 1950s, government, business, and science all vowed that a solution to the waste problem would be found. In a time of euphoria over the wonders of the atom and the promise of clean, cheap, and abundant nuclear power, there were few words of caution. And yet, when the final chapter is written on the great waste debacle, it may go down as the largest scientific and political blunder of the twentieth century. It will be decades before the toll can be tabulated, but a preliminary accounting suggests this much:

Nuclear waste will be stored for up to a century—if not forever—in some two hundred cities and towns throughout the country. Chunks of real estate will be rendered permanently uninhabitable in some states and placed off limits for much of the twenty-first century in others. Tens of billions of dollars will be spent to correct mistakes of the past and present, a massive financial burden that future generations will have to bear. Even worse, if these mistakes are repeated in the years to come, it is reasonable to assume that an as yet unknown number of men, women, and children will suffer from birth defects, genetic abnormalities, cancer, or other diseases, as some already have.

Perhaps all this will change. Perhaps physicists, geologists, and other scientists and engineers will resolve their differences, and government's regulators, administrators, and lawmakers will do the same, and all will unite in a concentrated campaign to develop and implement a safe and permanent waste-management process. But it is also possible, perhaps likely, this will not happen, at least not in the near future. Two bizarre proposals that were advanced in the 1950s suggest why it will not.

One called for waste to be planted in Antarctica, the other for it to be shot into outer space. Both were rejected as unsound, and for good reason. In the case of snow burial, the waste's intense heat could melt the polar ice cap and raise ocean levels. In the case of extraterrestrial burial, an accident during launch could contaminate vast areas of the United States, or if successfully sent aloft, the waste could rain back down on the earth. Nonetheless, both propositions have been revived in the 1980s, an indication of the lack of progress as well as the endurance of the out-of-sight, out-of-mind philosophy of waste management.

Given all this, the occasional warnings sounded over the last quarter-century by a minority of scientists and politicians may well prove correct. Back in January 1959, a time when nearly everyone championed the wonders of the atom and nearly everyone also disregarded its unwanted by-products, Abel Wolman, an expert in the young field, hinted at the gloomy possibility. Commenting on the absence of a technology to isolate nuclear waste, Wolman, an engineering professor at the Johns Hopkins University and a consultant to the AEC, told a subcommittee of Congress's Joint Committee on Atomic Energy, "I am not sure that there is a final solution."

Seventeen years later, in June 1976, after an extended investigation of waste practices, the House Committee on Government Operations echoed Wolman's frank assessment: "We may have to face the realization, even after determined and conscientious effort, that it just may not be possible to guarantee the containment of radioactive wastes over the ages until they are harmless to mankind and the environment. If this is the case, the implications of such a realization must then be considered in all their gravity."

1
Atomic Technology: Fantasy versus Reality

THE ULTIMATE ENERGY SOURCE

In the beginning, everyone, it seemed, was captivated by the atom, an extraordinary new energy source expected to provide an endless supply of clean power and to revolutionize life-styles. The atom, it was said, would even allow man to leave the earth and travel through space. To that end, in the late 1950s the Atomic Energy Commission began to test a nuclear rocket engine on a stretch of the Nevada desert called Jackass Flats. Government enthusiasts did not doubt the project's wisdom. Space, said one, "will be conquered only by manned nuclear-powered vehicles. Planning anything else is . . . flirting with obsolescence."

American astronauts eventually went to the moon six times. Unmanned spaceships landed on Mars twice. All the spacecraft were launched by conventional fuels. The atomic spaceship was a dismal flop. One test engine actually shook itself to pieces. There was always the nagging fear that such a vehicle's exhaust system would spew out radioactive residue as it circled the earth.

For years, about all that remained from the failed experiment was radioactive garbage scattered across Jackass Flats, including, according to a Department of Energy official, "little pieces of the fuel element [that] blew out the end of the rocket." Not until 1983 did federal cleanup crews pick up the trash. The atomic rocket to nowhere is only a memory, but the highly charged atmosphere that surrounded its development goes a long way toward explaining our nuclear-waste dilemma.

Throughout the 1950s and 1960s, experts in government, business, and science believed in an atomic solution to mankind's ills. More important, they believed they could inaugurate a commercial nuclear industry before the technology was perfected, before many questions had been answered. Not the least of these was what to do with the large volume of by-products that the industry would produce.

The public should know, said Rep. Chet Holifield, a Democratic congressman from California, in January 1959, that "this is a field where a permanent solution has not been found . . . that the problem of permanent disposal of high-level waste has not been solved."

Indeed not. It was as if the National Aeronautics and Space Administration had launched America's first orbiting spacecraft, *Friendship 7,* on February 20, 1962, with the understanding that the astronaut John H. Glenn, Jr., would continue to circle the earth until NASA had worked out the technology to bring him down. If the politicians and scientists in charge of nuclear waste had been running the space program, John Glenn would still be orbiting the earth today.

The cold war psychology that gripped America's leaders in the 1950s fueled this haste. Some were convinced that the United States, for public relations reasons, could not allow the Soviets to develop nuclear power first. Others felt that the nation had a moral obligation to devise peaceful applications of the atom to atone for the nuclear bombing of Japan. Still others were captivated by the atom's miraculous promise; they were positive it would become the ultimate energy source overnight.

Undersecretary of State Walter Bedell Smith trumpeted the obsession with communism when he told Congress's Joint Committee on Atomic Energy in June 1953, "It would be very damaging to the position of the United States if another country were to be first in this field of endeavor, and it would be especially damaging if the Soviet Union were to precede us in the development of atomic power. If this were to happen, the Soviet Union would cite their achievement as proof of their propaganda line that the United States is interested in atomic energy only for destructive purposes while the Soviet Union is interested in developing it for peaceful purposes."

During those same hearings, George W. Malone, Republican senator from Nevada, spoke for those with a mystic faith in the atom's magic: its commercial use could "change the course of history more than" the invention of the wheel. Members of Congress, federal officials, and scientists conjured up a fantasy world of commercial shipping fleets, locomotives, and automobiles powered by the atom, all before the year 2000. A dramatic increase in farm production would end world hunger for all time, thanks to the atom. And atomic excavation would level mountains, hollow out harbors, alter the flow of rivers, and perform other "feats of rearranging the contours of the earth."

Since much of the technical information relating to atomic energy was still classified because of military requirements, there was very little to cool fevered imaginations. But even those with access to the secrets engaged in making wild predictions. The AEC asserted that the atom would heat large office buildings, hotels, and apartment complexes; neighborhood reactors would heat individual homes. The nuclear life would be encouraged, it was said, by "the psychological desire of many Americans to elect to dwell in a community with new atomic heat." Lewis L. Strauss, AEC chairman from 1953 to 1958, declared that "our children will enjoy in their homes electrical energy too cheap to meter."

Newspapers, magazines, radio, and television all got caught up in the hysteria. "Our Atomic Program Is Expanding Rapidly: Plan for Atomic Airplane Is Only One of Numerous Signs Of Progress," declared a typical headline in the September 9, 1951, *New York Times*. The atomic airplane had great appeal, though the AEC made no secret that passengers in all probability would have to be exposed to some "acceptable" level of radiation.

Other forms of nuclear air travel also were envisioned. Gordon E. Dean, AEC chairman from 1950 to 1953, predicted that atomic-powered dirigibles would carry passengers about the country by the 1970s. "I can see no reason," Dean said, "why . . . such aircraft should not be available for commercial use." Special interests, from farmers to equipment manufacturers and electric utilities, were swept up in the atomic frenzy, along with other businesses and labor and religious organizations. Each group lobbied Congress and federal agencies, demanding that the atom be developed specifically to satisfy its needs.

There were some pessimists, voices crying in the wilderness. But their ranks were thin, their words of restraint routinely dismissed. Politicians who were reluctant to join the headlong rush to a nuclear economy were viewed as backward, if not unpatriotic. Business people who urged caution were warned that if they did not build nuclear power plants immediately, the government would build its own and compete with them. Scientists who suggested that still more work was needed in the laboratory were scorned. It was not that the dissenters failed to air their views in public. It was just that no one wanted to hear them, especially on the subject of some distant threat from radioactive waste.

Everyone listened when a waste specialist for the Dow Chemical Company told the Joint Committee on Atomic Energy in February 1957, "We feel it is important for all to know that this [waste] disposal problem has been taken care of by new technology recently demonstrated."

No one listened when a waste specialist for the AEC—one of the few dissenters in the commission—told the *Wall Street Journal* that same month, "We're merely sweeping the real problem under the rug."

Looking back on those days, Carroll L. Wilson, the AEC's first general manager, once explained the lack of interest this way: "It was not glamorous; there were no careers; it was messy; nobody got brownie points for caring about nuclear waste. The Atomic Energy Commission neglected the problem."

That no one took waste seriously was reflected in a popular idea of the time. Known as well injection, the scheme called for the toxic liquid to be poured into abandoned oil and gas wells or into new wells drilled expressly for that purpose. As unlikely as it may seem, this proposal gained wide currency in the 1950s. A study team from the American Petroleum Institute reported to Congress in February 1959 that "radioactive waste can be disposed of safely by injection, through deep wells, into porous rocks." This procedure would present some difficulties, the committee admitted, but it maintained, in a phrase soon to find its way into many future scientific reports, that "no insurmountable obstacles are indicated." The committee added that test drillings to a depth of 9,000 feet along the coast of North and South Carolina demonstrated that those two states would be ideally suited for waste dumping.

Although a few scientists clung stubbornly to this plan into the 1960s, it was abandoned in favor of solidification. Experience has shown that hundreds of millions of gallons of toxic waste pumped into underground nuclear sewers would have contaminated water supplies and land over a wide area.

Even those officials not especially enamored of well injection were unconcerned about the final resting place for radioactive waste. They placed their trust in science. After all, had not science split the atom, unleashing the most destructive force ever? Surely it could lock up the atom's waste.

Against this background in the 1950s, the federal government, persistently prodded by Congress, encouraged growth of the commercial nuclear establishment. Implicit in this growth was an understanding: pending discovery of a safe and permanent waste-management system, radioactive liquid that would remain deadly for thousands of years would be stored in tanks whose life span was uncertain, but probably limited to less than fifty years. In the event that the discovery was not made in fifty years, or before the first tank leaked, the liquid waste would be transferred to a new set of tanks. This ritual, a sort of radioactive musical chairs, was to continue—as it does today—until the permanent solution turned up.

Politicians and the public accepted on blind faith the scientific community's promise of a swift remedy. At a hearing of Congress's Joint Committee on Atomic Energy in February 1959, Herbert M. Parker, a General Electric Company official in charge of defense waste at the federal government's Hanford Reservation in Washington, expressed confidence that a technology would be developed to solidify the radioactive liquid. Declaring that the steel tanks would safely contain the waste for the next forty years, Parker told the committee, "That superior methods, such as binding of wastes in ceramics, or other more permanent forms of retention, will not be in place, and in place economically [in the next forty years] is inconceivable."

Nowadays government, industry, and science are as confident as they were in the 1950s that radioactive waste can be quarantined for more years than civilized society has existed. These experts no longer talk about finding a solution. They now insist the problem has been solved.

The National Academy of Sciences, a quasi-governmental organization of scientists and engineers that examines science-related issues for federal agencies, expressed this view in a January 1980 report. Its language was hauntingly similar to that used by the American Petroleum Institute to support well injection two decades earlier: "No insurmountable technical obstacles are foreseen to preclude safe disposal of nuclear wastes in geological formations. All necessary process steps for immobilizing high- and low-level wastes have been developed, and there are no technical barriers to their implementation."

In October 1981, Shelby T. Brewer, assistant secretary for nuclear energy in the U.S. Department of Energy, told a House Interior and Insular Affairs subcommittee, "Contrary to a sizable fraction of public belief, we already have the technology in hand or under development for safe disposal of nuclear waste."

In March 1983, the Philadelphia Electric Company, in a report to stockholders, quoted the president of the Atomic

Where High- and Low-Level Radioactive Waste Is Stored or Buried

	State	County	Nearest Town	Waste Type	Source*
1	Alabama	Limestone	Decatur	high	pp
2	Alabama	Limestone	Decatur	low	pp
3	Alabama	Houston	Columbia	high	pp
4	Alabama	Houston	Columbia	low	pp
5	Arizona	Navajo	Monument Valley	low	umt
6	Arizona	Conconino	Tuba City	low	umt
7	Arkansas	Pope	Russellville	low	pp
8	Arkansas	Pope	Russellville	high	pp
9	California	Stanislaus	Turlock	low	llb
10	California	Santa Clara	San Jose	low	llb
11	California	San Diego	Vista	low	llb
12	California	Orange	Orange	low	llb
13	California	Contra Costa	Richmond	low	llb
14	California	Alameda	Pleasanton	low	llb
15	California	Alameda	Pleasanton	low	llb
16	California	Sacramento	Clay Station	high	pp
17	California	Sacramento	Clay Station	low	pp
18	California	San Diego	San Clemente	high	pp
19	California	San Diego	San Clemente	low	pp
20	California	Humboldt	Humboldt Bay	high	pp
21	California	Humboldt	Humboldt Bay	low	pp
22	California	Alameda	Vallecitos	high	usg
23	California	Los Angeles	Canoga Park	high	usg
24	California	Alameda	Livermore	high	usg
25	California	Alameda	Livermore	low	usg
26	Colorado	Denver	Denver	low	llb
27	Colorado	Jefferson	Golden	high	usg
28	Colorado	Moffat	Maybell	low	umt
29	Colorado	San Miguel	Slick Rock	low	umt
30	Colorado	San Miguel	Slick Rock	low	umt
31	Colorado	Fremont	Canon City	low	umt
32	Colorado	Montrose	Uravan	low	umt
33	Colorado	Montrose	Naturita	low	umt
34	Colorado	Mesa	Grand Junction	low	umt

*Source Codes:
cbg	commercial burial ground
cp	properties once used by government agencies or contractors that remain contaminated
llb	low-level-waste broker
pp	commercial nuclear power plant
rp	reprocessing plant
umt	uranium mill tailings
usg	waste facility of U.S. government agencies or government contractors
tru	transuranic waste contaminated with plutonium

	State	County	Nearest Town	Waste Type	Source
35	Colorado	La Plata	Durango	low	umt
36	Colorado	Gunnison	Gunnison	low	umt
37	Colorado	Garfield	Rifle	low	umt
38	Colorado	Garfield	Rifle	low	umt
39	Connecticut	Hartford	Avon	low	llb
40	Connecticut	Fairfield	Ridgefield	low	llb
41	Connecticut	New London	Waterford	high	pp
42	Connecticut	New London	Waterford	low	pp
43	Connecticut	Middlesex	Haddam Neck	high	pp
44	Connecticut	Middlesex	Haddam Neck	low	pp
45	Florida	Hillsborough	Tampa	low	cp
46	Florida	Polk	Nichols	low	cp
47	Florida	Citrus	Red Level	high	pp
48	Florida	Citrus	Red Level	low	pp
49	Florida	St. Lucie	St. Lucie	high	pp
50	Florida	St. Lucie	St. Lucie	low	pp
51	Florida	Dade	Turkey Point	high	pp
52	Florida	Dade	Turkey Point	low	pp
53	Georgia	Appling	Baxley	high	pp
54	Georgia	Appling	Baxley	low	pp
55	Idaho	Bonneville	Idaho Falls	high	usg
56	Idaho	Boise	Lowman	low	umt
57	Idaho	Bonneville	Idaho Falls	high	usg
58	Idaho	Bonneville	Idaho Falls	low	usg
59	Illinois	Bureau	Sheffield	low	cbg
60	Illinois	Cook	Chicago	low	cp
61	Illinois	Cook	Chicago	low	cp
62	Illinois	Cook	Chicago	low	cp
63	Illinois	Cook	Tinley Park	low	llb
64	Illinois	Rock Island	Cordova	high	pp
65	Illinois	Rock Island	Cordova	low	pp
66	Illinois	Lake	Zion	high	pp
67	Illinois	Lake	Zion	low	pp
68	Illinois	Grundy	Morris	high	pp
69	Illinois	Grundy	Morris	low	pp
70	Illinois	Grundy	Morris	high	rp
71	Illinois	Cook	Argonne	high	usg
72	Iowa	Linn	Palo	high	pp
73	Iowa	Linn	Palo	low	pp
74	Kentucky	Rowan	Maxey Flats	low	cbg
75	Kentucky	Jefferson	Louisville	low	llb
76	Kentucky	McCracken	Paducah	low	usg
77	Louisiana	Jefferson	Kenner	low	llb
78	Louisiana	E. Baton Rouge	Baton Rouge	low	llb
79	Maine	Lincoln	Wiscasset	high	pp

	State	County	Nearest Town	Waste Type	Source
80	Maine	Lincoln	Wiscasset	low	pp
81	Maryland	Howard	Columbia	low	llb
82	Maryland	Prince Georges	Laurel	low	llb
83	Maryland	Calvert	Lusby	high	pp
84	Maryland	Calvert	Lusby	low	pp
85	Maryland	Montgomery	Bethesda	low	usg
86	Massachusetts	Middlesex	Natick	low	llb
87	Massachusetts	Plymouth	Plymouth	high	pp
88	Massachusetts	Plymouth	Plymouth	low	pp
89	Massachusetts	Franklin	Rowe	high	pp
90	Massachusetts	Franklin	Rowe	low	pp
91	Michigan	Van Buren	South Haven	high	pp
92	Michigan	Van Buren	South Haven	low	pp
93	Michigan	Charlevoix	Charlevoix	high	pp
94	Michigan	Charlevoix	Charlevoix	low	pp
95	Michigan	Berrien	Bridgman	high	pp
96	Michigan	Berrien	Bridgman	low	pp
97	Minnesota	Wright	Monticello	high	pp
98	Minnesota	Wright	Monticello	low	pp
99	Minnesota	Goodhue	Red Wing	high	pp
100	Minnesota	Goodhue	Red Wing	low	pp
101	Missouri	St. Charles	Weldon Springs	low	usg
102	Nebraska	Washington	Fort Calhoun	high	pp
103	Nebraska	Washington	Fort Calhoun	low	pp
104	Nebraska	Nemaha	Brownville	high	pp
105	Nebraska	Nemaha	Brownville	low	pp
106	Nevada	Nye	Beatty	low	cbg
107	Nevada	Nye	Beatty	high	usg
108	Nevada	Nye	Beatty	low	usg
109	New Jersey	Bergen	Westwood	low	llb
110	New Jersey	Salem	Salem	high	pp
111	New Jersey	Salem	Salem	low	pp
112	New Jersey	Ocean	Toms River	high	pp
113	New Jersey	Ocean	Toms River	low	pp
114	New Mexico	Los Alamos	Los Alamos	high	usg
115	New Mexico	Bernalillo	Albuquerque	high	usg
116	New Mexico	Bernalillo	Albuquerque	high	usg
117	New Mexico	McKinley	Ambrosia Lake	low	umt
118	New Mexico	Valencia	Grants	low	umt
119	New Mexico	Valencia	Grants	low	umt
120	New Mexico	Valencia	Grants	low	umt
121	New Mexico	McKinley	Church Rock	low	umt
122	New Mexico	San Juan	Shiprock	low	umt
123	New Mexico	Los Alamos	Los Alamos	low	usg
124	New Mexico	Bernalillo	Albuquerque	low	usg

	State	County	Nearest Town	Waste Type	Source
125	New York	Cattaraugus	West Valley	low	cbg
126	New York	Erie	Tonawanda	low	cp
127	New York	Erie	Tonawanda	low	cp
128	New York	Seneca	Romulus	low	cp
129	New York	Richmond	Port Richmond	low	cp
130	New York	Wayne	Rochester	low	cp
131	New York	Niagara	Lockport	low	cp
132	New York	Westchester	Peekskill	low	llb
133	New York	Kings	Brooklyn	low	llb
134	New York	Westchester	Buchanan	high	pp
135	New York	Westchester	Buchanan	low	pp
136	New York	Wayne	Ontario	high	pp
137	New York	Wayne	Ontario	low	pp
138	New York	Oswego	Scriba	high	pp
139	New York	Oswego	Scriba	low	pp
140	New York	Oswego	Scriba	high	pp
141	New York	Oswego	Scriba	low	pp
142	New York	Cattaraugus	West Valley	high	rp
143	New York	Niagara	Lewiston	low	usg
144	New York	Suffolk	Upton	high	usg
145	North Carolina	Mecklenburg	Cornelius	low	pp
146	North Carolina	Brunswick	Brunswick	high	pp
147	North Carolina	Brunswick	Brunswick	low	pp
148	North Carolina	Mecklenburg	Cornelius	high	pp
149	North Dakota	Stark	Belfield	low	umt
150	North Dakota	Bowman	Bowman	low	umt
151	Ohio	Cuyahoga	Cleveland	low	cp
152	Ohio	Ottawa	Oak Harbor	high	pp
153	Ohio	Ottawa	Oak Harbor	low	pp
154	Ohio	Montgomery	Miamisburg	high	usg
155	Ohio	Franklin	Columbus	high	usg
156	Ohio	Hamilton	Fernald	low	usg
157	Ohio	Pike	Piketon	low	usg
158	Oklahoma	Logan	Crescent	high	usg
159	Oregon	Columbia	Rainier	high	pp
160	Oregon	Columbia	Rainier	low	pp
161	Oregon	Lake	Lakeview	low	umt
162	Pennsylvania	Washington	Canonsburg	low	cp
163	Pennsylvania	Beaver	Aliquippa	low	cp
164	Pennsylvania	Indiana	Indiana	low	cp
165	Pennsylvania	Allegheny	Burrell Township	low	llb
166	Pennsylvania	York	Delta	high	pp
167	Pennsylvania	York	Delta	low	pp
168	Pennsylvania	Dauphin	Middletown	high	pp
169	Pennsylvania	Dauphin	Middletown	low	pp

	State	County	Nearest Town	Waste Type	Source
170	Pennsylvania	Beaver	Shippingport	high	pp
171	Pennsylvania	Beaver	Shippingport	low	pp
172	Pennsylvania	Allegheny	West Mifflin	high	usg
173	Pennsylvania	Armstrong	Apollo	high	usg
174	Pennsylvania	Allegheny	Cheswick	high	usg
175	Pennsylvania	Luzerne	Berwick	high	pp
176	Pennsylvania	Luzerne	Berwick	low	pp
177	South Carolina	Barnwell	Barnwell	low	cbg
178	South Carolina	Richland	Columbia	low	llb
179	South Carolina	Darlington	Hartsville	high	pp
180	South Carolina	Darlington	Hartsville	low	pp
181	South Carolina	Fairfield	Winnsboro	high	pp
182	South Carolina	Fairfield	Winnsboro	low	pp
183	South Carolina	Aiken	Aiken	high	usg
184	South Carolina	Aiken	Aiken	low	usg
185	South Carolina	Aiken	Aiken	high	usg
186	South Carolina	Oconee	Tamassee	high	pp
187	South Carolina	Oconee	Tamassee	low	pp
188	Tennessee	Hamilton	Daisy	high	pp
189	Tennessee	Hamilton	Daisy	low	pp
190	Tennessee	Anderson	Oak Ridge	low	usg
191	Tennessee	Anderson	Oak Ridge	high	usg
192	Tennessee	Unicoi	Erwin	high	usg
193	Tennessee	Anderson	Oak Ridge	low	usg
194	Tennessee	Anderson	Oak Ridge	low	usg
195	Tennessee	Anderson	Oak Ridge	low	usg
196	Texas	Brazoria	Friendswood	low	llb
197	Texas	Harris	Webster	low	llb
198	Texas	Travis	Austin	low	llb
199	Texas	Harris	Houston	low	llb
200	Texas	Harris	Houston	low	llb
201	Texas	Harris	Houston	low	llb
202	Texas	Galveston	Galveston	low	llb
203	Texas	Karnes	Falls City	low	umt
204	Texas	Karnes	Hobson	low	umt
205	Texas	Karnes	Falls City	low	umt
206	Texas	Potter	Amarillo	low	usg
207	Utah	Grand	Moab	low	umt
208	Utah	San Juan	Blanding	low	umt
209	Utah	San Juan	La Sal	low	umt
210	Utah	Emery	Green River	low	umt
211	Utah	San Juan	Mexican Hat	low	umt
212	Utah	Salt Lake	Salt Lake City	low	umt
213	Vermont	Windham	Vernon	high	pp
214	Vermont	Windham	Vernon	low	pp

	State	County	Nearest Town	Waste Type	Source
215	Virginia	Surry	Gravel Neck	high	pp
216	Virginia	Surry	Gravel Neck	low	pp
217	Virginia	Louisa	Mineral	high	pp
218	Virginia	Louisa	Mineral	low	pp
219	Virginia	Campbell	Lynchburg	high	usg
220	Washington	Benton	Richland	low	cbg
221	Washington	Stevens	Ford	low	umt
222	Washington	Stevens	Wellpinit	low	umt
223	Washington	Benton	Richland	low	usg
224	Washington	Benton	Richland	high	usg
225	Wisconsin	Manitowoc	Two Creeks	high	pp
226	Wisconsin	Manitowoc	Two Creeks	low	pp
227	Wisconsin	Kewaunee	Kewaunee	high	pp
228	Wisconsin	Kewaunee	Kewaunee	low	pp
229	Wisconsin	Vernon	Genoa	high	pp
230	Wisconsin	Vernon	Genoa	low	pp
231	Wyoming	Converse	Converse County	low	umt
232	Wyoming	Natrona	Powder Riv. Basin	low	umt
233	Wyoming	Natrona	Powder Riv. Basin	low	umt
234	Wyoming	Natrona	Powder Riv. Basin	low	umt
235	Wyoming	Carbon	Shirley Basin	low	umt
236	Wyoming	Carbon	Shirley Basin	low	umt
237	Wyoming	Fremont	Gas Hills	low	umt
238	Wyoming	Sweetwater	Red Desert	low	umt
239	Wyoming	Fremont	Riverton	low	umt

Source: Compiled from records of the U.S. Nuclear Regulatory Commission, U.S. Department of Energy, and state regulatory agencies.

High-level and low-level radioactive waste is stored either temporarily or permanently at more than 150 locations across the United States. The table shows commercial and government burial grounds, nuclear power plants, defense installations, abandoned nuclear facilities, uranium-mill-tailings sites, and properties owned by waste brokers who collect atomic garbage and hold it for several months to a year before shipping it to a burial ground. Not included are hundreds of hospitals and educational and research institutions where small quantities of low-level waste are stored. Nor does the table show places where companies have buried radioactive waste on their own properties.

Liquid high-level waste from nuclear weapons production has been stored temporarily for years in mammoth steel tanks at the federal government's Savannah River plant, Aiken, South Carolina, and the Hanford Reservation, Richland, Washington. Built forty feet deep in the earth, the tanks are encased in two to three feet of concrete and covered with earth. At Savannah River, two of whose tanks are above, there are fifty underground tanks with a capacity of 750,000 to 1,300,000 gallons each. Below, technicians at Hanford check intake pipes and monitoring devices above a similar tank farm there. *U.S. Department of Energy Philadelphia Inquirer / Nick Kelsh*

Industrial Forum, the nuclear-industry trade association, as saying, "Science has long known what the technical problems of waste management are and more than twenty-five years ago began developing a technology to deal safely with them. What's been missing until now, however, has been the political will to let science get on with the job."

SCIENTIFIC SOLUTIONS: SOLIDIFICATION

What, then, is the state of the technology that has been well in hand for years and that science has been waiting impatiently to implement? Consider what many have hailed as the perfect answer—solidification. From the 1950s on, government plans called for used fuel rods from power plants to be treated in a commercial reprocessing facility. There the rods would be dissolved in a chemical bath. Reusable uranium and plutonium would be recovered, and the remaining, highly concentrated radioactive liquid converted to a solid form and stored in an underground repository.

In January 1966, the AEC reported that in laboratory experiments "high-level radioactive waste has been solidified in stainless steel containers twelve inches in diameter and eight feet long. The conversion to a solid offered a much improved form for long-term storage [and] reduced the volume by approximately ten-fold."

As the 1960s gave way to the 1970s, government accounts of solidification took on the same self-assured tone that characterized most pronouncements on waste management. In its 1972 annual report to Congress, the AEC said without qualification, "From the outset, the wastes from commercial fuel processing will be treated by proven solidification processes yielding small volumes of waste contained in sealed canisters."

By 1975, federal officials had calculated the precise volume of liquid to be solidified each year and the area required to store it. Frank P. Baranowski, director of the Division of Nuclear Fuel Cycle and Production in the Energy Research and Development Administration, a forerunner of the Department of

Energy, told the Joint Committee on Atomic Energy in November 1975 that "the cumulative high-level waste from nuclear power in the year 2000 would fill a football field to a depth of about eight feet."

In November 1978, the Department of Energy reported that "the technology for processing waste into glass is advanced in the United States. Since 1966, over 50 million curies of radioactive materials have been incorporated into glass at Pacific Northwest Laboratory in a series of demonstrations" at the government's Hanford Reservation.

The numbers sound impressive. But at that rate, if the used fuel rods now stored at power plants were reprocessed, it would take more than 2,500 years to solidify the leftover liquid. Of course, the Hanford conversion was carried out only on a laboratory level. A commercial facility would operate on a production-line scale. Radioactive waste in a solid form would roll out of such a plant like cars off a General Motors assembly line. That, at least, is the scenario advanced by the experts.

The scenario is a fantasy. There never has been a nuclear-waste production line in the United States. The reason goes to the root of our failure to deal with radioactive waste. What works in a laboratory will not necessarily work in a factory, or work economically, a lesson that has been painfully learned in just about every phase of waste management.

The General Electric Company built a modern reprocessing complex at Morris, Illinois, only to find out during a dry run with nonradioactive materials that its sophisticated technology did not work. Today the GE plant sits idle, a stark reminder of the gulf that separates the nuclear scientist's laboratory from the real world.

There exists only one solidification facility in the world, a vitrification plant at Marcoule, France. It is owned by Cogema, a company established by the French Atomic Energy Commission to run France's atomic energy program.

Cogema boasts that Marcoule has "the only high-level waste solidification technique that is backed by more than twenty-five years of research and development, twenty years of pilot testing and five years of actual operating performance under commercial conditions." The plant started up in 1978. It has been cited time and time again by nuclear proponents in Congress, the federal energy bureaucracy, science, and industry as an example of state-of-the-art technology. The rhetoric, though, is far more persuasive than the reality.

A *Philadelphia Inquirer* analysis of available data on Marcoule's operating record contrasts sharply with the United States government's enthusiastic accounts, and offers some indication of what could be expected from a similar plant in this country. Marcoule's experience suggests that it would take nearly 1,200 years to solidify the radioactive liquid left over from a reprocessing of the used fuel rods that will have accumulated at reactors in the United States by 1990.

In other words, if Christopher Columbus and his crew had, on their arrival in the New World in 1492, built not one but two plants like the one at Marcoule, and if both had operated continuously since that time, they still would be turning radioactive liquids into solids into the next century. By then, enough additional used fuel rods would have backed up to keep the plants going for several thousand more years.

Of course, the United States could always build more plants, say, one in every state east of the Mississippi River, where most nuclear power stations are situated. Yet with twenty-six Marcoule-like installations from Florida to Maine, from Illinois to Pennsylvania, it would still take more than forty years to solidify the backlog of used fuel rods.

Even if such a system performed flawlessly, there would still be major unanswered technical questions about the French approach. The French have shrouded their nuclear development program in secrecy. They release only selective information that portrays the industry in the most favorable light. But there is one revealing document that suggests the French solidification process is not nearly as safe or as lasting as everyone originally said it was.

That is but one of the conclusions drawn from a carefully worded report released in December 1982 by a French scientific study commission, appointed by the Supreme Council for Nuclear Safety to assess that country's handling of used fuel rods. Understated in tone, the critical study attracted little attention in the United States. It is especially significant, though, given France's commitment to produce most of its electricity with nuclear power.

For years it has been assumed in both France and the United States that solidified waste from reprocessing would go directly to an underground repository. But the study—named for its chairman, Raymond Castaing, a member of the French Academy of Sciences—argues against burial at this time. The report states, "The group feels that, at all events, it is not possible for the time being to proceed with the definitive burial of wastes that can be classed as alpha wastes [a category including reprocessed solids]. . . . The group feels that any decision of principle calling ultimately for such irreversible burial would be premature in the current state of our knowledge."

Stripped of its polite phrasing, the Castaing Report says that high-level waste, which will remain lethal for thousands of years, must not yet be placed underground, because no one can be sure exactly what will happen to it there. This position runs counter to the accepted French wisdom and flies in the face of claims by the U.S. Department of Energy and the National Academy of Sciences that such waste may be stored safely in an underground repository forever.

SCIENTIFIC SOLUTIONS: SHALLOW BURIAL

If the forty-year quest to solidify high-level waste does not sound promising, consider the technology developed to rectify one of the industry's endless mistakes—shallow land burial of low-level radioactive waste in rainy regions. Since the early 1960s, most of this waste has been buried at six commercial dumps. At one, a twenty-acre nuclear graveyard near Sheffield, Illinois, 125 miles west of Chicago, trenches holding 3.1 million cubic feet of waste have been collapsing. Opened in 1967, Sheffield closed in 1978 after radioactive tritium showed up in nearby test wells.

From the late 1970s on, Sheffield's nuclear graves—some of them 25 feet deep, 55 feet wide, and 400 feet long—have been, as the Nuclear Regulatory Commission puts it, "subsiding." Large depressions and holes have appeared in fifteen of the twenty-one trenches, exposing waste. At one trench, records show that at least fifteen depressions and holes, some 10 feet deep, occurred over a thirteen-month period in 1979–1980. Water also began to collect. The operator of the site, the Nuclear Engineering Company, now US Ecology Inc., was ordered by a state court to pump water out of the most seriously affected trenches. In the meantime, radioactive tritium continued to leak out and by early 1982 had flowed off the property and had contaminated adjoining land.

As the trenches deteriorated, the NRC commissioned a study in 1980 to explore what might be done to halt the process. The answers came a year later in a 177-page report prepared by a research firm. Under the heading "Trench Stabilization Techniques," the consultants suggested any of the following: "Dynamic consolidation . . . Pile drivers and compaction piles . . . Blasting."

Roughly translated, those called for dropping giant weights on the nuclear graves, driving timbers into the earth to shake up the burial ground, or blowing it up with dynamite. The report explained each technology.

First, dynamic consolidation. "The method involves dropping five- to forty-ton weights from heights of twenty to one hundred feet according to a predetermined pattern evaluated for the particular site. A high-capacity crane is employed to lift and release the weight, which is dropped several times at one location before moving on to the next impact location. . . ."

Next, pile drivers and compaction piles. "The method involves driving wood piles, at close centers on a grid pattern, into the soil deposit to be densified. . . . Penetration of the pile into the trenches and the accompanying vibratory effects of the pile-driving operation may cause voids and containers to collapse and compact the less dense trench backfill soil and waste materials."

Finally, blasting. "Drive a pipe to the desired depth, usually two-thrids the thickness of the stratum to be densified. Lower an explosive charge to the bottom of the pipe. Withdraw the pipe. Backfill the hole. Fire charges."

The report acknowledged potential risks. In the case of pile driving, "the penetrating equipment may puncture the containers and be exposed to the waste materials contained in them. Consequently, radioactive gases may be released." In the case of blasting, the explosion may result in "the release of radioactive gases and worker exposure to these releases. The technique also requires strict control and expert personnel to handle the potentially dangerous material and operation."

Indeed it does. Although low-level cemeteries are frequently described as containing only slightly contaminated items, such as old gloves and laboratory coats, there are more-hazardous materials at Sheffield. These include thirty-four pounds of plutonium and seventy pounds of enriched uranium. Distributed through the atmosphere in an explosion, the plutonium would cause cancer or death in every American who breathed it.

SCIENTIFIC SOLUTIONS: TRANSPORTATION

If the scientific techniques proposed to take care of Sheffield seem bizarre, consider next the technology already in use in another phase of the waste business—the giant plastic bag for the transportation of radioactive used fuel rods. The plastic bag was tested in 1981, when eight used fuel assemblies were shipped from the General Electric Company plant at Morris, Illinois, to the nation's smallest nuclear generating station, the La Crosse plant of the Dairyland Power Cooperative in Genoa, Wisconsin, 250 miles to the northwest. The story, pieced together from NRC records and interviews with government and utility officials, goes like this:

In 1979, La Crosse had run out of space in its storage pool for the used fuel assemblies that are periodically discharged from a reactor's core. When the assemblies are removed, they are intensely hot and radioactive. To cool them and shield the surrounding area from radiation, they are submerged in a water basin resembling a large swimming pool.

While awaiting NRC approval to enlarge its pool's capacity, Dairyland was forced to find an interim storage location for eight used assemblies so that the plant could continue to generate electricity. The General Electric facility at Morris, which was built to reprocess used fuel rods but never operated, agreed to accept the assemblies temporarily and place them in its storage pool.

By May 1981, Dairyland had completed its expansion and was ready to take back the eight assemblies. Four trips would be necessary because only two assemblies could be transported at a time. They were to be hauled in a fail-safe metal cask that weighed twenty-five tons and was anchored on a flatbed tractor-trailer. Such casks have been described by the Atomic Industrial Forum as "the safest and most intensively designed shipping containers ever built by any industry." And well they might be. They must provide protection against extraordinarily high levels of radiation. Depending upon how long assemblies have been out of a reactor core, exposure to them could be fatal in seconds or minutes.

On May 26, 1981, two assemblies were lifted from the storage pool at Morris and loaded into the cask. As was customary, the cask was washed and scrubbed with abrasives to ensure that surface radioactivity was below the level permitted by the U.S. Department of Transportation. When it arrived the next day at La Crosse, surface contamination—although within federal limits—was still four times greater than when the cask had left Morris. No one had an explanation for the increase.

For the next shipment, on May 29, technicians scoured the cask anew. When it reached La Crosse, surface contamination had increased 136 times over the level when it had left Illinois, and was 14 times greater than that allowed by federal regulations. At La Crosse, workers repeated the cleaning exercise. An NRC report was confident that the new scrubbing efforts would succeed: "[Dairyland officials] stated that the decontamination procedures would be exceptionally thorough and would include the use of additional decontaminating agents acetone and an ammonia solution. These measures appeared successful in reducing the high contamination levels."

Nevertheless, when the tractor-trailer returned to Morris to pick up the thrid shipment, the cask showed excessive contamination. Morris workers used detergents and abrasives to reduce radioactivity to a lower-than-normal point. An NRC spokesman said, "They really cleaned it up."

They also put it through a test to see whether the reason for the contamination could be detected. On the second trip to La

A used fuel assembly en route from West Valley, New York, to Two Rivers, Wisconsin, in 1983. *Wide World (AP)*

Crosse, the truck had passed through a violent storm, and there was speculation that the rain might have agitated the radioactivity. So Morris technicians simulated a rainstorm by spraying the cask with a fire hose, then waited eight hours to see whether radioactivity levels rose. When they did not, the third shipment was sent on its way.

Despite these efforts, the cask arrived at La Crosse registering a new record for surface contamination. Readings now were thirty-six times greater than federal regulations allowed. The NRC asked Dairyland to postpone the fourth shipment until actions could "be taken to ensure that contamination levels" were reduced. After a day of pondering the dilemma, officials of the federal government, the transportation company, and the nuclear plant came up with a novel solution. They wrapped the twenty-five-ton cask in a sheet of polyethylene plastic. The NRC gave orders for a "chase car" to follow the truck, periodically take radiation readings, and repair the plastic, if necessary.

When the cask arrived at Morris, "no removable contamination was detected on the outer surface of the plastic cover," according to the NRC. It was then loaded with the last two fuel assemblies, washed, and covered with the plastic. No contamination was found when the truck reached La Crosse the next day. As for what caused the rise in radioactivity, that remains a mystery. Federal officials speculated that a combination of moisture and road vibrations might have stirred up radioactive particles on the cask's surface, but that was only a theory.

These, then, are a few of the technologies for dealing with radioactive waste:

• Solidify high-level liquid waste with a French system that leaves it unsafe for burial and that is so slow it would take nearly 1,200 years to process the volume accumulated by 1990.
• Blow up low-level burial grounds to correct sunken trenches and stop radioactivity from seeping off the site.

• Put plastic bags around used-fuel transportation casks to halt the emission of radioactivity while the casks are traveling along the nation's highways.

If these were isolated incidents, they might be dismissed as aberrations. In fact, they represent the best thinking of the nuclear-waste field. Lest there be any doubt about the state of the technology, it is worth looking at a once widely accepted scientific axiom that proved incorrect. This one involves the land burial of plutonium. The practice began in the 1940s and continued through the 1970s. During all those years, the experts certified it as perfectly safe.

Plutonium is one of the most poisonous substances produced by man. One ounce could kill 20,000 people. Scientists said that plutonium could be dumped in the ground like any other garbage, that it would adhere to soil particles and never move. In 1974, about thirty years after the federal government and industry began sprinkling plutonium into burial plots in Colorado, Idaho, Illinois, Kentucky, Nevada, New Mexico, New York, Ohio, Oklahoma, South Carolina, Tennessee, and Washington, the AEC reported that all was going well. Its study claimed that plutonium deposited at a burial ground at Maxey Flats, Kentucky—with a guarantee it would move no more than half an inch over the next 24,000 years—remained securely in place. The AEC declared, "Deep well water samples at the perimeter of existing licensed burial sites have not shown any detectable plutonium, indicating that the plutonium already buried has remained immobile and therefore constitutes no potential hazard."

A study that same year by the Kentucky Department for Human Resources found that the plutonium—far from "immobile"—had seeped off the burial ground. Rather than moving only half an inch in 24,000 years, it already had moved hundreds of feet in less than 10 years, contaminating neighboring properties and stream beds. Later studies by the Environmental Protection Agency confirmed the state's findings. No one was certain whether the plutonium had traveled deep underground, along the earth's surface, or both. No matter. It had moved. A 1977 report to the Kentucky legislature by an engineering firm calculated that airborne releases of plutonium were "over ten times that presently allowed by NRC from nuclear power facilities."

Since the Maxey Flats discovery, the plutonium that could never move has been found to be moving at other burial grounds. At West Valley, New York, test wells showed in December 1983 that kerosene mixed with plutonium had traveled more than fifty feet. Back in the late 1960s and early 1970s, the plutonium-contaminated kerosene had been blended with a dry substance known for its absorptive qualities. It was assumed that this material would soak up the kerosene and that the plutonium would hold fast in the soil. It didn't work. Still, the experiment was noteworthy. The absorptive material—another of the scientific community's innovative technologies for controlling radioactive waste—was kitty litter.

2
The Politics of Neglect

ANARCHY IN WASHINGTON

With the possible exception of the income tax, no other modern-day issue is so firmly mired in Washington politics as that of nuclear waste. That explains why the nuclear field has had one failure after another, from reprocessing, once considered the linchpin of a nuclear society, to low-level burial grounds, which should have been the easiest of all waste to look after. It also explains why the United States began the mass production of waste without the technology to control it permanently, and why lawmakers have alternately ignored the subject and enacted all the wrong kinds of legislation.

Congress, the White House, and the bureaucracy, unable to think beyond the next election, have played politics so long with radioactive waste that neglect by default has become official policy. They have repeatedly misled the public by giving overly optimistic assessments of existing technology and announcing ambitious programs that had little chance to succeed. They have initiated projects and then scrapped them, and they have based policies on faulty assumptions. Three legislative and administrative decisions, representative of policy-making overall, may serve to characterize the past and foreshadow the future.

In a report to the Atomic Energy Commission nearly two decades ago, a National Academy of Sciences committee warned that burying low-level waste above the water table posed "unacceptable long-term risks." The report said, "The committee thinks that the current practice of disposing of . . . solid wastes directly into the ground above or in the freshwater zones, although momentarily safe, will lead in the long run to a serious fouling of man's environment. Such methods represent a concept of easy disposal that has had and will continue to have great appeal to operators, but we fear that continuation of the practices eventually will create hazards that will be extremely difficult and expensive to eliminate."

The government disregarded the panel's warning. Since then, at three of the six commercial dumps, radioactive materials have drained off the sites and contaminated neighboring properties. The three dumps are now closed. Nonetheless, in 1982 the Nuclear Regulatory Commission formally approved the burial of radioactive waste above the water table. "A wide range of locations are potentially available for use as a near-surface disposal facility," the NRC said, defining "near-surface" in its regulations as "the uppermost fifteen to twenty meters of the earth." In future nuclear cemeteries, waste will be buried at depths ranging from forty-nine to sixty-six feet—generally above or near the water table.

Where will these landfills be? All over the place. The first are due to open before the end of the 1980s, products of another Washington policy reversal. An NRC task force had warned in 1977 that "undisciplined proliferation of low-level sites must be avoided." To prevent a rash of burial plots in individual states, the task force urged a much stronger federal role in their development and operation. Congress spurned the recommendation and in December 1980 enacted legislation that turned over responsibility for commercial burial tracts to the fifty states and ordered the opening of additional dumps. If the law is complied with, as many as two dozen dumps in as many states will be established, some in geologically unsuitable regions.

In a similar vein, the AEC in 1970 banned the shallow

burial of plutonium and other long-lived radioactive materials, known as transuranic waste, on federal land. The decision to end the nearly three-decade-old practice came with the grudging recognition that such waste, because of its long-lived radioactivity, should be isolated deep underground. (Plutonium loses only half its radioactive strength in 24,000 years.) But the AEC failed to extend the ban to privately run burial grounds. Operators placed plutonium in trenches at West Valley, New York; Sheffield, Illinois; Maxey Flats, Kentucky; Beatty, Nevada; and Richland, Washington.

Four years later the NRC proposed a similar prohibition at commercial cemeteries: "Because of the increased quantities of such wastes expected to be generated, the long half-life of transuranics and their high radioactivity, it was considered that such wastes in the future should be stored and disposed of at government-owned facilities."

What happened? The regulations were never implemented. From 1976 to 1979, federal records show, forty-four pounds of plutonium was placed in shallow graves at the Richland commercial dump. Nearly two-thirds of it came from the United States government or its contractors. The government that outlawed plutonium burial on federal land, because of its potential health hazard in 1970, continued to bury it at a commercial dump until 1979.

If the government sometimes dumps waste where it shouldn't, quite often it has no records to show where waste has been stored temporarily, where it has been dumped permanently, or where it has contaminated properties. Private companies can bury it on their own land. In many cases, the government does not know which companies are doing so, what kind of waste they have discarded, or where it is. In still other cases, the government has lost or destroyed records identifying properties where waste was produced, and then has spent years trying to find them.

The records are faulty in part because Congress divided responsibility for waste management among the states and a variety of federal agencies. Twenty-six states have enacted laws to comply with those of the United States government; they thus regulate some waste without federal supervision. In the other twenty-four states, the same kinds of waste are controlled by the federal government. All fifty states regulate certain other nuclear materials and enforce some protective guidelines. Because of this jumble of regulatory and enforcement responsibilities, there is no central record-keeping system, and the scores of federal and state agencies go their own ways in dealing with waste.

The fragmented lines of authority among four federal agencies alone—the Department of Energy (DOE), the Environmental Protection Agency (EPA), the Nuclear Regulatory Commission (NRC), and the Department of Transportation (DOT)—underscore the anarchy. The EPA sets environmental and public-health protection standards covering radioactive waste. The DOE enforces some of the standards set by the EPA. The NRC also enforces some. The NRC regulates low-level waste generated at some government installations. The DOE regulates low-level waste generated at other government facilities. The EPA and the NRC share responsibility for regulating radioactive materials emitted into the air. The EPA is responsible for waste dropped in the ocean. The NRC and the DOE are responsible for developing waste repositories on land. The NRC regulates high-level waste at power plants. The DOE regulates high-level waste at government installations. The DOT regulates waste carriers.

This regulatory maze allows waste to be trucked about the country and stored in various locations without any single agency being responsible. It also allows a company to operate in one state on the basis of a license granted by another state. The SouthWest Nuclear Company, headquartered in Pleasanton, California, about fifty miles southeast of San Francisco, is one of the country's largest waste brokers. It collects radioactive garbage nationwide for delivery to commercial dumps. Yet a 1983 NRC computer printout of all federally licensed nuclear businesses shows no record of the company's existence. That's because SouthWest is licensed by the California Department of

Health Services, not by the NRC. Since California is one of the twenty-six states whose laws comply with federal rules, the NRC permits any company licensed by it to operate in any of the twenty-four noncomplying states, such as Pennsylvania and New Jersey.

One of SouthWest's clients is the Department of Defense. When a cargo of low-level waste from military bases in West Germany arrived at a terminal in New Jersey in August 1983, SouthWest arranged for its transshipment to the company's Pleasanton warehouse. The waste was loaded onto a Home Transportation Company truck, which hauled it to a depot in Bucks County, Pennsylvania, where it was unloaded and stored for several days before it was sent on its way to the West Coast.

Pennsylvania authorities never knew that the waste was in the state. When asked about it, William P. Dornsife, chief of the division of nuclear safety in the Department of Environmental Resources' bureau of radiation protection, said, "I'm not aware of any shipments coming from out of country, coming through Pennsylvania. And having no regulatory responsibility, we have no direct knowledge of it. You would have to talk with the Nuclear Regulatory Commission to find out . . . why the material was there." The NRC does not keep such records. Nor does the state of California, which licenses SouthWest, the company that arranged for the waste shipment. Nor does the Department of Transportation, which regulates Home Transportation Company, the company that brought the radioactive waste to Bucks County.

In a perverse sort of way, there is some logic to this regulatory labyrinth. Washington did take care of its own, even if it neglected everyone else. Although the splintered system virtually assured future accidents, it guaranteed that no one agency or official could be held accountable. The legislatively mandated disorder also made it impossible to determine how much waste there is, who is producing it, where it is, and what is happening to it. About all that can be said is that an estimated 10,000-plus businesses, institutions, and government agencies work with radioactive materials and that each produces waste.

MILL TAILINGS—PLAYING BOTH SIDES

Even when the government knows who produces waste and where it is, it cannot agree on what to do with it. Nothing better illustrates this confusion than the way Congress and the regulatory agencies have treated uranium mining waste.

From the 1950s through the early 1970s, the AEC said that mini-mountains of uranium mill tailings, centered largely in nine western states, were harmless. The millions of tons of tailings, a sandlike material, were left over from the processing of uranium ore. Although the tailings still contained 85 percent of the radioactivity that had existed before the removal of the uranium, the AEC saw no danger. Even after tailings reached the Animas River in Colorado in 1959, contaminating drinking water, the AEC remained undisturbed. "No immediate health hazard exists as a result of the discharge of the mills' effluent into the Animas," the commission said.

Despite mounting evidence to the contrary, the AEC held this position throughout the 1960s. The tailings were officially innocuous. Dr. Peter A. Morris, director of the commission's division of operational safety, told a Senate Public Works subcommittee in May 1966, "The evidence available at the present time does not support a conclusion that the uranium tailings piles represent a radiation hazard to their environment. . . . We find it difficult to conceive of any mechanism whereby the radioactive material which is now so widely dispersed could become so concentrated as to exceed applicable standards for protection against radiation."

The AEC's general counsel, Joseph Hennessey, was more emphatic. "It has been the commission's position," he declared, "that the radioactivity resulting from the uranium in the piles is unimportant."

If the mill tailings had been confined to remote areas, far from people, there might have been some logic to the commission's position. But the tailing residue has threatened public safety in many places.

In Salt Lake City, Utah, mill tailings were later found under homes, businesses, and a fire station. At a plumbing supply store, radiation levels "exceeding the surgeon general's guidelines were detected inside the building," according to a 1979 report by the Department of Energy. In Grand Junction, Colorado, hundreds of homes were either built of or built over mill tailings. The broad-jump pit at the high school was filled with tailings. So, too, were children's sandboxes. A Colorado health official said that radiation levels in more than six hundred homes and businesses were "sufficiently high to pose a health risk."

In Shiprock, New Mexico, more than 1.5 million tons of tailings were spread over seventy-two acres of the Navajo Indian Reservation. One mound stretched across twenty-six acres and reached a height of forty feet. The Navajo Engineering and Construction Authority taught Indian students how to operate earth-moving equipment there. Radiation readings ranged from two to twenty-three times normal background levels.

In Canonsburg, Pennsylvania, about twenty miles south of Pittsburgh, mill tailings were scattered over eighteen acres. The tract, bordered by single-family homes, is believed to be the largest piece of land contaminated by tailings east of the Mississippi River. During the 1940s and 1950s, a plant at the site extracted uranium and radium from various ores, under contract with the AEC. The company discharged radioactive liquid through a sewer system into a swamp, which in turn drained into a nearby creek. When the plant closed in the 1950s, it buried thousands of tons of the radioactive debris on-site. The Pennsylvania Railroad Company—with the AEC's approval—hauled thousands of tons more to a railroad landfill in Burrell Township in Indiana County, Pennsylvania, about fifty miles northeast of Canonsburg. In the 1960s, the Canonsburg site, which the AEC had certified as radiation free, was developed as an industrial park. Neighborhood children over the years played in a pond where radioactive sludge was dumped. The pond was later filled and converted to a ball field. It was placed off limits in 1977, when a survey team found radiation readings above permissible limits. Radiation levels inside buildings in the industrial park, on the land, and in soil and water samples all exceeded federal guidelines. Residential properties on an adjoining street also were contaminated.

While the AEC held the line on the mill-tailings question, other government officials acknowledged a hazard—but only a small one. In a 1977 memorandum to the AEC's Atomic Safety and Licensing Board, Dr. Walter H. Jordan, physicist and retired assistant director of the Oak Ridge National Laboratory, wrote, "Deaths in future generations due to cancer and genetic effects resulting from the radon from the uranium required to fuel a single reactor for one year can run into the hundreds. It is very difficult to argue that deaths to future generations are unimportant. But it can be shown that the number is insignificant compared to those due to the radon contribution in natural background."

Recognizing that a large segment of the public might not find hundreds of deaths per reactor to be "insignificant"— especially if many of the victims were unaware they had been exposed to radiation—Congress enacted the Uranium Mill Tailings Radiation Control Act of 1978. What happened next is a case study of the results of divided regulatory authority and congressional waffling.

The act gave the EPA until May 1980 to set health and safety standards for mill tailings. Once the EPA established standards, the Nuclear Regulatory Commission would draw up regulations implementing them. But the EPA procrastinated. In October 1980, the NRC went ahead and issued regulations based on what it believed the EPA guidelines should be. The NRC imposed limitations on the level of radioactivity emitted by the mill tailings and ordered them covered with earth and rock.

Uranium-mining companies said they were already struggling in a depressed market and could not afford to comply. Officials in states where the companies operated lobbied their congressional delegations to block the rules. Congress caved in and in December 1981 barred the NRC from spending any of its appropriated funds to enforce the regulations. The about-

face on mill tailings is one of many policy reversals that explain
why a fickle Congress has never dealt effectively with waste.

The record of Pete V. Domenici, the Republican senator
from New Mexico, parallels that of many lawmakers. When
Congress debated the mill tailings bill in 1978, one of the disputed points was how much money the federal government and
the states would each contribute to the estimated $200 million
mill-tailings cleanup program. The Carter administration proposed that the federal government provide 75 percent of the
funds and the states the other 25 percent. The western states
and Pennsylvania did not like that idea very much. They believed Washington should pick up the full tab. Senator
Domenici, whose home state had four mill-tailings dumps, offered legislation that provided for full federal funding. "Why
shouldn't the federal government pay for the whole thing?"
Domenici asked his colleagues. "This was the federal government's responsibility in the first place." When finally passed,
the act did not authorize 100 percent federal financing, but it
came fairly close. It ordered the Department of Energy to pay
90 percent of the costs, the states the other 10 percent.

Three years later, Senator Domenici and his western-states
colleagues introduced legislation designed to prevent the NRC
from enforcing its mill-tailings regulations. Mining was in trouble. Now Domenici and other lawmakers were more concerned
about the economic health of mining companies that would be
affected by the rules, which the New Mexico senator described
as "completely impracticable." Reeling off statistics on mill and
mine closings and falling production, Domenici declared, "I
have pointed out that our domestic uranium industry is on its
knees, that it is in the essential security interest of the United
States to maintain a viable domestic industry, and that the
future of that industry is clouded to say the very least." Lest
anyone think special interests were at work, Domenici added,
"[I]t is not simply because the present status is so poor that I
am offering this amendment, but because I believe that without
some action now, the domestic industry will not recover, nor
will it be able to meet our future needs."

Thus, in three years, Domenici and other congressmen sought to protect the public—the act said the tailings "may pose a potential and significant radiation health hazard"—and then to protect the mining companies that had created the health hazard. They also first argued that the federal government should pay the full cost of cleanup and then blocked enforcement of the rules. This allowed mining companies to continue practices that made the cleanup legislation necessary. The response was similar to that of New York lawmakers who sought legislation to allow construction of a reprocessing plant at West Valley and then secured federal funds to clean up the plant when it failed.

As it turned out, the mining industry had little to fear from federal regulatory agencies. Three years late, in September 1983, the EPA announced its standards to restrict emissions from tailings and their seepage into groundwater. They allowed for radiation releases ten times greater than those permitted by the NRC. But the NRC had already decided that its initial rules were perhaps overly restrictive.

Within thirty minutes after the EPA administrator William D. Ruckelshaus signed the standards on September 30, 1983, both the American Mining Congress, representing industry, and the Environmental Defense Fund, a public-interest group, had initiated legal actions challenging them in federal courts at opposite ends of the country. The Environmental Defense Fund considered the rules too lax and filed its lawsuit in the U.S. Circuit Court of Appeals in Washington, D.C., a court it believed would be sympathetic to the public interest. The American Mining Congress considered the rules too stringent and filed in the U.S. Circuit Court of Appeals in Denver, a court likely to favor industry.

The outcome of the litigation will eventually be of special significance to the East Coast. The mining industry has expanded its search for uranium from the sparsely populated West to the densely populated East. Rich ore deposits have been identified in Virginia. If the radioactive waste practices of the West are introduced in the East, millions of people will be

exposed to additional health risks. In any event, six years after
Congress enacted a law that called for regulation of waste from
the uranium-mining industry, there were no regulations. Instead, the federal government continued to spend hundreds of
millions of taxpayers' dollars correcting mill-tailings mistakes.
As 1984 began, the Department of Energy moved to demolish
the industrial park in Canonsburg, Pennsylvania, as well as a
number of contaminated homes in the surrounding neighborhood.

Because the legislative branch of government has shirked its
lawmaking obligations, the courts are being called on increasingly, as in the mill-tailings controversy, to settle disagreements
among the states, the federal government, the nuclear industry,
and public-interest organizations. But the subject does not lend
itself particularly well to judicial decision making. The courts
have neither the expertise nor the resources to formulate nuclear policies. Nonetheless, they are doing so, and as a result the
legal system is laying its own chaos over that spread by Congress and the states. A pair of unrelated cases in 1981 and 1983
in federal courts in New York and in Nebraska symbolize the
problem. First, New York.

A total of 750 used fuel assemblies from commercial reactors were stored at a reprocessing plant in West Valley, New
York, after it closed in 1972. The assemblies had been shipped
there by utilities in four states under contract with Nuclear Fuel
Services Inc., the plant operator. The assemblies remained in
the storage pool after Nuclear Fuel Services left the reprocessing business and turned the plant over to the New York State
Energy Research and Development Authority in 1982. The
state agency, perhaps fearful that the presence of fuel rods at
West Valley might lead to its selection for a national high-level
radioactive waste storage center, sued the utilities to compel
them to take back their assemblies. The state argued that the
power companies did not have a contract with New York and
that therefore the assemblies represented "a continuing tres-
pass."

The utilities maintained that it would be safer not to move

the assemblies. The Jersey Central Power & Light Company, for one, contended that "transportation of nuclear fuel, no matter how carefully done, inherently involves more risk than allowing it to remain at West Valley." This was ironic because in the past, when others sued utilities to block similar fuel shipments, the utilities insisted that the hauling of assemblies from one location to another was perfectly safe. That contradiction aside, the U.S. District Court in Buffalo agreed with New York State and in June 1983 ordered the utilities to begin removing the assemblies. The first shipment left West Valley in October 1983.

In 1967, the General Electric Company contracted to supply nuclear fuel for Nebraska's Cooper power plant and to assume responsibility for the used assemblies. At the time, GE intended to reprocess the assemblies in a new plant at Morris, Illinois. But the Morris facility did not work, and no reprocessing was carried out there. The Nebraska Public Power District sued GE to force the company to transfer used fuel assemblies from the Cooper reactor, twenty miles south of Nebraska City, to Morris. Under an agreement reached in the U.S. District Court in Lincoln in June 1981, GE must move the assemblies to its Morris plant. The first shipment was made in December 1983.

Here, then, is nuclear-waste policy as laid down by the federal courts: under a New York court order, used fuel assemblies are being removed from a closed reprocessing plant and trucked to electric utilities. Under a Nebraska court agreement, used fuel assemblies are being trucked from an electric utility to a closed reprocessing plant. Although both court actions may be legally appropriate, good law does not necessarily make for good or consistent nuclear policy.

The interstate juggling of fuel rods is only part of a larger pattern of governmental neglect. Neither federal nor state agencies have made adequate provisions for the long-term care of nuclear waste or properties contaminated with it. This, too, is the product of misguided federal policies. In 1959, the AEC, which then administered all low-level burial grounds, said that private companies would not be permitted to enter the business until long-term care of the graveyards had been arranged. Would the businesses and institutions that created the garbage be responsible for it, or would the companies that dumped it for profit, or the taxpayers of the twentieth and twenty-first centuries?

An AEC official told Congress that "because of the type, level of activity and half-life of the radioactive wastes, it may be necessary to maintain land burial areas for an extended period of time, perhaps hundreds of years." He added that "the feasibility of a commercially operated burial ground under AEC licenses is largely dependent upon resolution of this problem."

Brave words. But before the commission could assign responsibility—which in fact remains unassigned—it bowed to pressure from private companies and began to issue licenses to open burial grounds without adequate provisions for long-term maintenance.

Although several states, including Illinois, Kentucky, New York, and South Carolina, established special funds to pay for perpetual care, the revenue collected from burial ground operators amounts to only a few million dollars, while the combined cleanup costs could eventually run into billions. States without burial grounds are no better off. With few exceptions, neither they nor those with dumps have set aside funds to clean up nuclear manufacturing facilities.

This is especially shortsighted. Most nuclear companies, aside from electric utilities and some industrial corporations, are small businesses such as research laboratories, trash collectors, and manufacturers. Many rent or lease their equipment and buildings. Some are run out of family homes by means of a telephone answering service, or from buildings no larger than a multicar garage. Almost without exception, they have limited financial resources. Even the major corporations, such as Exxon and Gulf Oil, have formed nuclear subsidiaries with limited assets for which the parent companies assume no financial responsibility. Consider Nuclear Fuel Services, a Getty Oil

Company subsidiary that managed low- and high-level radioactive wastes at the former reprocessing plant in West Valley, New York.

During a hearing before a House Science and Technology subcommittee in June 1977, George E. Brown, Jr., a Democratic representative from California, questioned Ralph W. Deuster, president of Nuclear Fuel Services, about the company's financial resources for cleaning up the West Valley plant.

Brown—"What if you were stuck for a judgment for $100 million? Could you satisfy it? Does the corporation have that kind of assets?"

Deuster—"No, it does not."

Brown—"It was set up just for the purpose of operating this particular facility, was it not?"

Deuster—"Yes, it was, basically."

The Department of Energy has since assumed control of West Valley and has begun a twenty-year project that could cost taxpayers more than $1 billion if the property is restored to its original state. Getty Oil Company had assets of $9.9 billion in 1982 and profits of $691.6 million. Nuclear Fuel Services, Getty's subsidiary, will contribute about $9.4 million toward removal of radioactive debris from its former plant, about 1 percent of the potential cost.

In failing to require private businesses to allocate funds to eliminate radioactive contamination from their land and buildings, the state and federal governments have at least been consistent. The federal government has not set aside funds for its own properties. The Department of Energy watches over about four hundred buildings that once housed radioactive materials. The structures have been sealed or fenced in and kept under surveillance to prevent intrusion and accidental radiation exposure.

The Energy Research and Development Administration calculated in 1977 that it could cost $30 million a year for the next one hundred years—or a total of $3 billion—to remove all traces of radioactivity from the facilities. The General Accounting Office dismissed that figure as too low, saying, "We do not believe this is a credible estimate." The GAO proved correct. Two years later, in June 1979, Worthington Bateman, deputy undersecretary in the Department of Energy, told a House Interior and Insular Affairs subcommittee that "the current estimated cost of solidifying the liquid waste at the [government's] Savannah River" plant alone was about $3 billion. If the government proceeded to clean up all defense high-level waste, Bateman thought, it would be "very easy to imagine a future . . . [of] multi-billion-dollar programs per year."

The price tag caught Morris K. Udall, Democratic representative from Arizona and the committee chairman, by surprise. "I had no idea that what was involved was that expensive," said Udall, who as the architect of much nuclear-waste legislation is considered one of Capitol Hill's better authorities on the subject. In two years, the projected cost of the government's cleanup program soared from a multibillion-dollar project over a hundred years to a multibillion-dollar project annually.

Such estimates assume that the government really intends to rid its properties of radioactivity. In all probability, some government land and buildings will be contaminated forever. Commenting on the future of the Hanford, Washington, facility, and of one in Nevada, a DOE official told a House Science and Technology subcommittee, "The Hanford site has an enormous amount of waste on it. My guess on that particular site is that it is going to be a partially restricted use site for as long as man is around. . . . I think you will have those [sites] that can be cleaned up, but I suspect that there will be major federal facilities like the Nevada Test Site that are going to be dedicated as monuments to humanity and restricted for a long, long time."

There is little doubt that many more tracts of land in a number of states will be designated as "monuments to humanity" in coming years. This is especially so when one considers that the level of radioactivity in the defense waste that has contaminated government installations is only a fraction of that in the commercial waste. Of the 16.2 billion curies of all nuclear waste now in storage, the military accounts for only 1.5 billion curies, 9 percent of the total. The commercial nuclear industry, mostly electric utilities, accounts for the remaining 14.7 billion curies, or 91 percent of the total.

Congressmen and federal officials have often sought to give a contrary impression. During a House Armed Services subcommittee hearing in March 1981, Samuel S. Stratton, a twelve-term Democratic representative from New York, had this exchange with Secretary of Energy James B. Edwards:

Stratton—"Mr. Secretary, I understand that something like 99.9 percent of the waste problem is from defense. The commercial waste matter is a relatively small percentage of the total. Is that correct?"

Edwards—"I don't know the exact figures, but you are close to the proper figure. . . ."

Stratton—"It occurred to me if the American people understood that percentage, they might be less traumatized by the idea of nuclear electric reactors around the country which, as I say, are providing such a minor percentage of the waste problem."

Stratton and Edwards could not have been further off the mark. For every 100 million curies of defense waste, there are nearly 1 billion curies of commercial waste. By the year 2000, that gap is expected to grow another 50 percent.

Regardless of whether it comes from military or from commercial operations, 99.9 percent of all radioactive waste ever produced is kept in stopgap facilities. Indeed, science, government, and industry have given new meaning to the word "temporary." Defense waste, some of it dating back to the first atomic bombs, is stored temporarily in 169 underground steel tanks, each with a capacity of from 500,000 to 1 million gallons, at the Hanford Reservation in Washington; in more than 100,-000 fifty-five gallon barrels stacked in long rows, one atop another, at the National Engineering Laboratory in Idaho Falls, Idaho; and in fifty underground steel tanks, each with a capacity of from 750,000 to 1.3 million gallons at the Savannah River plant near Aiken, South Carolina.

Most defense waste—and these tanks, barrels, and sites represent only a partial inventory—as well as the commercial waste, is now safely contained. But it is housed in facilities that were designed and built to accommodate it for only a few years, in some cases a few decades. By government default, these facilities have become permanent storage centers. As a result, the risk of an accidental release of radiation is growing.

The current concern over toxic-waste dumps will pale into insignificance if similar mistakes are made, and a few already have been, in the management of radioactive waste. It should be remembered that forty years ago this waste did not exist, that twenty years ago it was of small quantity, and that what there is today is only a fraction of what the future will yield. For these and other reasons, today's political decisions and governmental policies will determine whether the country will one day face multiple radioactive Love Canals and Times Beaches.

OFFICIAL DECEPTION

It would be one thing if Congress and the regulators were merely overwhelmed. But there is a darker side to the federal record. In the 1940s, the government allowed a federal contractor to pour 37 million gallons of radioactive liquid waste into shallow wells at Tonawanda, New York. It kept the well dumping a secret for thrity-five years, until the New York State Assembly Task Force on Toxic Substances in 1980 uncovered documents describing the practice.

The Linde Air Products Company had produced the waste while processing uranium ore at a federally owned plant for the Manhattan Engineering District, the government entity that was building the atomic bombs. Confronted with a growing volume of waste and no place to store it, Linde got government permission to dump it in wells on plant property. Although Linde deemed the waste harmless, it offered a peculiar reason to justify its disposal system—if the waste should contaminate area properties, it would be difficult to trace it back to the Linde facility. In a letter seeking the Manhattan Engineering Dis-

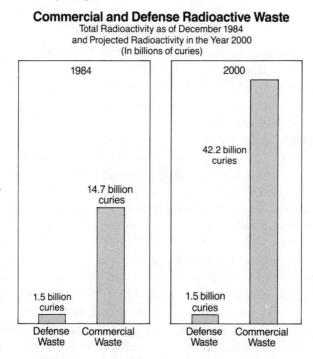

Commercial and Defense Radioactive Waste
Total Radioactivity as of December 1984
and Projected Radioactivity in the Year 2000
(In billions of curies)

Source: Compiled from U.S. Department of Energy records.

Of the 16.2 billion curies of radioactive waste now in storage in the United States, 14.7 billion curies were produced by the commercial nuclear industry, mostly atomic power plants. Only 1.5 billion curies were produced in the manufacturing of nuclear weapons. By the year 2000, according to Department of Energy projections, the radioactivity in accumulated commercial waste will total 42.2 billion curies, or twenty-eight times greater than the level in defense nuclear waste.

trict's concurrence in the scheme, a Linde executive wrote on March 29, 1944, "Our Law Department advises that it is considered impossible to determine the course of subterranean streams and, therefore, the responsibility for any contamination could not be fixed. Our Law Department recommends that this method of disposal be followed." The government agreed.

Years later, the New York legislative committee reported that "both Linde and Manhattan Engineering District officials were aware that this method of disposal would permanently contaminate Linde's wells and probably the wells of Linde's neighbors in the surrounding region. In fact, this method of disposal was selected precisely because the source of the underground contamination could not readily be traced back to Linde or the Army."

It is possible, perhaps, to excuse this incident as one that sprang from the necessities of war and the early ignorance about radiation. A decade later, however, the government's secrecy policy on radiation mistakes remained in place—as it does today. In the late 1950s, the AEC withheld information about radioactive liquid that had leaked out of its underground storage tanks at the Hanford, Washington, nuclear installation. During an appearance in January 1959 before a subcommittee of the Joint Committee on Atomic Energy, an official of General Electric, then responsible for managing Hanford's waste, testified, "No environmental hazard will exist as long as the tanks maintain their integrity. . . . We have never detected a leak from any of these tanks, so that we are in turn persuaded that none has ever leaked." A year later, the AEC asserted in its annual report that "waste problems have proved completely manageable." The commission said that "in more than a decade of tank storage at Hanford, no leaks have been detected."

In fact, the Hanford tanks had started leaking two years earlier, in 1958. Thus began the steady deterioration of a tank farm that the AEC once said would last four to five decades. But the public did not learn that Hanford's tanks were leaking until years later. The AEC detected some leaks soon after they occurred. Others went unnoticed for weeks. In 1973 alone,

Radioactive waste from the Manhattan Project, which manufactured the first atomic bombs, is still stored temporarily in this silo in Lewiston, New York. *Philadelphia Inquirer / Nick Kelsh*

115,000 gallons of high-level waste drained into the ground
from one tank. Nearly 100 gallons of the lethal liquid poured
out every hour for forty-nine days before it was discovered. The
repeated incidents of escaping waste contradicted the AEC's
1960 claim to Congress that "an inventory is maintained of
the contents of each tank, and the liquid level is watched carefully."

A government report in 1980 identified 20 of the 156 tanks
as "confirmed leakers," and 38 others were classified as "of
questionable integrity." A supervisor in charge of monitoring
the tanks, a man who had quit in 1978, charged that Hanford
officials had covered up information about the leaks. But the
DOE Inspector General's Office concluded otherwise: "Had
there been any officials desiring to minimize publicity about
tank leaks, they would have had no real need to engage in
conduct which might be considered questionable. This is because Hanford's existing waste management policies and practices have themselves sufficed to keep publicity about possible
tank leaks to a minimum." The inspector general was saying
that nothing was covered up, because it was official government
policy not to disclose information about radioactive-waste mistakes.

But the government has resorted to far more questionable
practices than the mere withholding of information. This is
especially true when it comes to formulating standards to determine how much radiation the public will receive without its
consent. These regulations will take on a growing importance
as radioactivity in waste grows geometrically, for the extent to
which waste is sealed off from the environment—or more precisely, how much escaping radioactivity is deemed acceptable
—will be determined according to the radiation-protection
rules.

On the subject of permissible levels of radiation, the federal
government's record is consistent. It discredits and terminates
research projects that suggest all is not as well as claimed. It
conceals mistakes and issues misleading statements. Reports
that disease and death may be attributable to radiation doses

the government considers harmless are repudiated. Dissent is not tolerated.

Sometimes the pressure is applied subtly, as Dr. Samuel Milham, Jr., found out. A staff physician for the Washington State Department of Social and Health Services, Milham made a study of more than 500,000 males who died in that state from 1950 to 1971. He concluded that workers at the Hanford nuclear plant were more likely to die of cancer than other Washington state males. Before he published his findings, Milham met with AEC officials. As he later told a congressional committee, "The impression I got at the meeting with AEC was that release of my findings might cause concerns and problems in the industry. . . . I got to thinking [that] politically, and for a lot of reasons, it would probably be better in the long run not to publish it then."

Milham later published his study in an abbreviated form. Others have not been so fortunate. Federal employees who questioned the safety of radiation-protection standards have been ostracized and pressured to quit. In 1969, Dr. John W. Gofman, associate director of the government's Lawrence Livermore Laboratory in Livermore, California, and Arthur R. Tamplin, a physicist at the laboratory, challenged the radiation regulations at a scientific conference. On the basis of their studies, they told the scientific gathering that "if the average exposure of the United States population were to reach the allowable [level of radiation annually] . . . there would, in time, be an excess of 32,000 cases of fatal cancer plus leukemia per year, and this would occur year after year."

Although both had expressed their views privately within the AEC, Tamplin said, the conference marked the first time the issue had been raised in public. He described what happened next in testimony before a House Interstate and Foreign Commerce subcommittee in January 1978: "All hell broke out. I had a group at that time at the laboratory of thirteen people. Within a short period of time, the group was cut down to two people and then the other person was fired."

Gofman, a physician as well as a physicist, and the codiscoverer of uranium 233, was at work on a cancer research project. The government terminated the project, Tamplin said, and Gofman left the laboratory. "But I stayed on," Tamplin testified, "essentially as a non-person. I had no assignments, but I had an office and I could get my paycheck every month, but I was never given any assignment in the laboratory." In time, Tamplin also quit.

Others who disapproved remained in their jobs and buckled to official pressure. They amended scientific papers at odds with the government's position. Dr. Karl Z. Morgan, who was for twenty-nine years director of the health physics division at the Oak Ridge National Laboratory in Oak Ridge, Tennessee, described the practice as follows when he testified before the same congressional subcommittee:

"It is very difficult to determine with certainty how much of this suppression . . . and actions against freedom of speech go on, because in a laboratory, a manager of an operation doesn't accuse you of what he has in mind. He will pick out some little minor detail of a paper, why you shouldn't present that paper, why it is not appropriate or timely. So I am convinced that much more of this goes on. Furthermore, there are not many people that wish to make an issue so they will lose their job and would no longer have support for their family and no chance of getting another job in their profession."

It should not be too surprising that a government that suppresses or discourages scientific misgivings about established policies has, again and again, approved waste-management programs that turned out to rest on faulty assumptions. At West Valley, New York, for example, the experts predicted that waste buried in trenches would be immobile, so firmly fixed that if it had been planted there 5,000 years ago, it would still be there today.

In an August 1964 report to the AEC, Nuclear Fuel Services, which planned to operate the burial ground, assured the commission that waste could be safely contained at the site. The silty condition of the soil, the company said, meant that water would not drain through the radioactive garbage and contaminate area farms and communities. "We have now had considerable experience," the company said, "in working with this material in various excavations in the course of constructing the plant and in the operation of a low-level waste burial operation." The company said its calculations showed that "something over 5,000 years" would pass before any leached radioactive material even reached a ravine on the property.

As it turned out, the experts miscalculated by 4,990 years. Less than a decade after the first waste was buried, radioactive runoff was a serious concern. Tritium and other substances had flowed off the property. Plutonium was also moving, but years would go by before anyone noticed. New York State officials later summed up the situation: "By 1975, so much water had infiltrated the trenches that they began to overflow, resulting in the discharge of radioactively contaminated water into nearby streams which flow into Lake Erie, a source of drinking water for hundreds of thousands of people."

On still other occasions, federal agencies have disclaimed responsibility for waste projects they approved and that later went awry. In July 1967, the U.S. Geological Survey, after a study of land and water conditions at the proposed low-level burial ground at Sheffield, Illinois, concluded that the site was appropriate for such a use. "Based on data supplied to the Atomic Energy Commission," the Geological Survey said, "the geologic and hydrologic conditions of the site . . . appear to be suitable for burial of low-level solid radioactive waste."

Sheffield eventually turned out not to be suitable after all. Radioactive waste seeped out of the burial ground and onto neighboring properties. In April 1980, thirteen years after it had said the location was adequate for nuclear-waste burial, and two years after the dump had closed because it was not adequate, the Geological Survey asserted that it was really not the agency's responsibility to say whether it was adequate. In a letter to a concerned resident who lived near the burial ground, a Geological Survey official wrote, "It is not our responsibility to make any determinations as to adequateness of the site. This is the responsibility of the regulatory agencies both of the state and federal government."

The AEC took a similar approach when uranium mill tailings became a public-health issue, suggesting that the states—not the commission or federal government—were responsible for the results of the mining activities the AEC had licensed for years. A commission official explained to a Senate Public Works subcommittee in May 1966, "We would like to say that if there is a long-term problem, we think there should be a long-term solution. And as I said . . . gradually, the mills, the licensing authority, is being turned over to the states. And, moreover, the hazard from radiation, if there is one, comes from radium, which the commission does not regulate, but which the states do."

If there is a lesson to be learned from the West Valleys, Sheffields, and Maxey Flats of America's throwaway nuclear society, it is that even the short-term behavior of radioactive waste is unpredictable. The long-term threat of waste that will remain hazardous over thousands of years is thus incalculable. The most serious danger is not that someone will be exposed to it directly at a waste-storage center or in a transportation mishap. Far more likely, the waste will slowly work its way into the food chain, the water supplies, and the air people breathe, and will thus expose large segments of the population indirectly.

Although much less likely, there is also always the possibility of a nuclear-waste accident like that near Kyshtym, in the Soviet Union, in 1958. To this day, the Soviets have never acknowledged that the accident occurred. No one knows precisely what happened. About all that's certain is that there was an explosion and that rivers and a large land area, covering tens of square miles, possibly hundreds, were contaminated in the Ural Mountains. The people who lived there were permanently relocated.

Zhores A. Medvedev, an exiled Soviet scientist living in Great Britain, first disclosed the incident to the Western world in 1976. At the time, he wrote that "the explosion poured radioactive dust and materials high up into the sky. . . . Strong winds blew the radioactive clouds hundreds of miles away. It was difficult to gauge the extent of the disaster immediately, and no evacuation plan was put into operation right away. Many villages and towns were only ordered to evacuate when the symptoms of radiation sickness were already quite apparent. Tens of thousands of people were affected, hundreds dying, though the real figures have never been made public."

American and British nuclear experts initially dismissed Medvedev's story as fiction. The head of Britain's Atomic Energy Commission labeled it "rubbish," suggesting it would have been impossible for radioactive materials to have spread over such a large area without the West's knowledge. But the contamination has since been confirmed by a variety of independent sources. The most recent verification comes from a March 1983 report prepared for the DOE's Office of Nuclear Waste Isolation by Frank L. Parker, a professor of environmental and water resources engineering at Vanderbilt University and a former waste-management official at the Oak Ridge National Laboratory. Parker, who conducted a search of available Soviet literature and interviews, wrote that people who visited that section of the Ural Mountains "found the area devastated— they are not allowed to drink the water, they are not allowed to fish, they are not allowed to stop, the area has been evacuated."

Medvedev conjectured that the contamination resulted when a nuclear-waste burial ground, where the Soviets had been dumping high-level atomic garbage, including plutonium, exploded, showering the countryside with radioactive debris. Parker offered another explanation. "At present," he said, "the best supposition is that there were many releases of wastes to the river system over time, plus an explosion in the fuel reprocessing plant." Whatever the precise cause, the contamination of Kyshtym is attributable to a radioactive-waste mistake.

That such a mistake has not yet occurred in this country is due more to luck than to superior technology. The United States, like the Soviet Union, continues to rely on makeshift storage methods in the absence of a permanent waste-management system.

3
The Failure
of Reprocessing

THE VISION

The birth of commercial nuclear power was based on a single assumption—that used fuel rods from reactors would be recycled into fresh fuel in a reprocessing plant. It sounded simple enough. Reactors would discard fuel rods by the hundreds of thousands each year. The rods would be dissolved in a chemical solution. Then the reusable uranium and plutonium would be recovered and fashioned into more fuel. The dangerous liquid waste that remained would be converted into a solid form and placed in an underground repository, where it would be isolated from people and the environment for thousands of years.

Without reprocessing, experts in government and industry agreed, there could be no large-scale nuclear society. In fact, nuclear power plants could not even be built unless reprocessing costs were factored into their design. Richard W. Cook, deputy general manager of the AEC, told the Atomic Industrial Forum in October 1957 that the recovery of uranium and plutonium from used fuel rods "must be obtained at a low unit cost if economic nuclear power is to be achieved; the cost of processing must be considered early in the conceptual design of the reactor."

In January 1959, a reprocessing specialist from the Oak Ridge National Laboratory told a subcommittee of Congress's Joint Committee on Atomic Energy, "[W]e have estimated that there will be possibly twenty chemical [reprocessing] plants. . . . [They] can be centrally located so that the shipping distances [from reactors] are not greater than 200 to 500 miles."

The AEC, charged with promoting the growth of nuclear power, later predicted the establishment of reprocessing plants everywhere. "It is not unreasonable to foresee a day," the commission reported in 1965, "when large nuclear power sites may have their own integrated reprocessing plants."

Whatever the number and location of reprocessing facilities, the buildup of fuel rods at power plants was to be avoided. Edward J. Bloch, director of the AEC's production division, advised the Joint Committee on Atomic Energy in May 1958 that used fuel rods could not be allowed to pile up at reactors across the country. "There are some problems in letting any quantity of [fuel rods] accumulate in storage," Bloch said.

Today, a quarter-century later, fuel rods are doing just that. While the nuclear-power industry has spent more than $100 billion for plants and equipment, reprocessing, the necessary centerpiece of American nuclear planning, has crashed—an economic, technological and environmental failure. The AEC's vision of a reprocessing plant connected to every reactor complex did not become a reality. Nor did the Oak Ridge National Laboratory's more modest expectation of twenty such facilities.

Only three commercial plants were ever built. One at Morris, Illinois, never opened, because the owners discovered that it would not work. Another, at Barnwell, South Carolina, was too costly to be finished without government help. The third, and only operating, plant, at West Valley, New York, sputtered along for six years before shutting down in 1972, leaving behind 572,000 gallons of highly radioactive liquid waste and a possible billion-dollar cleanup bill for American taxpayers. With a touch of understatement, the House Committee on Government Operations later concluded that "all seem to have made

an inadequate technological assessment of the waste disposal
problem."

The short life and uneasy death of the West Valley plant
illustrate the failures of reprocessing. On a sunny day in June
1963, with the noontime temperature hovering at 70 degrees,
nearly a thousand people gathered in a cow pasture on the edge
of West Valley, about thirty miles south of Buffalo, for a historic groundbreaking. They were there to celebrate the advent
of the world's first privately owned reprocessing plant, to be
built by Nuclear Fuel Services, a company jointly owned by W.
R. Grace & Company and American Machine & Foundry.

Gov. Nelson A. Rockefeller presided over a grand cere-
mony. The audience assembled around a blue-and-gold striped
tent. A miniature dirigible carried a "Welcome guests" greet-
ing. The crowd included the customary assortment of local,
state, and federal officials, corporation executives, bankers,
chamber of commerce leaders, high school bands, and the curious residents of nearby farms.

Miss Buffalo, Miss Southern Tier, and Miss Southern Erie
County showed in a pageant how reprocessing would work. A
succession of dignitaries spoke with unstinting praise of the
industry to be born on the former farm. J. Peter Grace, president of W. R. Grace & Company, hailed the project as one that
"in the end may well prove to be the most important industrial
advance of the second half of the twentieth century." Rodney
C. Gott, president of American Machine & Foundry, said it
would provide "a prototype for similar centers all over the
world."

A beaming Governor Rockefeller, campaigning for the
1964 Republican presidential nomination, was equally optimistic. "We are launching a unique operation here today which I
regard with pride as a symbol of imagination and foresight on
the part of your state government," said Rockefeller, who had
personally led the drive to bring the new nuclear industry to
New York. "Because of its unique status," Rockefeller said,
"the plant will be one of the prime sources—and the only
non-government source—in the United States of uranium fuel,

plutonium and a wide variety of potentially valuable radioactive byproducts." He added that "many visitors from all parts of the United States and abroad will be attracted to it." At a wave of the governor's hand, a crane operator pressed a button, driving a sixty-foot steel pile, painted blue and gold to match the state's colors, into the ground, to signal the start of construction.

The groundbreaking was not only a political triumph for Nelson Rockefeller. It was also the culmination of a vigorous government campaign to encourage private investment in reprocessing. Throughout the late 1950s, the federal government sought to sell industry on the golden opportunity, a chance to take advantage of this once-secret technology, which it had engineered and was generously making available. No one was buying.

Kenneth E. Fields, the AEC's general manager, told Congress in October 1957 that technical information on reprocessing had been sent to 108 corporations to determine how many might consider going into the business. Only 18 responded and none was interested. "Among the factors which made the investment in chemical reprocessing unattractive," Fields said, were the questionable economics and "the unknowns in the storage and disposal of radioactive wastes generated by the new chemical processes. . . ." Both the AEC and Congress persisted, but industry remained steadfastly opposed. During a Joint Committee on Atomic Energy hearing in February 1960, Rep. Chet Holifield explained the continued reluctance. The AEC "tried to get private industry into . . . fuel reprocessing for years," Holifield said, but "private industry cannot afford to do it. . . . It just simply is not economic."

By the early 1960s, the government had worn down corporate resistance by making the reprocessing business irresistibly easy to enter, especially for Nuclear Fuel Services. The AEC made it easy when it gave the company the reprocessing technology developed to produce plutonium for nuclear weapons. It also gave Nuclear Fuel Services a five-year, multimillion-dollar contract to reprocess used fuel rods from the government's own stockpile, and established a captive utility market for the company by announcing that it would no longer accept fuel rods from commercial reactors, as it had from the first plants. New York State pitched in by acquiring the 3,345-acre West Valley property and leasing it to Nuclear Fuel Services. The state also agreed to assume full responsibility, after the lease expired, for the contaminated plant, the adjoining low-level-radioactive-waste burial grounds, and all the high-level waste generated. Finally, the AEC, New York State, and Congress all ignored the question of what to do with the liquid waste. They merely permitted it to be stored temporarily in underground steel tanks until a permanent solution could be found.

At dedication ceremonies marking West Valley's opening in June 1966, federal officials were every bit as ecstatic as state officials and business leaders had been three years earlier. Presi-

Aerial view of the Nuclear Fuel Services reprocessing plant at West Valley, New York. *U.S. Department of Energy*

dent Lyndon B. Johnson hailed the facility as "a splendid example of government-industry cooperation to bring the benefits of the peaceful atom to our country. It is another instance where the United States government is following the sound policy of turning over to private industry a service for which industry has shown a competence and willingness to perform."

Glenn T. Seaborg, the AEC's chairman, called the plant "an important milestone in the history of the peaceful atom. It will have a significant role in the growth of our nation's economy and should make an important contribution toward a more effective system for the international control of nuclear energy."

WHAT WENT WRONG

Time would prove wrong just about every prediction made about West Valley. From the day it started up, in 1966, until it closed, in 1972, West Valley operated at only one-third of its stated capacity, reprocessing about 640 metric tons of used fuel rods. Actually, that figure exaggerates the plant's record. More than half the fuel rods came from an AEC production reactor and thus were far easier to reprocess than those from utility reactors. Even at the inflated operating ratio, it would have taken the plant a century to reprocess the fuel rods stored at power plants in 1984—and more than five hundred years to reprocess the rods that will have accumulated by the year 2000.

Chronic equipment breakdowns and accidents involving radioactive contamination plagued the plant. Pipes and pumps became clogged with radioactive debris. The ventilation system carried radioactive particles into the lunch room and laundry room. On one occasion, forty-two ruptured fuel rods were placed in a storage pool, where they leaked radioactivity into the water. These fuel rods were retrieved, encased in concrete, and then buried—this even though the government insisted then, as it does now, that dumping high-level waste in the ground is not permitted. A General Accounting Office investigation later concluded that "although this action was not spe-

cifically allowed by the AEC license, AEC was aware of it."
Nuclear Fuel Services said the burial was carried out "at the
direction of the AEC Savannah River Operations Office and in
accordance with AEC security procedures." During the
cleanup of the ruptured fuel rods, Nuclear Fuel Services reported to the AEC that about 165 pounds of uranium was
"unaccounted for."

Spontaneous fires broke out at the plant. Radioactive gases
were released to surrounding communities. Radioactive liquid
seeped out of the burial ground and drained into nearby
streams. One yardstick of the plant's contribution to the countryside came from measurements of nuclear materials in the
Cattaraugus Creek at the time it shut down and seven years
later. Between those two dates, the level of radioactive tritium
found in the creek plunged 98 percent. That of strontium 90
plummeted 99 percent. Radioactive iodine 129 was found in
milk samples from area dairy farms while the plant was running, but was not detected after it closed.

Because of the plant's design, equipment that failed had to
be repaired directly by hand rather than by remote control, as
in government installations. As a result, West Valley was the
country's "dirtiest" plant, one whose workers received a larger
cumulative dose of radiation than any others. Conditions became so bad that Nuclear Fuel Services hired hundreds of
transients each year, many of them from among Buffalo's
unemployed, to repair equipment and perform maintenance
chores in contaminated areas. Some worked just until they
received a radiation dose of three rems, the maximum allowed
by the government for a three-month period. A number of the
temporary workers, who were as young as eighteen, received
the maximum dose in a matter of minutes and were promptly
replaced by a fresh supply of transients. For Nuclear Fuel
Services, there was little choice. Its only other option was to
assign its own, skilled employees to the repair and maintenance
tasks, then lay them off after they had accumulated the allowable radiation dose.

A report by the Nuclear Regulatory Commission, which

along with the Department of Energy took over some of the AEC's functions when that agency was abolished, shows that from 1969 to 1971, the plant's last full year of operation, the number of workers who received annual radiation doses ranging from 1.25 to 12 rems soared by 206 percent, from 186 to 570. As a general rule, a worker is permitted to receive no more than 5 rems a year, although under certain conditions the maximum dose may be 12 rems.* If every American received 1 rem over the course of a year, about 46,000 people could be expected to die eventually of cancer caused by this exposure.

One of Governor Rockefeller's rosy predictions in 1963 did come true. "Many visitors from all parts of the United States and abroad" flocked to West Valley. They went there to ponder how to solidify 572,000 gallons of simmering, high-level radioactive liquid waste, stored deep underground in two steel tanks that in time would deteriorate. They went there to speculate why a steel pan, installed beneath one of the tanks to trap any leaking liquid and prevent it from seeping into area water supplies, developed a crack—a defect that rendered the pan useless but remained unnoticed for several years.

They went there to study how to scrape out the sludge, with a highly concentrated radioactivity measured in millions of curies, that had settled on the bottom of one of the tanks. They went there to puzzle over why water had collected in 750-foot-long trenches, where 2.3 million cubic feet of so-called low-level waste—some of it lethal—had been buried with scientists' assurance that this would never happen.

They went there to assess the options in dealing with the forty-two radioactive fuel rods and other high-level waste that had been buried. And, finally, they went there to mull over the disposition of the reprocessing plant itself. Should it be decontaminated, dismantled, and trucked, piece by piece, to nuclear cemeteries in other states, or should it be entombed in concrete, a radioactive sepulcher?

In many respects, the equipment breakdowns were the

---

*A rem is a standard unit for measuring the biological effect of radiation.

greatest surprise of all. The technology was supposedly perfected. After all, the government had reprocessed fuel rods at
its defense installations since the early 1940s, although all of its
waste, too, was kept in temporary storage. But government and
industry both erred drastically when they assumed that fuel
rods from power plants could be treated like those from military reactors. The two are quite different. The military rods are
used in reactors designed especially to produce plutonium for
weapons. They are left in the reactors only long enough to turn
out the amount of bomb-grade material desired. Utility fuel
rods, by contrast, because they are used to generate electricity,
stay in reactors for a much longer period, leading to a larger
buildup of waste by-products. These by-products make commercial waste far more radioactive than defense waste. Coupled
with differences in the composition of the fuel rods, this renders
commercial reprocessing more difficult and costly, something
the operators of West Valley were the first to learn.

After the plant opened in 1966, it took the owners of Nuclear Fuel Services, W. R. Grace & Company, which held 78
percent of the stock, and American Machine & Foundry, which
held 22 percent, little more than a year to discover that reprocessing's real economics would not match paper projections.
Grace conceded in a report to stockholders in 1968 that "start-
up problems occurred and had more impact on production than
would have been the case with a less complex process. The
result was a loss for the year." Nonetheless, the company remained outwardly confident. "The problems encountered to
date in the operation of this plant have been solved and there
is every reason to expect more reliable operation in the future,"
it reported.

Grace's optimism was unfounded. Without saying it had
failed to achieve a "more reliable operation," Grace told its
stockholders in 1969 that it intended to get out of the reprocessing business that it had entered amid great fanfare and promises
three years earlier. The company explained its decision this
way: "We have often expressed the belief that management not

only needs to recognize new opportunities for profitable growth but also should identify operations or businesses which are no longer compatible with the company's long-range objectives. In accordance with this belief, several units have been sold or are the subject of negotiations for sale. . . . Contemplated sales in 1969 include the remaining . . . interest in Nuclear Fuel Services."

That year, the Getty Oil Company acquired the stock of Nuclear Fuel Services and became the new owner of the world's only private reprocessing plant. Getty brought a fresh enthusiasm to West Valley. Within months, the company announced plans to expand reprocessing capacity to "three tons per day" in order "to keep pace with the increasing construction of nuclear-powered generating plants."

But Getty fared no better than its predecessors. After it had reprocessed all the fuel rods for which it had contracts, Nuclear Fuel Services shut down the plant in 1972. At the time, the company said that it intended to enlarge capacity from 300 to 600 metric tons a year—essentially the same production increase announced in 1969 and never implemented—and to make other modifications to improve waste handling, reduce worker exposure to radiation, and remedy operating defects.

The planned two-year shutdown came just as the government imposed tougher requirements on nuclear facilities. While the company studied the cost of complying with the revised regulations, work on the modernization program stalled. Finally, in 1976, Nuclear Fuel Services informed the New York State authorities that it intended, as the terms of its lease provided, to turn over all radioactive waste at the site to the state and get out of the reprocessing business.

West Valley should have served as a lesson. Instead, federal officials ignored the record and continued to talk of reprocessing as a viable, ongoing business. It was essential to keep up the pretense. To do otherwise would have been to admit that what they had been saying publicly for two decades was not true. Perhaps never in recent American history have so many government officials talked of programs as though they existed when, in truth, they did not, and when there was little expectation they would.

In April 1973, a year after West Valley closed, Frank K. Pittman, director of the AEC's division of waste management and transportation, assured a Senate Appropriations subcommittee, "Every bit of commercial waste generated [from reprocessing] will be solidified and placed in an easily manageable form right from the very beginning. Federal regulations require that the solidified waste be shipped to the AEC for permanent management within ten years of its generation. The first few canisters will be delivered in 1983. . . ."

In May 1976, one month after Nuclear Fuel Services decided to abandon the business, Elliot L. Richardson, chairman of the Federal Energy Resources Council, gave this account of government waste plans to a Joint Committee on Atomic Energy subcommittee: "Our present assumption, Mr. Chairman, is that the processing up through to the stage of waste solidification would be private. As I understand it, there would be a

The idle control room of the defunct reprocessing plant at West Valley. *Philadelphia Inquirer / Nick Kelsh*

financial return to the commercial energy-related industry through the reprocessing of the [used] fuel. . . ."

All seemed to believe that if they said it often enough their dreams of reprocessing and solidification would come true. But they didn't. And that could have been anticipated. As Congressman Holifield accurately noted in 1960, private industry was not the least bit interested in reprocessing. That it became interested was a testimonial to the persistence of the AEC and to the smorgasbord of benefits it offered.

After the collapse of West Valley, reprocessing advocates focused their hopes on the Barnwell Nuclear Fuel Plant in South Carolina. Unveiled in 1968, Barnwell was supposed to reprocess five time more fuel rods than West Valley. This goal was originally announced by the Allied Corporation, the diversified chemical, oil, gas, aerospace, and electronics conglomerate. Eventually, the company picked up two equally impressive partners, the Gulf Oil Corporation and the Royal Dutch/Shell Group. The three made up Allied–General Nuclear Services, in which Allied held a 50 percent interest and Gulf and Shell 25 percent each.

Construction started on the main plant in March 1971, with much the same promise and governmental assistance that had given rise to West Valley. The 1,587-acre site was carved out of the federal government's neighboring Savannah River plant property, the huge nuclear-weapons complex that boasted the state's largest payroll. At the groundbreaking, South Carolina's Gov. John C. West, a Democrat, was every bit as optimistic as the Republican Rockefeller had been eight years earlier. "Today we mark the beginning of a project which makes the State of South Carolina the nuclear capital of the United States and the free world," the governor said. He added, "[T]he most deadly weapon ever created by man is being converted for the benefit of mankind. Under these fine hands, we will begin to reap the truly great potential of nuclear energy."

Four years and $250 million later, Barnwell was about 90 percent complete when it became clear that it would never survive as a commercial undertaking. Although all the build-

ings were erected, the waste-storage tanks built, and the reprocessing equipment installed, two required auxiliary components
had yet to be added—separate facilities to solidify both the
liquid waste and the extracted plutonium. To rescue its faltering
investment, Allied-General quietly began talks with government officials early in 1975 to try to secure federal funds to
finish the plant. The secret negotiations are spelled out in a
series of memoranda and letters between the company and the
Energy Research and Development Administration.

ERDA staff members looked favorably on a proposal that
called for the government to invest up to a quarter of a billion
dollars. Under the plan, the agency was to build the facilities
and take full responsibility for solidifying the liquid waste and
plutonium. During their private talks, ERDA officials and Allied-General executives agreed, according to a memorandum
dated May 8, 1975, that Barnwell should "be designated as a
demonstration plant" and thereby be "exempted from licensing
regulatory requirements." In another memorandum, dated
May 19, 1975, energy planners justified a federal subsidy for the
private venture by saying that ERDA was "providing encouragement to preserve the nuclear option in the future national
energy picture."

Government and industry were talking out of both sides of
their mouths. In public, reprocessing and waste solidification
were called proven technologies. In private, it was said the
technologies had yet to be demonstrated. An ERDA official, in
a September 5, 1975, letter to the president of Allied–General
Nuclear Services, summarized as follows the understanding
reached by the agency and the company following a series of
meetings: "No private investor will commit funds for construction of such facilities without assurance of significant participation by ERDA until all parts of the fuel cycle have been well
demonstrated. . . . Each demonstration system would include
all steps, i.e., reprocessing [including waste solidification].
. . . There must be a production scale demonstration of waste
solidification, and ERDA must provide for acceptance of the
solidified waste."

The government bailout eventually fell through. Because of this and continuing uncertainty about the passage of final federal regulations, the plant was never finished. Even if it had been completed, there is some doubt whether Barnwell would have been an advance over West Valley. In fact, there are contrary signs. A report by the Argonne National Laboratory in September 1981 offered this comparison: "Because of the fundamental philosophical, dimensional and fabrication details for the design, full scale operation of the [Barnwell] plant would be accompanied from the moment of start-up by inordinately high operation and maintenance risks. With respect to operation and maintenance, the [Barnwell] design and construction is unfortunately no better than that of the Nuclear Fuel Services plant [at West Valley] in the event of mishaps in the liquid handling parts."

Although the report noted that Barnwell's owners were confident that the plant would function properly, it said that "independent groups which have reviewed the [Barnwell plant] are fearful that it could suffer the same fate as Nuclear Fuel Services' West Valley plant and give the industry a further black eye. Specifically, they fear that the first serious contamination in the liquid section at the facility might require that the entire plant be written off from further fuel reprocessing and, perhaps, other uses as well."

In closing, the Argonne report unwittingly touched on a question that government and industry might well have addressed in the earliest days of the nation's waste planning. After itemizing the technical and economic liabilities of the South Carolina facility, the report concluded, "Thus, the question arises as to whether the [Barnwell plant] should ever be completed and permitted to start up."

To be sure, Barnwell has its supporters. When parts of the critical Argonne study appeared in a Department of Energy booklet distributed publicly in January 1982, federal energy officials rushed to the plant's defense. Shelby T. Brewer, assistant secretary for nuclear energy, dismissed the reported shortcomings in a two-page letter sent to recipients of the publica-

tion. Saying that the opinions expressed in the article were
"inappropriate for this publication and their inclusion was the
result of an incomplete staff review," Brewer declared, "[A]ll
things considered, I do not believe there are any intrinsic defi-
ciencies in the Barnwell plant design that will preclude its
successful operation, and I am confident that any problems
which may develop can be overcome."

Similar support has come from the engineering community.
In an article published in *Nuclear Engineering International* in
August 1982, three officials of Bechtel National Inc., a part of
Bechtel Group Inc., the San Francisco–based global engineering and construction company, described Barnwell's importance as follows: "The most expeditious and cost-effective approach to re-establishing commercial reprocessing is to
complete Barnwell. The reality is that Barnwell exists." Bechtel
was the company that designed Barnwell, and it was the general
contractor at West Valley.

In the end, the arguments of DOE officials, Bechtel executives, and others with a vested interest came to naught. Reality
caught up with Barnwell just as it had with West Valley. If the
definitive history of radioactive waste is ever written, July 31,
1983, will probably go down as the official date of death for
commercial reprocessing. On that day, federal funds ran out for
research projects that had been carried out at the Barnwell
Nuclear Fuel Plant, keeping the facility alive in the hopes that
someone, somewhere would acquire it for the purpose for which
it was built. That was not to be.

After nearly two years of frantic negotiations, would-be
buyers—foreign utilities, a consortium of American utilities,
and major corporations—all dropped out of the bidding. A
Department of Energy official, seeking to put the best possible
light on the last days of an industry that did not survive its
infancy, said during the summer of 1983, "We had had hopes,
and in fact the secretary of energy is on record as having said
that we stand ready to negotiate with any industry entity which
chooses to come forth with a proposal on preserving the plant.
. . . As of today, we have no such proposal. We're not aware

that any specific proposal is in the offing. . . . I think it's fair to say with each waning day the prospects would appear to be decreasing."

George T. Stribling, vice-president of regulatory and public affairs for Allied–General Nuclear Services, the company that owns Barnwell, said the plant started in 1983 with about 300 employees. "We're down to something well under 150 now," he said in November, "and all of the people here have been given notice of the dates beyond which their services will not be required, so that we'll be down to probably less than ten people by year-end. . . . Barring something unforeseen, we will have a padlock on the door, and all cleaned out, by [then]."

And so it was. In the summer of 1984, a skeleton staff of three was all that remained at the Barnwell Nuclear Fuel Plant.

4
The Bid
to Revive Reprocessing

BOMB FACTORIES

On May 18, 1974, India detonated an atomic bomb 330 feet underground in the Thar Desert, a remote section of Rajasthan State along the Pakistan border. The explosion was of roughly the same magnitude as that which leveled Nagasaki and killed 35,000 persons. It enrolled India as the sixth member of the once-exclusive world nuclear-weapons club. Indians generally applauded their government's achievement; the rest of the world denounced it. In time, the nuclear blast would have far greater consequences in the United States than in India.

For two decades Americans had listened to their leaders speak of two distinctly different atoms—the peaceful atom and the warlike atom. The United States, the politicians said, would keep tight control over the warlike atom so that it could never become a basic weapon in every nation's arsenal. At the same time the United States would export the peaceful atom to all the friendly countries on earth so that they, too, could enjoy the benefits of nuclear energy. It was perfectly safe to do this, they said, because there was no connection between the peaceful atom and the warlike atom.

India's bomb, built with a reactor, fuel, and technology

supplied by Canada and the United States to enable the impoverished Indians to generate badly needed electricity, obliterated the semantic illusion. The Indian Atomic Energy Commission had obtained the plutonium for the bomb by reprocessing fuel rods. In doing so, it graphically demonstrated that every nuclear power plant is a potential bomb factory.

Mitchell W. Sharp, Canada's external affairs minister, summarized the feelings of a bitter Canadian government. "All of this assistance," he said, "was intended to help India in meeting the critical energy needs of the Indian people and was provided to, and accepted by, India on the basis that it would be used for peaceful purposes only."

David E. Lilienthal, the first chairman of the AEC, cited America's contribution to the spread of nuclear weapons when he testified before the Senate Committee on Government Operations in January 1976: "The tragic fact is that the atomic arms race is today proceeding at a more furious and a more insane pace than ever. Proliferation of capabilities to produce nuclear weapons of mass destruction is reaching terrifying proportions. And now, the prospect of the reprocessing or recycling of nuclear wastes to produce weapons material from scores of atomic power plants is close upon us. . . . The fact is that we, the United States, our public agencies and our private manufacturers, have been and are the world's major proliferators."

Proliferation began with the best of intentions. President Dwight D. Eisenhower delivered his landmark "Atoms for Peace" speech at the United Nations in December 1953, offering to unlock the secrets of nuclear technology for the world. As with many of the government's early nuclear decisions, little thought was given to the consequences of the new policy. Gerard C. Smith, a special AEC assistant at the time and later the Department of State's top disarmament negotiator, described reactions to Eisenhower's proposal during a talk in April 1982. Recalling that he was asked to read the president's speech to other government officials, who had not had advance notice, Smith said, "One knowledgeable [AEC] commissioner remarked that it was 'a thoroughly dishonest proposal.' Later, when Molotov [Soviet deputy premier Vyacheslav Molotov] protested to a dubious John Foster Dulles that the proposal would result in the spread worldwide of stockpiles of weapon grade material, I had to explain to Dulles that Molotov had been better informed technically than he. Subsequently, the Soviets asked how we proposed to stop this spread. The best we could reply was 'ways could be found.' "

By the 1970s, the nuclear threat extended beyond the possibility that any number of countries could, like India, assemble and explode their own atomic bombs. At least half a dozen other nations began to acquire the technology to build weapons after the Indian test—from Argentina and Brazil, in South America, to South Korea, in the Far East. With the projected worldwide growth in nuclear power plants, stockpiles of plutonium would accumulate accordingly if the used fuel rods were reprocessed as planned. Its routine shipment from one country to another in a global nuclear-reprocessing economy would offer a tempting target for terrorists.

A Ford Foundation study in 1974 warned that plutonium could be used as an explosive device or poisonous agent. "In criminal hands," the foundation said, "plutonium could be a danger not only as material for a bomb, but also in a relatively simple radiation dispersal device. Because it is so extremely toxic, the amounts that could pose a threat to society are very small. A few ounces, or even a fraction of an ounce, of the stuff could be a deadly risk to everyone working in a large office building or factory, if it were effectively dispersed."

Most members of Congress publicly professed an interest in halting the spread of nuclear materials. Yet few were willing to enact legislation curbing the sale of the technology. They reasoned that if American companies did not peddle nuclear systems to anyone who would buy them, businesses in other countries—notably France and West Germany—would willingly do so. As a result, the United States, France, and West Germany all continued to push the sale of nuclear technology after the Indian bomb test.

But on October 28, 1976, five days before the presidential election, President Gerald R. Ford, trailing his Democratic rival, Jimmy Carter, in the polls, announced a sudden reversal in policy. Declaring that "avoidance of proliferation must take precedence over economic interests," President Ford ordered a temporary ban on commercial reprocessing. "I have decided," he said, "that the United States should no longer regard reprocessing of used nuclear fuel to produce plutonium as a necessary and inevitable step in the nuclear fuel cycle." Ford's policy shift was a slightly weaker version of one that Carter had called for in a speech delivered months earlier. The belated decision did not help him on election day.

Three months after President Carter moved into the White House, he extended Ford's ban and wrote the obituary for the Barnwell Nuclear Fuel Plant. "We will defer indefinitely the commercial reprocessing and recycling of the plutonium produced in the United States nuclear power programs," Carter said, adding that Barnwell "will receive neither federal encouragement nor funding for its completion as a reprocessing facility."

The atomic community made much of Carter's decision, suggesting that the policy turnabout was by itself responsible for the industry's failure. In fact, industry representatives have long complained that constantly changing regulations killed private reprocessing. They mention, for example, the 1970 order that required conversion of liquid waste to a solid form. This ruling came too late to affect West Valley, which is why 572,000 gallons of liquid waste remain to be dealt with there. Later still, federal officials announced that the plutonium extracted from fuel rods also should be solidified. That requirement was cited by Barnwell's owners as a reason for seeking federal assistance to complete the plant.

Some regulations may have been overly restrictive. But many were necessary and long overdue. Solidification, especially, was a step that many believe industry should have taken on its own, since storage of liquid waste was always considered an interim measure. In any event, long before regulations became a source of industry carping, reprocessing had proved an economic failure.

Although Carter's deferral seemed to be the end of commercial reprocessing, its advocates still had hopes for Barnwell. To that end, Barnwell's owners secured a multimillion-dollar federal contract to study systems to safeguard plutonium and prevent its diversion or theft. The research work allowed Allied-General to maintain the plant for the next four years.

Then in January 1981, President Ronald Reagan, who was friendly to reprocessing and had fewer concerns about weapons proliferation, took office. Nine months later, he reversed the nation's reprocessing course once again and promised government assistance. "I am lifting the indefinite ban which previous administrations placed on commercial reprocessing activities. . . . In addition, we will pursue consistent, long-term policies concerning reprocessing of spent fuel from nuclear power reactors," the president said, "and eliminate regulatory impediments to commercial interest in this technology, while ensuring adequate safeguards."

IMPOSSIBLE ECONOMICS

So it was that the Reagan administration reverted to a policy of the 1950s, when government first encouraged industry to invest in reprocessing. There was one major difference, though, between the two periods. In the 1950s, everyone had hopes—if no practical experience—that commercial reprocessing would succeed. By the 1980s, the evidence was indisputable that reprocessing was not economically viable.

West Valley had proven that. W. R. Grace, American Machine & Foundry, and Getty Oil all lost money at it. If anything, the economics of reprocessing have deteriorated further since that time. A *Philadelphia Inquirer* analysis of the plant's performance, together with other available data, indicates that for reprocessing to be a successful business in 1984 uranium derived from it would have to sell for upward of $400 a pound. Since uranium mined from the earth sells for $23 a pound on the spot market—and imports have been limited to prop up the price—there would be no buyers for reprocessed uranium. In that sense, the tons of uranium in used fuel rods are like the tons of gold in seawater. The gold is certainly valuable, but the cost of extracting it far outweighs the value.

By the time of Reagan's reversal, even Barnwell's owners had stopped claiming that a private company could earn a profit at reprocessing. James A. Buckham, executive vice-president of the company, told a House Science and Technology subcommittee in March 1981 that "whatever Barnwell's future role, it seems clear that federal ownership is an essential prerequisite to further development." A month later, another executive, Brian D. Forrow, senior vice-president and general counsel for Allied, was equally grim during an appearance before a Senate Energy and Natural Resources subcommittee. "The crucial question today is whether reprocessing can take place under private ownership," Forrow said. "In our judgment, the answer to that question is an unequivocal no, not only for Barnwell's present owners, but also for any other private investors." More recently, Buckham said flatly in a May 24, 1983, letter to the DOE, "We share your view that the Barnwell Nuclear Fuel Plant is a vital national asset, but as you know we do not believe [it] can be completed and operated on a commercial basis."

Given that background, it was really no surprise when electric utilities declined to invest in Barnwell as a source of uranium after President Reagan took office. A spokesman for the Commonwealth Edison Company in Chicago, the nation's largest generator of nuclear electricity, explained, "If you could get a hundred utilities together, if there were a hundred interested, each utility would have to justify its contribution based on expected return of investment. And the way the math works now, that's just not there. Even if I only had to invest $20, if I'm looking at a zero return and nothing but risk, how can I justify that to my ratepayers? It doesn't matter into how many small pieces you cut it, the point is that the return's got to be there."

Just how bad is the math? At the time that West Valley shut down in 1972, Nuclear Fuel Services charged $23,400 for a metric ton of reprocessed uranium, according to court records. (A metric ton is 2,204.62 pounds.) Four years later, the company said that in order to reopen the plant it would have to charge $1,010,300 for a metric ton of uranium—a price increase of 4,218 percent.

The figures may be easier to understand if they are applied to a more familiar form of energy, such as crude oil. In 1973, oil produced in the United States sold for an average of $3.89 a barrel. (A barrel contains forty-two gallons.) By 1984, crude oil had risen to $29 a barrel. But if its price had risen at the rate of that for reprocessed uranium, crude oil in January 1984 would have sold for $168 a barrel. And that may understate the case because the uranium price was set in 1976, before the country entered an era of double-digit inflation. Adjusted for inflation, the $1,010,300 charge announced in 1976 would be more than $1,800,000 in 1984. If the price of crude oil had risen at the same rate, it would be $297 a barrel. Gasoline would be selling for $29 a gallon.

Advocates of reprocessing use another set of numbers. They argue that a plant could operate profitably if mined uranium sold for something less than $50 a pound. This is hard to reconcile with the reprocessing facility at La Hague, France, which charges more than $300 a pound and is, in addition, supported by the French government. Reprocessing's backers insist, too, that West Valley's performance is not a proper yardstick. A newer and larger plant like Barnwell would be more efficient. But that is what supporters said about West Valley. In documents filed with the AEC prior to its opening, Nuclear Fuel Services predicted a gross annual profit of $4.6 million. Instead, the company suffered multimillion-dollar losses.

Despite overwhelming evidence that commercial reprocessing could not be profitable, the Reagan administration nonetheless mounted a campaign to revive the industry. Until he left office in 1982, Secretary of Energy James B. Edwards, a one-time oral surgeon and former Republican governor of South Carolina who once acknowledged that he was "not an expert on energy matters," was the administration's biggest booster of Barnwell. Following the secretary's lead, the DOE staff pressed for nuclear-fuel reprocessing by private industry, while conceding that it was not a comercially attractive business.

Shelby T. Brewer, assistant secretary for nuclear energy, outlined the contradictory policy during an appearance before members of two Senate committees in October 1981. Pointing out that the department's strategy was to encourage reprocessing "as a private sector venture," Brewer said, "[I]ndustry must play the central role. As you know, the administration's policy is that reprocessing is appropriately a private sector responsibility." Brewer then had this exchange with James A. McClure, Republican senator from Idaho:

McClure—"What are the incentives for reprocessing?"

Brewer—"There are three principal incentives. One is to recover the fissile material, plutonium and uranium. We need the plutonium to carry out the breeder program and indeed to deploy the breeder when the economics are right for that. You will recover the uranium, and the enriched uranium left in the fuel can be recycled for further use in light-water reactors. You also decongest the spent fuel congestion."

McClure—"Are those incentives sufficient to lead to commercial activity?"

Brewer—"Those are national incentives. They are not the sort of incentives a private corporation doing bottom-line accounting would account for."

Indeed they are not. Brewer's statement that uranium from reprocessing could be recycled for further use in existing reactors was a big selling point in the late 1950s and early 1960s. It has no economic merit today. The reason: the United States is awash in uranium, and the last thing the industry needs is a fresh supply from a more expensive source. That would be roughly akin to a municipality's building a desalinization plant to make ocean water drinkable, rather than tapping existing reservoirs and groundwater supplies.

Even the Edison Electric Institute, the electric-utility trade group, which supports Barnwell as a "national asset" for the future, concedes there is a glut. "There's so much uranium around because of delays and cancellations [of new power plants]—around meaning above the ground—that utilities are selling to each other off of inventories," said Steven P. Kraft, a spokesman for the institute.

So much is around that uranium mining has fallen on its hardest times ever. An official of the DOE, the same department that has been lobbying for Barnwell to open and turn out more uranium, had this response when asked what was happening in the uranium-mining business: "There's just nothing. It's as simple as that. The mines are closed down or on standby. The mills [that process the ore] are closed down or on standby. There are a few that are operating, but few." Gulf Oil symbolizes the industry's plight. In its 1982 annual report to stockholders, Gulf said that "demand and prices slid to seven-year lows" and that the company's only "remaining uranium mine at Mount Taylor, New Mexico, was placed on standby status in November [of 1982] due to the depressed state of the uranium market." Conditions have not changed since then. Gulf told stockholders in March 1984 that the company had contracts to supply twenty million pounds of uranium through 1991 and that its inventory and supply agreements were "sufficient to cover all but approximately four million pounds of this commitment." The Mount Taylor mine was still closed, and would be for the foreseeable future.

Nothing like this had been expected. As recently as 1975, a task force assembled by the Energy Research and Development Administration warned that the uranium industry might not be able to satisfy the anticipated surge in demand. Noting that "there is an increasing concern over the adequacy of uranium supplies by the mid to late 1980s," the task force said that industry would have to step up its exploratory drilling to find all the uranium that would be needed. "In addition to the pronounced increase in drilling rates required," the task force concluded, "the mining and milling industry must open up hundreds of new mines as well as build about sixty new mills over the same time frame. It is estimated that this will require capital investment of [about] $18 billion."

The grandiose forecast was predicated on energy growth

rates of the past. But the oil crises of the 1970s rendered those calculations meaningless. The demand for electricity, on the rise for years, suddenly flattened as the public began to conserve. Utilities found their customers rebelling at rate increases to finance nuclear plants. On top of that, more and more communities became suspicious of plants to build reactors in their midst, especially after the accident at the Three Mile Island plant at Middletown, Pennsylvania, in March 1979. Suddenly, the boom in nuclear power was over. No more new plants were commissioned. Many that had been ordered were canceled by cost-conscious utilities. Some under construction were scrapped.

As a consequence, the predicted demand for uranium never materialized. According to DOE statistics, uranium production in 1982 plunged to its second-lowest level since 1958. A total of 10,000 tons was mined, down 35 percent from 15,600 tons in 1981. And that was down 22 percent from the peak output of 20,000 tons in 1980.

LURE OF THE BREEDER

When a uranium shortage became a uranium glut, federal officials changed tactics in their drive to open Barnwell. They began to talk of buying the other by-product of reprocessing, plutonium, for the breeder reactor. A breeder is an old and cherished dream of the nuclear establishment. It operates much like existing reactors except that it runs on plutonium rather than uranium and is designed to generate more fuel than it uses. Hence the name. Some politicians and a hard core of scientists have been enthralled by the notion of an endless energy machine since the earliest days of atomic power. But because it would be fueled by plutonium, a breeder would create safety and environmental hazards that do not exist at conventional nuclear plants. Not only could such a facility explode; it would turn out enough plutonium each year to manufacture dozens of atomic bombs.

Back in the 1950s, when the AEC pushed reprocessing, it

also extolled the breeder. Federal officials envisioned breeders supplying most of the nation's electricity before the century was out. They endorsed the idea in part because they were sure uranium supplies were insufficient to keep conventional reactors going. Walter H. Zinn, director of the Argonne National Laboratory outside Chicago and a dedicated breeder proponent, cautioned the Joint Committee on Atomic Energy in July 1953 that "a power industry based on the outright consumption of [uranium] would have only a brief life, for the supply of uranium on present projection is inadequate."

During those years, some electric utilities lobbied Congress to allow commercial development of atomic power in general and of the breeder in particular. A consortium of more than two dozen utilities, industrial corporations, and engineering and construction companies urged the Joint Committee on Atomic Energy in July 1953 to let it develop a breeder with private capital. Walker L. Cisler, president of the Detroit Edison Company, told the committee that "if the present work shows a breeder reactor can be commercially competitive, and the law permits, the group intends, with private funds, to design, construct, test and operate a full-sized breeder reactor."

The consortium eventually built a modest-scale breeder, the Enrico Fermi, about thirty miles south of Detroit. The reactor started up in 1963, several years behind schedule, but operated only intermittently because of continuing mechanical problems. When the cooling system jammed in October 1966, the reactor core partially melted, as had the core in the government's first test breeder a decade earlier. A plant engineer later described the incident as the time "we almost lost Detroit." That was the end of industry's brief flirtation with the breeder, at least using its own money. The damaged core was shipped years later to a federal installation—as the damaged core from Three Mile Island will be. Thousands of gallons of radioactive sodium from the Detroit breeder are still sitting in barrels, awaiting final disposition.*

---

*See page 335 for detailed note.

Fermi's failure did not discourage supporters. Although industry would never finance another on its own, it was willing to make a modest contribution if the federal government put up most of the money. The Joint Committee on Atomic Energy was still preaching the miracle of the breeder, and Congress in 1972 authorized construction of a test reactor. Under an agreement struck with electric utilities, industry would contribute $250 million and the government would pick up the rest of the $700 million tab, plus all cost overruns. The plant, to be built on the Clinch River in Tennessee, was expected to begin operation in 1980.

Construction was never started, as one technical obstacle after another cropped up. When President Carter deferred commercial reprocessing in 1977, he also canceled the breeder, calling it "a large and unnecessarily expensive project which, when completed, would be technically obsolete and economically unsound."

After President Reagan took office and ended the reprocessing ban, he also revived the breeder, describing it as "essential to ensure our preparedness for longer-term nuclear power needs." Faced with mounting congressional opposition, Reagan marshaled support. The chief arm-twister was Howard H. Baker, Jr., the Republican Senate majority leader, whose home state of Tennessee would benefit from the project. Work resumed at Clinch River in 1983. But in May of that year the House voted to cut off funds, and in October the Senate beat back an attempt by Baker and Senator McClure of Idaho to rescue the venture with a $1.5 billion appropriation.

Breeder enthusiasts may yet make one more attempt to win federal funds. Although success appears unlikely, Clinch River has died and been resurrected before. The government has already spent more than $1.5 billion on it. About 90 percent of the hardware has been purchased. The site is cleared and a hundred-foot-deep pit the size of three football fields has been dug. This is history's most expensively engineered hole in the ground. It will cost an additional quarter of a billion dollars or so to terminate the project.

Like so many others in Washington, President Reagan was captivated by the alchemist's lure of a power plant that breeds more fuel than it burns. But, in fact, the statistics on this crucial selling point, even if they measured up to all the claims of partisans, are not impressive. For years, France has been committed to nuclear development at any cost. Although this commitment is just beginning to show signs of wavering, France is building its own breeder, called the Super Phénix.

If everything works as French and American experts say it will, thirty years after Super Phénix begins generating electricity, it will have produced enough additional plutonium to start up a second breeder. At that rate, if the United States put not one but three breeders into operation, it would take 120 years for those plants to multiply to forty-eight. And that number is overstated because the initial units would have been scrapped by then, their useful working lives long past. By way of comparison, during the 25 years from 1958 to 1983, the United States placed seventy-seven conventional reactors in service.

Since the price of Clinch River was first calculated, costs have soared. Projections have ranged from $3.2 billion by the DOE to $9 billion by the General Accounting Office. The utilities, which originally agreed to pay for 36 percent of the project, have resisted any further investment—at least without government guarantees—so that industry's share has shrunk to 8 percent or less. Whether the experimental breeder would cost $3.2 billion or $9 billion, it would be the single most expensive, most heavily subsidized energy-producing plant in the nation's history.

Several years ago, analysts at an international nuclear conference estimated that a conventional reactor would remain cheaper to operate than a breeder unless the price of uranium averaged $181 a pound over the reactor's lifetime. That works out to nearly eight times more than the spot-market price of $23 a pound. What's more, the $181 was figured in 1978 dollars. In 1984 dollars, the price would be $280.

Standing alone, the numbers mean little. But consider what happens when the same economic conditions are applied to crude oil, which supplies 43 percent of the country's total energy needs. Suppose that Congress provided a multimillion-dollar subsidy to a company called the All-American Breeder Oil Company to produce crude oil from some exotic new source. Using the uranium-price projections, the All-American Breeder Oil Company would sell its oil for $353 a barrel—that is, if it could find any buyers, since the average market price of conventional crude oil in early 1984 was $29 a barrel.

REAGAN'S RESCUE ATTEMPT

If a breeder is not economical, if none will be built before the twenty-first century or ever, if there is a uranium glut, if private industry refuses to invest in reprocessing without a subsidy—then why has the Reagan administration labored so feverishly to open the Barnwell Nuclear Fuel Plant? The most likely answer is some combination of the following reasons:

• To aid Barnwell's owners, who invested $362 million in the facility only to find it too expensive to complete.

• To aid American reactor manufacturers, namely, the General Electric Company and the Westinghouse Electric Corporation, whose sales in the United States have dried up and who have encountered stiff resistance in foreign markets.

• To meet the needs of the Department of Defense, which under President Reagan's planned military buildup will require large volumes of plutonium for nuclear weapons.

• To assist other countries where resistance to nuclear power has so hardened that new plants cannot be built until a reprocessing industry is established to handle the used fuel rods.

First, the state of domestic manufacturers. From 1970 through 1975, Westinghouse sold thirty-one reactors; General Electric, twenty-four; the Babcock & Wilcox Company, seven; and the Combustion Engineering Company, nineteen. In the next six years, through 1981, Westinghouse sold two reactors and Babcock & Wilcox sold one. General Electric, the other major builder, sold none. Overall, domestic sales of nuclear power plants plummeted 96 percent, from eighty-one to three, between the two periods.

John F. Welch, Jr., chairman and chief executive officer of General Electric, was blunt when he met with Wall Street analysts for a question-and-answer session in December 1981. Asked whether GE would enter the nuclear business if it were just starting up, Welch replied with a firm no. The company summed up the future in its 1982 annual report: "GE does not anticipate recovery of the domestic nuclear steam supply systems market in the foreseeable future."

The picture is much the same for overseas markets. From 1970 to 1975, Westinghouse sold twenty reactors to foreign utilities, and GE sold fifteen. From 1976 to 1981, Westinghouse sold seven reactors abroad, GE and the others none. Thus, foreign sales fell 80 percent, from thirty-five to seven reactors. The Atomic Industrial Forum reported the ongoing dismal results in its 1983 annual worldwide survey. "As in the previous year," the trade association said, "United States reactor manufacturers were shut out, with no new orders originating in this country and no United States manufacturers winning a foreign contract."

Although there is little likelihood of a resurgence in reactor sales in this country—indeed, cancellations continue to trickle in—there remain large, untapped markets abroad. To promote nuclear power in foreign countries, and with it the sale of American technology, federal officials have offered a variety of inducements. One of them is reprocessing.

The United States government, which promised reprocessing to American utilities in the 1950s, to persuade them to build nuclear power plants, has been making the same offer to foreign countries. Three members of President Reagan's cabinet—Secretary of Energy Edwards, Secretary of State Alexander M. Haig, and Commerce Secretary Malcolm Baldridge—sent a diplomatic cable to the Mexican government in January 1982 offering broad-based support for the development of nuclear power there. "We ascribe very high priority to working with Mexican authorities to develop a stable and long-term framework within which United States industry and the United States government can provide nuclear fuel, reactor components and other equipment, services, technology and manpower training and development," the cable said.

The three cabinet officers outlined a variety of nuclear services that the United States would make available. They urged the purchase of American-made reactors because United States companies have "an unsurpassed capability to assist the Mexican program." And they invited Mexico to reprocess its nuclear fuel at Barnwell or to acquire an interest in the plant. "We are encouraging the establishment by the private sector of a commercial reprocessing industry within the United States," the cable continued. "Such reprocessing services may become available to other countries in the future, and we would welcome Mexico's interest in acquiring such services or in becoming a close partner in United States ventures."

Other Reagan administration officials fanned out around the world to sell American technology. W. Kenneth Davis, deputy secretary of energy, accompanied manufacturers and engineers on a sales trip to Yugoslavia. Reporting on that trip and the administration's overall efforts on behalf of nuclear power, Davis told a business conference in St. Charles, Illinois, in April 1982, "I have just returned from Yugoslavia, where I participated in a nuclear seminar with Yugoslav officials, aimed at convincing them that the United States is the best possible partner for their nuclear power development plans. . . . We had a constructive seminar and while there, we invited Yugoslav representatives to visit the United States to see first hand our capabilities." Davis reiterated the administration's commitment to reprocessing, declaring that "foreign partners should be encouraged to participate as appropriate in commercial reprocessing ventures within the United States. The prospect of such participation could be an important selling point to potential cutomers for American made nuclear reactors."

What would happen to the radioactive waste that would be

produced if Mexico, West Germany, and Yugoslavia took up the United States' reprocessing offer? A State Department spokesman, when asked about that, replied, "If we did in fact agree to reprocess fuel for some other country, I assume we would handle the waste products the way we already are handling those in our government program." That means that the federal government, which has been storing high-level radioactive waste temporarily for forty years, would take in high-level waste from foreign countries and store it temporarily, too.

There is, of course, an option other than reprocessing that could be offered to foreign buyers of American reactors. As the same State Department spokesman said, "Another alternative would clearly be simply to take back the spent [used] fuel, but do nothing with it, simply store it." That is what electric utilities have been doing since the first reactor started up in 1957 at Shippingport, Pennsylvania, all the time waiting for the government to devise a permanent-storage plan.

Although the United States does not need more nuclear waste, or more used fuel rods, or more uranium, it could use more plutonium to make more bombs. There are but two obstacles to that use of commercial reactor fuel—one technological, the other political. Both could be overcome.

Over the years, Congress has maintained that civilian and military uses of nuclear power must be kept separate, in order to set an example for the rest of the world. Not until 1982, however, did lawmakers prohibit the reprocessing of commercial reactor fuel to produce plutonium for the military. Even then, the ban was accomplished through a parliamentary maneuver, with an amendment tacked onto NRC appropriations bills. Some believe the policy could be reversed if Barnwell were to start up. They reason that if Barnwell began reprocessing used fuel rods, its operators would have to store the plutonium for the day it would be needed by commercial breeder reactors, if they are ever built.

In the meantime, if the DOE, which operates all nuclear production facilities for the Department of Defense, found it difficult to meet military requirements for plutonium, the growing stockpile at Barnwell would offer an attractive alternative that could be tapped for "national security" interests. On this point, the Department of Defense has maintained a consistent policy. From the birth of commercial nuclear power, the military has said that plutonium in used fuel assemblies should be made available for the production of atomic bombs. Robert LeBaron, assistant to the secretary of defense in charge of atomic energy and chairman of the AEC's military liaison committee, staked out that position during an appearance before the Joint Committee on Atomic Energy in June 1953. At the time, Congress was debating what course the nation should follow in developing the peaceful atom. "We should arrange our program," LeBaron testified, "so that . . . we can be ready to convert as much civilian inventory into military use as may be necessary in times of national emergency."

Nearly three decades later, Deputy Secretary of Defense Frank C. Carlucci restated that view in a letter dated March 29, 1982, to John G. Tower, Republican senator from Texas. "The option to use civilian plutonium in the weapons program should not be foreclosed," Carlucci wrote, "because we may need to provide for a sudden, unforeseeable increase in need resulting from an overriding national security requirement or from a calamitous interruption in the plutonium production complex." He added, "I note that this option remains open to all other nuclear weapons states."

Carlucci could have put his lobbying skills to better use on hesitant lawmakers, for in Senator Tower he had not just an ally but a frenzied partisan. The Texas senator believed not only that used fuel assemblies should be turned into bombs but also that Congress should enact a law requiring it, if the practice would be cost-effective. "We could solve much of the commercial nuclear waste problem by this approach," he told his Senate colleagues on March 30, 1982, "if the government would simply take the spent commercial fuel for reprocessing in defense facilities."

Other members of Congress, although not as vocal as Tower, agree with this strategy. "The United States has always kept available the option to use commercial nuclear facilities and products for military purposes, should our national security interests so dictate," the Senate Armed Services Committee reported in March 1982. A year earlier, the committee had fretted over a looming shortage of plutonium to upgrade warheads. "The committee remains concerned," it said in a July 1981 report, "over the availability of the special nuclear materials that will be needed for weapons production and modernization in future years." To produce enough plutonium to get through the 1980s, the Senate panel said, would require the start-up of two currently closed production reactors, one at the Savannah River plant near Aiken, South Carolina, the other at the Hanford Reservation near Richland, Washington, as well as the government reprocessing plant at Hanford.

Beyond the 1980s, the committee warned, "one or more new production reactors" to make plutonium will be required. But the DOE does not expect to have another one in operation until 1994, and that, the senators said, "may be too late." They offered another solution, one favored by President Reagan: "With the decision of the administration to pursue commercial reprocessing, it may be technologically feasible to separate weapons-grade materials during reprocessing using laser technology. . . . The committee has included additional authorization for a pilot facility that would demonstrate the technological feasibility of laser isotope separation."

This is what lies behind the thinking: the ideal weapons material is plutonium 239. Fuel rods in a nuclear power plant produce several forms of plutonium in addition to 239, including plutonium 240, an isotope not especially suited for advanced weaponry. At present, there is no established process for isolating the bomb-grade plutonium 239 from other forms of plutonium. For several years, scientists have been experimenting with a laser technology that could be applied to reprocessed civilian-reactor fuel to separate out the desired plutonium 239. If the laser works as expected—Exxon Corporation developed a similar technology for uranium—then it can be employed along with the Barnwell reprocessing plant to satisfy military plutonium demand for years to come. There is enough plutonium 239 in used fuel rods already stored at power plants to produce more than 10,000 atomic bombs. By the turn of the century, there will be enough plutonium in the accumulated rods to manufacture many times that number of bombs.

THE MYTH OF FOREIGN REPROCESSING

To buttress the case for a greater federal commitment to reprocessing, Barnwell boosters cite successes in Europe and Asia. They are fond of saying that the United States is losing its technological leadership to countries that have built active reprocessing industries. The argument is eerily reminiscent of the 1950s. Then it was intended to prod utilities to build nuclear power plants. Now it is designed to appeal to the American ego, to shame those who would allow the United States to finish lower than first in a global reprocessing race. This time the race is with America's allies rather than the Russians.

Dr. Chauncey Starr, vice-chairman of the Electric Power Research Institute, the research arm of the electric-utility industry, lamented the loss of leadership during an appearance before a House Science and Technology subcommittee in June 1980. "We have destroyed the appearance of the United States as being the technological leader in the nuclear field," Starr said. "Our technical professionals are no longer a party to the international discussion that goes on in the development of advanced nuclear technologies. . . . We are looked at internationally as a second-rate nuclear power in nuclear technology."

During those same hearings, Tom Corcoran, Republican representative from Illinois, said it was time the United States followed the lead of everyone else. "Just as all the other countries in the world that use nuclear power commercially have opted for reprocessing," he said, "I believe that the United States should do likewise." Corcoran was especially impressed with the French operation. "The La Hague [reprocessing] facility," he said, "will have enough extra capacity in 1985 through 1995 to service twenty foreign reactors each year for a ten-year period."

Two years later, in September 1982, W. Kenneth Davis,

deputy secretary of energy, reaffirmed the foreign commitment. Davis was an executive at Bechtel Group Inc.—which designs and builds reprocessing plants, including both Barnwell and West Valley—before he was recruited by the Reagan administration. He told a Senate Governmental Affairs subcommittee, "I think we have to bear in mind that the Japanese are doing reprocessing, the western Europeans are doing reprocessing. . . . They are interested in reprocessing for perfectly sound reasons from the point of view of economics and technology."

At that same hearing, Richard T. Kennedy, under secretary of state for management, asserted that "the Japanese and Europeans have gone full bore with their programs of reprocessing. . . . That is a fact. It is there, you cannot ignore it."

The Atomic Industrial Forum, in a report distributed to the news media in March 1983, ticked off a list of countries with active reprocessing programs—Great Britain, France, West Germany, Japan, and India. The Japanese plant at Tokai Mura, the nuclear-industry trade association said, had a "210-metric-ton-per-year capacity." The French facility at La Hague, operated by Cogema, had a capacity of "400 metric tons per year . . . with 1,200 more scheduled to come on line in 1987."

This image of reprocessing plants worldwide busily dissolving used fuel rods daily to recover uranium and plutonium—a picture drawn sharply by American promoters—disappears on closer inspection. In truth, reprocessing in Great Britain, France, and Japan has been no more successful, either technically or economically, than it was at West Valley.

Japan's reprocessing plant has never achieved 10 percent of its design rate. Shut down because of equipment failures and accidents far more days that it has run, Tokai Mura has been unable to match even West Valley's dismal performance. On February 15, 1983, the reprocessing complex resumed operations following an extended shutdown. Three days later, it closed once again because of radiation leaks and remained closed for the rest of the year. West Germany does not have an operable commercial reprocessing plant, and will not have one this century. A plant in Belgium, little more than a test facility, has been closed for years. But it is the French plant, which Americans often cite, that best tells the story of reprocessing abroad.

La Hague, located on the English Channel about fifteen miles northwest of Cherbourg, is the site of frequent and serious accidents. Radioactive waste is dumped in the ocean—a practice long ago banned in this country because of its potential health and environmental consequences. Radiation releases to the surrounding area have occurred on a number of occasions. A power failure in April 1980 led to a breakdown in the cooling system for high-level-waste storage tanks. Loss of cooling power for one day could result in an uncontrolled chain reaction and an explosion. Plant operators pressed emergency generators into service and restored power before having to resort to their last line of defense—turning fire hoses on the tanks to keep them cool. When plutonium leaked onto the floor of a building, the French took a page out of the United States handbook of innovative waste-handling technology that includes plastic bags, exploding burial grounds, and kitty litter. To clean up the plutonium spill, the French proposed shoveling mud on the floor. The mud would absorb the plutonium, they said, and then could be vacuumed up.

A single statistic places the highly touted French system in its proper perspective. La Hague's experience suggests that a similar plant in this country would take nearly three centuries to clear up the backlog of used fuel rods that will be stockpiled by 1990. By then, naturally, there would be enough additional rods in storage to keep the plant going for another thousand years or so. The life of a reprocessing plant is no more than forty years.

La Hague has never come close to operating at its existing capacity. Even so, it is being expanded. The expansion is being financed by electric utilities in other countries. During the late 1970s, when the rest of the world became enchanted with reprocessing, as the United States had in the 1960s, Belgium, Japan, the Netherlands, Sweden, Switzerland, and West Germany entered into contracts with France to reprocess their used fuel rods. The agreements provided for most of the reprocessing to be carried out in the 1990s and for the leftover radioactive waste to be returned to the source countries.

But France may well be building a white elephant on a scale never before seen. Far more telling than the reprocessing accidents and operating failures is the changing attitude of other nations toward the industry. This is a trend that advocates in the United States have ignored. One after another, countries with nuclear-power programs have begun to turn away from reprocessing. Sweden, once as committed as France, has decided to bury its used fuel rods. Although it has already shipped some fuel rods to La Hague, where they are being stored before reprocessing, a Swedish nuclear official said that his country "should take home spent fuel . . . and store it in Sweden without reprocessing." Sweden's parliament has voted to dismantle the country's reactors in 2010. Finland has opted to store used fuel rods rather than to reprocess them. The West Germans, too, are considering this alternative—but in China rather than in West Germany. Desperate for foreign currency, and with land to spare, China has offered to store fuel rods from West Germany and other European countries.

Japan's government and utilities also began to reexamine reprocessing in 1983 to determine whether it should be delayed. While economics have become a major consideration, as they were in this country, the Japanese also are concerned because they, like the Americans, have yet to devise a permanent storage system for high-level waste. Because of the country's relatively small land area and a high population density, radioactive waste storage is a very volatile issue in Japan. One proposal, to dump the atomic garbage in the ocean, was scrapped following protests by Pacific Islanders.

Other nations are not far ahead in perfecting reprocessing technology. Rather, they are lagging far behind the United States in discovering the industry's multiple failures and liabilities. In the 1980s, Japan, Sweden, and West Germany just began to learn the lessons Americans had learned at West Valley in the 1960s and early 1970s. What's more, none of these nations, given current projections, will ever produce the volume of high-level nuclear waste—or the level of radioactivity—that the United States generates. Not even France. France generates a larger percentage of its electricity with nuclear power, but it still has less than half the total nuclear generating capacity of this country. Should nuclear power continue to grow abroad at its past rate—a shaky assumption—none of those countries will face the kind of waste buildup that already exists in the United States until sometime in the next century.

Curiously, while American reprocessing enthusiasts claim that the French have cornered the world market, the French are lobbying hard to encourage resumption of the industry in this country. If France has assumed world dominance in the technology, then why should it care whether the United States trails far behind? Tom Corcoran, the Illinois congressman, provided the answer following a tour of overseas facilities in 1980: "The French are concerned that if the United States does not get in with a heavy commitment to nuclear power, many of the European nations will have to undergo increased public pressure and questioning on the safety of their programs. This is because the population will be concerned with the question: If it is safe, why is not the United States doing it?"

Other European governments share France's concern with what they perceive as the American public's unfounded preoccupation with radiation protection and nuclear-waste-management controls. Their attitude is due in no small part to the cavalier way Europeans treat radioactive waste. Because they have been accustomed to dealing with much smaller volumes, they have not had the same concerns about pouring it into the ground or the ocean. At the Windscale reprocessing works along the west coast of Great Britain, the British government ran a 1½-mile steel pipeline out into the Irish Sea. For some three decades the plant has pumped radioactive liquid waste through the line, discharging an estimated half-ton of plutonium and a variety of other radioactive materials into the ocean.

Windscale has been harder hit by accidents than West Valley, and although the New York facility was the dirtiest—most radioactive—in the United States, the British plant has won that distinction for the world. A reactor fire in October 1957 rained radioactive iodine over hundreds of square miles. Farmland was contaminated and milk supplies had to be dumped. A mistake by operators in November 1983 sent high-level waste flowing into the ocean. While the government said there was no cause for concern, it nonetheless recommended that people avoid a long stretch of beach after radioactive seaweed and trash began drifting ashore. Between 1957 and 1983, there were frequent fires, radiation releases, and other mishaps. Now epidemiological studies indicate that the incidence of leukemia in the vicinity of the facility is higher than normal. This is in addition to the thyroid cancers that earlier accidents have admittedly caused. In the ocean, marine animal and plant life has been contaminated. Levels of radioactivity in some fish run several hundred times above average.

European nations fear that if the United States enacts tough radiation protection standards, they will be compelled to do the same. They have thus taken the highly unusual step of intervening in American regulatory proceedings.

The NRC has proposed a strict rule for the containers that will hold high-level waste stored underground. The canisters must be designed to last 1,000 years. Both Great Britain and the Netherlands have protested. It is not disputed that such waste will remain hazardous for many thousands of years. Nevertheless, Great Britain declared that the "rule is unsatisfactory and should not be adopted in its present form," and complained that the 1,000-year requirement was "very likely to lead to criteria which are too restrictive, thus causing more expenditure on high-level waste disposal than is warranted by radiological protection consideration." The Netherlands called the packaging rule "an irrational requirement" and argued that the container was "not a key component" of a waste-management system.

Both governments had strong allies in the United States, including the DOE, which cited their objections to bolster its argument that containers need not hold radioactive waste for

1,000 years. The EPA also opposed a long-lived container. It argued that "careful selection of site characteristics" would do the job just as well, although the government's record on site selection has been marked by one failure after another. The final regulations have yet to be implemented. When they are, it may be possible to assess the influence of foreign governments on American radiation protection standards.

The debate over the life expectancy of waste containers and the security of geological formations is not an academic exercise. The question goes to the heart of the waste problem. Virtually every medium so far chosen to contain radioactive waste—whether high level or low level—has failed, from leaking tanks at Hanford to burial plots at West Valley, Maxey Flats, and Sheffield. Decisions made today regarding container types will become very important to future generations. Never has such a large volume of lethal material been buried.

COSTLY CLEANUP AT WEST VALLEY

To appreciate the magnitude of the reprocessing blunder, it is worth returning for a moment to West Valley, New York. Once the focal point of reprocessing's hopes, West Valley today is the scene of a massive environmental cleanup. The DOE has taken over the site as a "demonstration project" under a bailout plan sought by New York State and approved by Congress. In 1959, the state's political leaders asked Congress to let them build the reprocessing plant. They returned to Capitol Hill in 1980 to get upward of a quarter-billion tax dollars to correct the mistakes. Under the terms of the agreement, the federal government will pay 90 percent of the cost and New York 10 percent.

Taxpayers were not supposed to get stuck with this bill. A "perpetual care" fund was set up in 1963 to provide the public long-term protection from the waste buried there. To establish the fund, Nuclear Fuel Services was to make annual payments to the New York State Atomic Research and Development Authority, owner of the property. In a 1964 report, the New York agency said the fund "by 1980 is estimated to be $4 [million] to $7.5 million, depending upon the volume and type of wastes accepted for storage. . . . [The fund would be] sufficient, utilizing current proven technology, to provide for the perpetual surveillance and maintenance of the waste stored at the center. . . ."

The authority considered many of the waste products to be an asset rather than a liability. Of the high-level liquid waste then going into tanks, it said in a subsequent report, "Many of these so-called 'waste' products are of great potential value to aerospace, medical and industrial programs, and substantial research and development efforts are under way to provide for their reclamation and productive utilization."* In yet another report, the authority said that money accumulating in the perpetual-care fund "will be available . . . for the employment of new, more advanced [waste storage] techniques as they may be developed by the Atomic Energy Commission, the authority or others."

New York's nuclear-energy specialists, who had worked closely with the AEC, were correct on only one count. By 1980, the perpetual-care fund totaled $4.5 million, well within the range they had estimated sixteen years earlier. There were, though, a few complications. Nuclear Fuel Services, then preparing to abandon West Valley, was spending $3 million every year to look after the stored waste. At that rate, the perpetual-care fund would be exhausted in less than two years. The DOE had spent nearly $4 million on the first in a series of studies on what to do with the facility. And government estimates placed the cost of dismantling the plant, removing all waste, and restoring the property to its original, radiation-free state at more than $1 billion. The cost of dealing with the high-level radioactive liquid waste alone—getting it out of the underground tanks, converting it to a solid form, and taking it away for storage—was put at $300 million.

---

*This view was widely held by nuclear experts in the 1950s and 1960s. Dr. Edward H. Teller, a pioneer in the atomic field, said in November 1957 that "in the end . . . these radioactive byproducts will turn out to be useful and will not be considered as waste at all."

For added measure, there are no economically recoverable products "of great potential value" in West Valley's waste. Nor did the AEC, the New York State Atomic Research and Development Authority, or anyone else develop "more advanced [waste storage] techniques."

Under Congress's federal aid program, formally entitled the West Valley Demonstration Project Act, the DOE and its contractor, Westinghouse Electric, will "demonstrate" the technology for solidifying liquid waste. Government and industry have maintained for nearly two decades that this technology was already proven. Over the next several years, work will center on devising a method to extract and solidify the 572,000 gallons of liquid waste in the two underground storage tanks—560,000 gallons in one tank, 12,000 in the other. The two tanks contain an estimated three dozen different radioactive substances, including enough plutonium to make several atomic bombs. The radioactivity inside the two tanks is about 39 million curies.

To solidify the liquid, the DOE and Westinghouse also must figure out how to remove the sludge that has settled on the bottom of the tank holding 560,000 gallons. No one knows the exact composition or consistency of the sludge, although it is believed that most of the radioactive materials have settled in it, making the removal task more difficult. What's more, no one is certain of the sludge's depth. A Nuclear Fuel Services calculation placed it at just under five feet. According to a government report, the company measured the sludge by dropping a bottle tied to a string into the tank and noting "the point at which the string went slack."

DOE officials are enthusiastic about the solidification prospects. They have every reason to be. West Valley will only repeat solidification experiments conducted at Hanford two decades ago. It is a fairly straightforward process to turn radioactive liquid into a solid form under controlled conditions, when cost is no object. It is not possible to do so in a full-scale commercial operation.

In addition to removing the sludge and solidifying the liquid waste, the DOE and Westinghouse will also decontaminate the reprocessing plant itself. At some point, a decision will be made either to dismantle the facility piece by piece and cart it to a burial ground in some other state or to seal off the building and grounds for hundreds of years. Also to be determined at some future date is whether the radioactive garbage buried at the site will be dug up and moved to another state or whether it will be left in place.

In the meantime, the cleanup proceeds as company after company goes about its assignment at the taxpayers' expense. For example, Rockwell International Inc. studied how to secure samples of the liquid in the underground tanks, how to measure better the volume of the sludge and how to identify the various radioactive materials in it. The General Atomic Company studied the planned transportation systems "to assure that the waste transportation approach complies with regulations" and that radiation exposure of workers and the public is held to "the lowest reasonable achievable" level. The Burns & Roe Industrial Services Corporation studied the potential use of

Radiation monitoring at the closed Nuclear Fuel Services reprocessing plant, West Valley, New York, eleven years after the shutdown. *Philadelphia Inquirer / Nick Kelsh*

existing buildings on the site to solidify the liquid waste and evaluated "options for decontamination" of the buildings after the project is completed. The engineering firm of Dames & Moore worked on an environmental safety analysis of the property, including "a position paper on seismology and earthquake engineering, geology and geohydrology activities."

The DOE plans to complete solidification of the liquid waste in the early 1990s. If that happens, it will be the first waste-management project ever finished on schedule. In any event, two early statistics fairly well sum up the state of commerical reprocessing. From 1982 to 1984, the DOE spent $62 million on the preliminary stages of the cleanup. That is almost two times what it cost to build the entire West Valley complex. And, assuming that the solidification deadline is met, the government will have spent two years to clean up a reprocessing plant for every year it operated.

Although reprocessing as a commercial industry is dead in the United States, many adherents continue to speak of it as a proven technology that actually exists. In October 1983, the Philadelphia Electric Company distributed reprints of an article by Bernard L. Cohen, a University of Pittsburgh physics professor who formerly worked at the Oak Ridge National Laboratory and other government nuclear-research facilities. Cohen criticized the news media for provoking unwarranted hysteria over nuclear power, radioactive waste, and radiation.

Declaring that journalists had misinformed the public through "their highly unbalanced treatments and their incorrect or misleading interpretations of scientific information," Cohen singled out radioactive waste as an example. "Another favorite article [of journalists] is the so-called unsolved problem of disposal of high-level radioactive waste," Cohen stated. In fact, he wrote, "the solution planned for high-level waste is well known and very simple: High-level waste will be converted into rocks and put where natural rocks are, deep underground."

Not so. Converting waste "into rocks" has been the answer on paper ever since the 1950s. But it is not now a reality and perhaps never will be. In addition to the technological and environmental problems that remain unsolved, the economic difficulties of commercial reprocessing are currently insurmountable.

What, then, does the future hold for those millions of used fuel rods now accumulating at nuclear power plants? The government is promoting burial with the same confidence it once displayed in promising reprocessing. It will bury the fuel rods intact in an underground repository. And, as with reprocessing, it insists that the technology for a repository is well in hand. The DOE says, "More than twenty years of research support DOE's confidence that the mined geologic disposal system can meet the goal of effectively isolating highly radioactive wastes from the environment. . . . Isolation of the waste will be effective for 10,000 years."

5
The Buildup of High-Level Waste

CONGESTED STORAGE POOLS

When the Atomic Energy Commission ardently pressed electric utilities to build nuclear power plants during the 1950s, one promised subsidy proved more enticing than all the others. This was the federal government's unprecedented pledge to assume full responsibility for used fuel rods. The government did not accept mountains of ashes from coal-burning power plants or, for that matter, the waste products of any other industry. The promise was critical to the birth of nuclear power, for it relieved utilities of a nagging problem: what to do with the radioactive fuel rods that each plant would in time discharge by the tens of thousands.

Up to one-third of a reactor's fuel rods must be removed each year because of the buildup of radioactive waste. The rods, or metal tubes, are about half an inch in diameter and measure from twelve to thirteen feet in length. They are filled with pellets of uranium 235 about the size of a pencil eraser, bundled together and placed in a metal container called a fuel assembly. Depending upon the type and design of the reactor, the number of rods in an assembly may vary from 63 to 264. Similarly, the number of assemblies in a reactor varies according to the generating capacity of the power plant. There are 72 in the Dairyland Power Cooperative unit near La Crosse, Wisconsin, and 764 in the Tennessee Valley Authority's units near Decatur, Alabama.

The production of waste is part of the burning or fissioning process. When a neutron strikes the uranium nucleus in the rods, the nucleus splits in two. This produces additional neutrons that shatter more uranium nuclei, setting off a chain reaction involving billions of atoms. This is called nuclear fission. It releases radiation and heat that creates steam to power a generator that in turn produces electricity. During the fissioning, waste products—strontium 90, cesium 137, iodine 129, and scores of others—accumulate inside the rods. Because they also absorb neutrons, an increasingly smaller portion of the uranium is split and the chain reaction slows. The fuel rods then must be replaced even though they still contain 90 percent of their original uranium. For this reason, industry has always referred to the rods not as waste but rather as spent fuel. Like so many industry terms, the designation is misleading, since it implies the rods are harmless or spent, when they are in fact lethal.

As the fuel assemblies are withdrawn from a reactor's core, they are intensely hot and radioactive. Anyone who walked by a single assembly would receive a fatal dose of radiation. To absorb the heat and to shield the surrounding area from radiation, the assemblies are stored underwater in forty-foot-deep, steel-lined pools made of reinforced concrete several feet thick. When nuclear power plants were built, utilities relied on the federal promise to take title to the assemblies. They therefore designed their storage basins to hold only a few years' worth.

From the late 1950s onward, everyone assumed that the assemblies would go to a reprocessing plant where the unused uranium and plutonium would be recovered and fashioned into fresh fuel. The leftover liquid waste would be solidified and sent to an underground repository where it would be sealed off from the public forever. But things did not work out that way. The government reneged on its agreement to take the fuel assemblies. The private reprocessing industry that it said would take them failed.

As for the underground repository, during the 1960s federal officials had said one would open in the early 1970s. None did. Then they said a repository would open in the late 1970s. None did. Then they said a repository would open in the early 1980s. None did. Then they said a repository would open in the late 1980s. None will. Although the repository was always intended for the burial of solidified reprocessed waste, it could also accommodate the used fuel assemblies themselves.

That utilities would need a repository or some other storage arrangement was evident in the numbers. In 1960, there were no used fuel rods in the country. A decade later there were only 36,000. But by 1980, more than 3.4 million rods had been crammed into utility storage pools. That number was expected to swell to nearly 14 million in 1990 and to 30 million at the turn of the century.

Fuel assemblies being loaded in a reactor core. *U.S. Department of Energy*

By the late 1970s, after the first decade of explosive growth, power companies had become alarmed about their mounting inventory. Much of the increase was attributable to the opening of new plants, but plants old and new were disgorging rods that would have to be kept in pools for the foreseeable future. The government's assurances that it would take care of the rods had evaporated. As storage pools were filling up, utilities were left with these options, short of shutting down their expensive plants: squeeze more assemblies into the pools through processes called reracking and rod consolidation, transfer the assemblies to pools in newer plants with more space, or place them in casks for dry storage on site.

In reracking, entire fuel assemblies are moved closer together in the pool. Rod consolidation is a condensed form of reracking in which the individual fuel rods are bunched closer together. Dry casks are massive steel and lead vaults capable of holding from twenty to fifty used fuel assemblies. To date, neither rod consolidation nor dry cask storage has been tested or licensed by the NRC. But more than two-thirds of the nation's utilities have reracked their pools at least once, wedging the assemblies closer together, according to the NRC. There is a practical limit to this approach. Furthermore, some pools cannot be expanded, because of seismic conditions. Others are limited by weight restrictions. A single assembly from one type of reactor in use weighs about 1,400 pounds. At some plants, fifty assemblies may be removed from a reactor during refueling, adding more than 70,000 pounds to a pool.

Finally, there is an element of danger. Although this is considered a remote possibility, a reracked pool could in theory suddenly lose its cooling power. Heat would build up quickly, melt the rods holding the uranium fuel pellets, and release hydrogen. The hydrogen would explode, rip open the building enclosing the pool, and shower the surrounding countryside with radioactive debris. Both the Department of Energy and the utility industry dismiss this possibility, but it was a failure in the reactor's cooling system at Three Mile Island that led to the worst commercial nuclear accident.

While the NRC routinely approves requests to rerack storage pools, it has been sitting for several years on a rod-consolidation application from the Maine Yankee Atomic Power Company, the first utility that sought to employ the technique. The state of Maine opposes the plan, contending that the additional rods would increase radioactive contamination in an accident.

The storage pool at Maine Yankee's Wiscasset plant was three-fifths full in the fall of 1983. It was licensed to hold a maximum of 953 assemblies, and unless capacity is enlarged the plant will be forced to close in 1987. Reracking alone, a Maine Yankee spokesman said, would increase storage capacity to about 1,500 assemblies, and rod consolidation would boost it to 2,400. That would provide enough space, the spokesman said, to "take us just about to the end of the plant life, which is 2008." Rod consolidation, an as yet unproven space saver, would work like this, according to a utility representative:

The core of the Maine Yankee reactor holds 217 assemblies. Each assembly contains 176 individual fuel rods. To consolidate the rods, the top would be lifted off each assembly, a metal box about eight inches square and twelve feet long. Rods would be removed one by one and inserted in a new metal casing the same size as the assembly, only closer together, thus permitting the storage of many more rods in the same space. Although the technology has yet to be approved by the NRC, "the actual process of doing it, taking individual rods out of a fuel assembly and putting new ones in, has been done many times," the Maine Yankee spokesman said. "We've done it in our own pool. For instance, we have a fuel assembly that's got a leaking rod, let's say. We pull that one out, slip a new one in its place. So the procedure for doing it is down pretty pat. It's been done for different reasons."

Rather than consider rod consolidation or reracking, some utilities bought time by moving assemblies from pools at their older plants to those at reactors just starting up. From 1977 to 1981, the Carolina Power & Light Company shipped 304 assemblies from its Robinson plant at Hartsville, South Carolina, to its Brunswick plant at Southport, North Carolina. But the practice has been criticized by a few federal officials who envision highways crowded with tractor-trailers ferrying fuel assemblies from one plant to another. When the Duke Power Company in Charlotte, North Carolina, sought permission to transfer assemblies, the NRC's Atomic Safety and Licensing Board rejected the request.

The board concluded that such transfers do not "reduce or eliminate waste." It said, "Transporting spent fuel elements about the country does not significantly alter their form or change their quantity. A juggler with many balls in the air may

The chart shows the total number of used fuel assemblies stored and expected to be stored at nuclear plants through 2020.

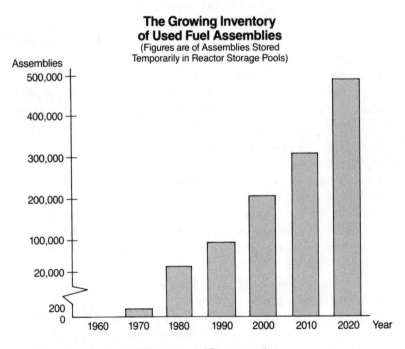

The Growing Inventory of Used Fuel Assemblies
(Figures are of Assemblies Stored Temporarily in Reactor Storage Pools)

Source: Compiled from U.S. Department of Energy records.

give the illusion of purposeful motion, but the number of balls for which he or she is ultimately responsible is not changed." The board's decision was later overruled by an NRC appellate panel.

THE NUCLEAR WASTE POLICY ACT OF 1982

Against this background—some utilities shipping assemblies from one plant to another, most just jamming more into existing pools—Congress finally took up the waste issue in 1980. The lawmakers also felt some sense of urgency as a result of Three Mile Island. The accident there a year earlier had produced a large volume of high-level radioactive waste that had to be shipped somewhere. The near meltdown not only undermined confidence in the nuclear industry but also focused public attention on the lack of a permanent repository for such waste. So it was that in July 1980 the Senate passed the first comprehensive nuclear-waste bill—thirty-eight years after the government had begun producing radioactive garbage. The House passed its own waste bill, which differed dramatically, in December. The two chambers were unable to resolve their differences before the year ended.

During the months that followed, the politics of nuclear waste hardened lines in both the House and the Senate. Two Senate committees reported out separate bills. One of the measures was pushed through the Senate Energy Committee by James A. McClure, Republican senator from Idaho. Committee members were directed to vote before the staff had finished writing the bill and before they knew all its provisions. It was an ominous sign of the legislative future of nuclear waste. Two House committees also reported out separate bills. No floor action was taken on the conflicts between the bills. For the second consecutive year the issue died.

In June 1982, two years after it had passed its first waste bill, the Senate enacted a second. The House passed its own bill in December. As before, there were striking inconsistencies between the two pieces of legislation. It appeared that, confronted

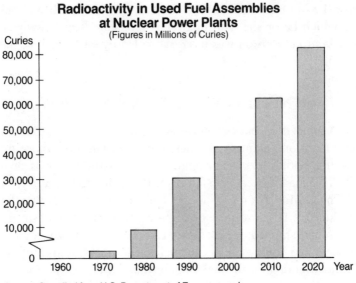

**Radioactivity in Used Fuel Assemblies
at Nuclear Power Plants**
(Figures in Millions of Curies)

Source: Compiled from U.S. Department of Energy records.

The chart shows the rise in radioactivity in used fuel assemblies stored at nuclear power plants from the advent of commercial power in the late 1950s to the present, and the projected growth to 2020.

with other pressing matters, the House and Senate would once again be unable to resolve the discrepancies before year's end. Normally, conflicting bills are sent to a conference committee made up of members from both houses to work out a compromise. But the differences were so great and the time so short that it was widely believed no bill would be acted upon before adjournment, just as had happened in 1980 and 1981. The *Washington Post* reported on December 20 that "the long, drawn-out discussion about the farm legislation virtually precluded Senate consideration this year of a controversial nuclear waste-disposal bill. . . . " Less than twenty-four hours later, the Nuclear Waste Policy Act of 1982 sailed through Congress.

Two lawmakers, McClure and Morris K. Udall, Democratic representative from Arizona, and their committee staffs put together a final bill and rushed it through a lame-duck session of Congress in ninety minutes, hours before the start of the Christmas vacation. During the afternoon of December 20, the Senate, with many of its members absent and with debate limited to a total of fifteen minutes, approved seventeen unprinted amendments. Some were lengthy and, to the uninformed, obscure, prompting a congressman to observe that "there is not one senator who could tell us what is in this bill."

The Senate forwarded the revised legislation to the House with orders to pass it or defeat it without further change—or, as a disgruntled representative put it, to "take it or leave it." The House took it. With one-third of its members not bothering to vote and the other two-thirds unfamiliar with the Senate's amendments, the House rubber-stamped a 30,000-word bill that contained provisions it had previously rejected as unsound.

Supporters in both houses characterized the bill as a momentous piece of legislation. Carlos J. Moorhead, Republican representative from California, declared, "[W]e have a good bill, one that will adopt a permanent policy for this country and one which I think will work." Senator McClure stated that "this bill is a truly comprehensive approach to the ultimate solution to disposition of the large and varied quantities of nuclear waste existing today in the United States and nuclear waste which will be created in the years and decades ahead." President Reagan joined in the praise when he signed the bill into law in January 1983. "The step we are taking today," the president said, "should demonstrate to the public that the challenge of coping with nuclear waste can and will be met."

In truth, the act is a case study in everything the federal government has done wrong for forty years. A political masterpiece of special-interest legislation, it creates only the illusion of a federal policy. As might be expected when Congress enacts a measure few of its members understand, the bill was a Christmas tree festooned with favors for private groups and influential politicians. It offered a little something for everyone and a catalog of excuses for not doing what government had promised since the 1960s—building a repository.

For electric utilities, which must have a waste-management program to satisfy regulatory authorities, it offers a fixed date by which a repository will be built. For those states that have been targeted as potential repository sites, it offers a veto that will enable them to block construction. For advocates of reprocessing, some of whom would like to see reactor fuel used to make weapons, it offers hope. For opponents of reprocessing, who want to keep civilian nuclear power separate from the weapons program, it offers a chance to do just that. For members of Congress who envision a temporary storage facility as a pork barrel project for their districts, it offers that potential, should their constituents like the idea. For states that do not want existing storage facilities turned into fuel-rod dumps, it offers a guarantee that they will not be.

These provisions, only a sampling of the act's contents, obviously are contradictory. But it gets worse. Congress's grand plan to deal with high-level radioactive waste also contains the following provisions:

• The federal government will build a "test and evaluation facility," a sort of minidemonstration plant for fuel-rod-burial technology, according to a specific timetable—unless it decides not to build such a plant. In that case, it will not know whether the technology works until after it opens a multibillion-dollar repository, if it builds one.

• The demonstration plant, if built, will be used to discover whether a particular rock formation will contain radiation from fuel rods—although the rock formation tested need not be similar to the one where the government builds a repository.

• The government may build the demonstration plant, carry on all the research designed to show that it has the burial technology well in hand, and then never build a repository.

• To overcome public distrust, the government will hold public hearings at prospective repository sites to describe in detail the tests that will be conducted there and to obtain comments from residents—except in those locations where the government will conduct the tests first and hold hearings later.

If all that sounds like an odd way to deal with deadly waste, consider the act's timetables. The secretary of energy was required to nominate five sites for a repository in 1984, and by January 1, 1985, to recommend three to the president for further study.* Then, by March 31, 1987, the president must recommend one site to Congress, and by January 1, 1989, the NRC must either reject the location or issue a construction permit. This means that all the design and engineering work for the mammoth underground storage depot must be finished long before January 1, 1989. But research at the demonstration plant may not even begin until 1990. And that assumes that a demonstration plant will be built. Although federal energy officials insist it will be, some uncertainty remains.

What difference does any of this make? During a limited experiment at the government's Nevada Test Site near Las Vegas, eleven used fuel assemblies from the Florida Power & Light Company's Turkey Point plant were sealed in holes drilled in granite 1,400 feet underground. According to a DOE spokesman, the assemblies measured thirteen feet in length and were fifteen inches square. Each contained more than two hundred individual fuel rods and weighed about 1,400 pounds. It took workers more than a day to bury each assembly.

If that same schedule were followed at a repository, it would take most of the twenty-first century just to bury the used fuel rods currently stored at power plants. By the year 2000, accord-

---

*As is customary in nuclear-waste matters, the government is running behind schedule. By election day in November 1984, the DOE had yet to select the five candidate sites. A spokeswoman said that the DOE might designate more than five, possibly all eight. Interested parties would then have sixty to ninety days to comment. Public hearings would be held in the affected areas. Under that timetable, it would be impossible for the DOE to comply with the law requiring it to recommend three sites to the president by January 1, 1985. That suggested three possibilities: first, the DOE had its candidates in mind before the selection process even started; second, the DOE will fail to meet the schedule required by the law; third, a combination of the first two.

ing to government projections, 203,000 assemblies will be awaiting burial. At the Nevada Test Site pace, if the first assembly had been lowered into the ground when Joan of Arc was burned at the stake in 1431, and if crews had labored around the clock ever since, they would still be burying nuclear fuel assemblies.

Federal energy officials insist that repository burial would proceed at a faster clip than it had in experimental Nevada. Several repositories would be scattered about the United States. These officials estimate that one assembly would be lowered down a 2,000-foot shaft to the underground cavern every hour of the day. But production-line burial has never been tested—and will not be tested prior to the design of the repository. No one knows how it would function.

This is contrary to the often-stated intentions of government waste planners. For years they had maintained that a test-and-evaluation facility, or pilot-scale plant, would precede construction of a repository. Dr. Frank K. Pittman, director of the division of waste management and transportation in the former Energy Research and Development Administration, described the steps to a Joint Committee on Atomic Energy subcommittee in February 1975. Before building a repository in a salt formation, Pittman said, ERDA intended "to demonstrate its safety by placing a significant number of actual containers —maybe 1,000—into a salt bed in a way that we can get them back out again. . . . We would run the pilot plant operation for six or seven years, gathering information."

Six years later, ERDA's successor, the DOE, still planned to operate a test facility to demonstrate the technology and safety of a prospective repository. Sheldon Meyers, deputy assistant secretary for nuclear waste management, told a House Energy and Commerce subcommittee in June 1981, "We think it makes sense from an engineering point of view to develop and construct an operation for a limited period of time that would be the equivalent of a pilot scale repository which we are calling a test and evaluation facility. . . . We feel a test and evaluation facility is an important step in developing a full scale repository."

Even Congress's own advisory panel, created to pinpoint the consequences of technological programs, has warned of the folly of building a repository before testing the burial process. "It is almost imperative to obtain some hands-on experience at a pilot scale before attempting to design and construct a full-scale facility," Thomas A. Cotton, director of the Office of Technology Assessment, told a congressional committee in 1981. "It would be awkward at best," Cotton said, "to build a repository and discover that in practice it can only be loaded at half the design rate—after it is too late to change it."

It would be even more awkward to build a repository, load it with thousands of tons of radioactive waste, and discover that it leaked in 10 years rather than the 10,000 promised by government. That could create a health and environmental disaster without precedent. The federal government is awash in paper studies on repositories, but no one has the slightest idea what will happen when the largest concentration of deadly waste in history is dumped in a single location deep underground.

France's Castaing commission said in 1982 that plans for the permanent burial of nuclear waste should be deferred. This recommendation ran counter to accepted opinion in both Europe and the United States. "In the current state of knowledge," the commission said, "all the [used] fuel management strategies present uncertainties for the safety of long-term waste storage. . . . As long as the . . . uncertainties have not been dispelled, nothing irreversible should be done in terms of waste management."

On top of all the unanswered technical questions, the forty-year record of waste management by the United States government and industry gives little cause for optimism about projections concerning fuel-rod burial, a complicated and hazardous operation. Nor does it inspire confidence in government claims that high-level waste will remain securely in place once it is buried. After only twenty years, the failure rate for commercial low-level graveyards stands at 50 percent. And the waste in those dumps amounts to just 7 million curies—less than 1 percent of the 14.7 billion curies in used fuel rods awaiting burial.

FIELD DAY FOR SPECIAL INTERESTS

When Congress passed the Nuclear Waste Policy Act, it virtually guaranteed a continuation of this dismal record. While a number of sections could be singled out, five in particular are telling. They involve away-from-reactor storage facilities, monitored retrievable storage facilities, the transportation of used fuel assemblies, military waste, and, finally, the keystone of the legislation—permanent underground repositories. First, the away-from-reactor facilities, commonly dubbed AFRs by government and industry.

For some years, federal officials had planned to use the storage basins of three closed commercial reprocessing plants to house assemblies from power plants that were running out of space. After President Carter deferred reprocessing, he included in his National Energy Plan a proposal for "modification of an existing storage facility either in Barnwell, South Carolina; Morris, Illinois; or West Valley, New York," to take care of the fuel-rod overflow.

When it became clear that the proposed Nuclear Waste Policy Act would do just that, the congressional delegations from all three states lobbied to exclude them from consideration. Illinois and New York, in particular, were sensitive about being turned into high-level-nuclear-waste dumps for other states. Nearly 2,000 assemblies were stored at the Morris and West Valley reprocessing plants. Although some of the assemblies came from nuclear utilities within the two states, most came from other states.

California has long been a pioneer in tough environmental laws. It has banned further nuclear-power-plant construction until a safe waste-management system is assured. But while California considers nuclear waste to be an unwanted threat to its environment, it has no qualms about shifting the hazard to some other state. In doing just that, it has made good use of the Morris facility. Indeed, California has managed to transfer a larger percentage of its high-level waste beyond its borders than any other state has. Of the nearly nine hundred used fuel assemblies discarded by California's utilities, more than one-fourth are stored in Illinois.

Lawmakers from Illinois, New York, and South Carolina were so concerned about the use of reprocessing plants that they tried, without success, to eliminate the temporary-storage provision entirely. To muster support, they invoked an argument that has run through most congressional debate on radioactive waste. Reduced to its simplest terms, it goes like this: The technology for safe management of nuclear waste is perfected. The federal government must provide a storage facility for nuclear waste. That facility must be located in some other state.

Jack Kemp, the Republican congressman from New York, used a variation of that theme when he sought a special deal to prevent the selection of West Valley as a temporary storage facility. "I want to emphasize as well that my concern about the interim storage provisions of this bill," Kemp said, "does not stem from purely parochial interests. It is true that I strongly oppose allowing the West Valley site, in our community of western New York, to become a storage site. Congress is spending millions of dollars cleaning up the nuclear reprocessing plant at West Valley, precisely because the nuclear waste now stored there represents a real and very significant threat to public health. West Valley is not and would not be an appropriate storage site because of well-established geographical and geological factors."

Although both the House and Senate directed the DOE to provide away-from-reactor storage, the language was carefully phrased to eliminate Morris, West Valley, and Barnwell as prospective sites. Before voting on the measure, lawmakers from Illinois, New York, and South Carolina obtained assurances that the act would exclude their states. In the House, a query from one of them brought this response from Representative Udall, one of the bill's architects: "I too would like to give my assurances to the gentleman. After many years of work on nuclear waste legislation, we have been able to achieve a consensus bill that includes carefully drawn limited away-from-reactor storage provisions. These provisions preclude federal acquisition or use of private facilities in Morris, Barnwell, and West Valley for the limited away-from-reactor storage program authorized by the bill."

Not content with the legislative guarantee that barred Barnwell's selection as a temporary storage facility, and worried that some other section of the state might be chosen, South Carolina's two senators, the Republican Strom Thurmond and the Democrat Ernest F. Hollings, introduced another unprinted amendment to remedy that situation. Prior to the act's passage, the federal government could have opened a temporary storage center almost anywhere it chose to do so. But the Thurmond-Hollings amendment gave the states the right to veto a temporary facility. Anyone who followed the explanation of the amendment on the Senate floor could be excused if he or she came away with the impression that the two senators were looking after the collective best interests of all states.

"Mr. President, the senior senator from South Carolina and I have long been sensitive to the issue of states rights," Hollings said. "One might argue that this is the result of our southern heritage. However, it also might be because we have long recognized the need for federal-state cooperation if issues of national importance are ever to be resolved. I prefer to think the latter is the reason and that the amendment being offered on behalf of the senior senator from South Carolina and myself helps to make this a better bill." Actually, what the amendment did was give the states authority they had never had before—power to block the opening of even a temporary storage center for used fuel rods. South Carolina was among the half-dozen leading contenders for such a facility.

That Illinois, New York, and South Carolina lawmakers successfully worked out an arrangement to prohibit the storage

Used fuel assemblies cooling in a storage pool. *Philadelphia Inquirer/Nick Kelsh*

of used fuel assemblies at the reprocessing plant sites was especially significant. Illinois alone accounts for 16 percent of all used fuel assemblies in the country. A total of 6,199 assemblies from Illinois reactors are stored at power plants and at the Morris and West Valley reprocessing facilities. Illinois is, and will remain, the undisputed leader in the production of high-level radioactive waste. The state has more nuclear reactors (nine), generates more electricity with nuclear power (about 30 billion kilowatt hours), and has more nuclear plants under construction (seven) than any other state. New York State ranks third with 3,022 used fuel assemblies at power plants and West Valley. South Carolina ranks eleventh with 1,347 assemblies. The three states combined have produced 27 percent of all used fuel assemblies currently awaiting burial or storage in a temporary facility.*

While the congressional delegations from Illinois, New York, and South Carolina made certain that their states would not become even temporary nuclear-waste storage depots, other special interests carved out similar deals. Another clause slipped into the waste policy act banned the storage of fuel assemblies at defense installations. This eliminated facilities like the Hanford Reservation, which could easily accommodate all assemblies currently at power plants. As a result of the exclusions, the government, if it went ahead with AFRs, would have to select one or more new locations for temporary storage. One possibility allowed for in the act is the erection of a storage center at an existing nuclear power plant, which then would house fuel assemblies from other utilities.

In addition to underground repositories and AFRs, the act also provided for a so-called monitored retrievable storage cen-

---

*In addition to 5,240 used fuel assemblies stored at power plants in Illinois, another 753 Illinois assemblies were at the Morris reprocessing plant, and 206 were at the West Valley reprocessing center, as of November 1983. This brought the overall total of used assemblies produced in Illinois to 6,199. Similarly, in addition to the 2,901 assemblies stored at power plants in New York, one of that state's utilities had another 121 at West Valley, bringing New York's overall total to 3,022.

ter. Unlike a repository, where the fuel assemblies would be buried permanently, this facility, constructed either above or below ground, would allow assemblies to be removed sometime in the future, if that was deemed necessary. The act directs the secretary of energy to submit a detailed program to Congress for such a storage center, including three potential sites, by June 1985.

Why would the United States government consider monitored retrievable storage if it planned to seal the assemblies in an underground repository? Because four different factions in Congress, for four different reasons, wanted it. One group viewed the concept interchangeably with away-from-reactor storage and saw it as another guarantee that electric utilities would have a facility to take their assemblies. A second group strongly supported the resumption of reprocessing and wanted the assemblies stored so that they can be retrieved for that purpose. As the late Sen. Henry M. Jackson, Democrat from Washington, explained, "We must address the question of whether spent fuel will be stored until a reprocessing capability is established in this country, or whether some spent fuel will be disposed of."

A third group, consisting of delegations from several potential repository states, notably Louisiana, sought monitored retrievable storage as another obstacle to forestall construction of a repository in their states. And a fourth group wanted insurance in the event that federal energy officials—who have insisted for years that all the technology is at hand to build and operate a repository—turn out to be wrong. A staff member of the House Interior and Insular Affairs Committee, who followed the legislation through Congress, explained that "there is a core of monitored retrievable storage supporters who sincerely do believe . . . that we are so far from being able to solve the nuclear waste problem safely that we shouldn't even be trying to build a permanent repository at all right now." One of the strong advocates of the Nuclear Waste Policy Act, the committee aide said, supported monitored retrievable storage because it was "too overconfident to put all your eggs in a basket, that political or technical problems could just terminate the repository program and that you'd better have this backup answer in case things really get messed up down the road."

But monitored retrievable storage is a questionable backup. Many energy analysts agree that once such a facility opened, barring some cataclysmic accident at the retrievable center, a permanent underground repository would never be built. They say that it would be more economical—even if far more hazardous—to continue packing the used fuel rods into the retrievable storage center than to package and ship them to a repository. By the year 2000, a monitored retrievable storage system could have as many as 30 million used fuel rods crowded into one facility or in a series of facilities sprinkled about the country to reduce the concentration of high-level radioactive waste in any single location.

Whatever the case, the risks are clear. Nearly a decade ago, the Environmental Protection Agency rejected a proposal by the Atomic Energy Commission to build retrievable surface storage facilities (RSSF)—the 1970s version of monitored retrievable storage facilities (MRSF)—to solve the nuclear-waste dilemma. "It is highly unlikely," the EPA said, "that any of the RSSF concepts will prove to be an acceptable ultimate disposal technique for this waste."

Another special interest that received favorable treatment was the electric-utility industry. The act provided a firm commitment that the government would at long last accept responsibility for used fuel rods—as it had promised to do in the 1950s. Better still, a federal agency would arrange for their transportation. Like many other provisions of the act that reversed what had been the expected policy, the significance of this amendment escaped many lawmakers. The few who did recognize its importance were ignored.

For more than two decades, federal planning was based on the understanding that the United States government would take title to high-level radioactive waste or used fuel rods on delivery to a federal repository or temporary storage center. George W. Cunningham, DOE's acting program director for nuclear energy, explained the policy in a letter to electric utilities in December 1977. "Spent fuel transferred to the United States government," Cunningham wrote, "must be delivered to a government approved storage site at user expense. A one-time storage fee will be made to cover the full cost to the government of providing for interim storage and subsequent permanent disposal. . . . Fuel would be transferred, at owner expense and in owner provided casks. . . ." A March 1978 DOE report restated the intent, saying that "title [to the used fuel rods] transfers at the time of delivery." The GAO repeated the policy a year later, in a June 1979 report, in which it said the federal government will "accept and take title to spent fuel upon delivery to a government-approved storage site."

But when the waste policy act emerged from Congress, it specified that "the federal government will take title [to the used fuel rods] at the civilian nuclear power plant site." This seemingly innocuous change means the American taxpayer will assume financial responsibility for a multimillion-dollar utility business expense—the cost of providing insurance coverage and cleaning up any accident that might take place during shipment to a repository. The cost of a serious accident could run into the billions of dollars. On top of sparing utilities these expenses, the act shifts the burden of coordinating fuel shipments from the utilities to the government. Not only will the government work out the transportation arrangements; it also will provide the specially designed casks in which the fuel rods must be carried to prevent radiation from escaping.

In the brief period allotted to House members to debate the bill—but not to change any of its Senate provisions—some members questioned the wisdom of establishing yet another federal nuclear bureaucracy. "What we are going to set up in this bill is a new Federal Transportation Agency for Nuclear Waste," declared Edward J. Markey, the Massachusetts Democrat who was among the act's more vocal critics. "We are just going to hire a couple of hundred people to transport these nuclear wastes from the nuclear reactors to the repositories all around the country."

The bill's defenders dismissed those fears. Manuel Lujan, Jr., the Republican representative from New Mexico, said that private carriers working under government contract would haul the waste. "The same people that would transport it for the private utilities, if they owned it," Lujan said, "would be the same people that would transport it for the federal government. We do all kinds of jobs on a contract basis."

In fact, the ambiguous transportation clause suggests both possibilities. It states, "The secretary [of energy], in providing for the transportation of spent nuclear fuel under this act, shall utilize by contract private industry to the fullest extent possible in each aspect of such transportation. The secretary shall use direct federal services for such transportation only upon a determination . . . that private industry is unable or unwilling to provide such transportation at reasonable cost."

Although a nuclear transit network is still years away, the DOE has hinted that the federal waste-trucking company foreseen by Markey might become reality. The department said in a December 1983 report that it was "committed to have the necessary transportation capability in place when needed. Where the private sector cannot or will not provide the service required in a timely or cost effective manner, the department will seek approval to use government resources."

As was true of many other provisions of the waste policy act that the House had either previously rejected or never seriously considered, the transportation clause was contained only in the Senate bill. Several House committees, and the House itself, had approved bills that called for just the opposite, for utilities to deliver their radioactive waste to a repository. Why did the Senate believe that the government should direct the shipment of millions of used fuel rods about the country and that the taxpayer should pick up the tab for any accidents? J. Paul Gilman, a staff member of the Senate Energy and Natural Resources Committee, which helped draft the act, gave the following explanation:

"It gives, we believe, a greater assurance to the public that there will be a uniform program of safety-related transportation regulations . . . a coordinated and comprehensive program for the transport and ultimate disposal of waste and spent fuel. . . . The federal government can make certain assurances to states and the citizens of those states that a utility cannot. If you are concerned about liability, wouldn't you rather the liability rest with the federal government than with the utility? If you're concerned about whether or not a transportation accident would be appropriately cleaned up, and that sort of thing, aren't you trying to make sure to everyone's satisfaction that is done by placing it in the hands of the federal government?"

Whatever the merits of that argument, the government did not provide similar assistance for the trucking of chemical and other hazardous materials or of any other waste products.

A DOUBLE STANDARD FOR THE MILITARY

Yet another special interest achieved everything it wanted from Congress. That was the military establishment. For years, the armed forces and their supporters had played a game of legislative semantics, saying they wanted—and did not want—to mix defense and commercial radioactive waste. In a written response to questions raised by members of a Senate Armed Services subcommittee in March 1982, the DOE flatly rejected a suggestion that defense- and commercial-waste-management programs be combined. "The wastes are separate and different," the department said. "A merger would serve no useful purpose now. There are important considerations pertaining to the effective management of defense waste activities affecting nuclear weapons production and our national security that are essentially not involved in commercial waste management. . . . There is essentially no advantage to merging the programs."

Nevertheless, at hearings conducted by the same Senate subcommittee, the DOE objected to proposed legislation that would prohibit joint burial of defense and civilian waste. W. Kenneth Davis, deputy secretary of energy, told committee members that "the administration is opposed to legislatively foreclosing the option of disposing of defense wastes in a commercial repository." He added that "if national defense or security programs are not jeopardized, it might be appropriate to utilize a commercial repository with payment of disposal charges."

As inconsistent as these two positions may appear, there is a compelling logic to them, at least from the military's point of view. Once military waste was ready for interment, federal officials believed, it was then appropriate to combine it with civilian waste. But the military did not want to subject day-to-day defense-waste management to review by other federal agencies, such as the NRC. "We don't want the NRC to have anything to do with defense weapons production," Seymour Schwiller, a staff member of the House Armed Services Committee, once observed.

When Congressman Markey introduced an amendment to the original House bill, providing that defense and commercial waste be bound by the same regulations, it was roundly defeated. "Whatever residents live nearby this defense facility," Markey argued, "will suffer the exact same health consequences if there has been a mistake made . . . as they would suffer living nearby a civilian waste repository." Thomas M. Foglietta, a Pennsylvania Democrat and one of a handful of lawmakers who expressed support for the measure, said "the environmental, health, and safety concerns that surround nuclear waste disposal are every bit as much a factor when disposing of defense produced waste as with commercial civilian waste."

But the majority of the House members did not see it that way. Marilyn Lloyd Bouquard, Democratic representative from Tennessee, spoke for many when she said "the administration has a well-founded fear that requiring the licensing of any defense repository could be a national security problem in that [the] NRC is required to make most of the licensing related information . . . publicly available."

What would have to be disclosed is the way defense waste is handled. In other words, if it was being treated less safely than commercial waste, the military and Congress wanted to keep it that way. It was the secrecy of the military-waste system and the absence of an independent review or accountability process that allowed the government to conceal the fact that tens of thousands of gallons of high-level liquids drained into the ground at Hanford. No public mention of the incidents was made until years later. Perhaps more telling, the defense-waste-management system gave birth to commercial-waste practices that later proved costly failures.

A lawsuit is the best measure of the government's attitude toward this subject. The legal action was brought by the Natural Resources Defense Council and the Legal Environmental Assistance Foundation against the Department of Energy in the U.S. District Court in Knoxville, Tennessee. The two environmental groups, supported by the state of Tennessee, charged that the DOE had failed to comply with federal laws on hazardous wastes, including radioactive materials, at the Oak Ridge National Laboratory in Tennessee. As a result, land and streams near Oak Ridge have been polluted with radioactive substances like uranium, thorium, and plutonium and with other hazardous materials like cyanide, mercury, and beryllium.

The government's response to the charges was straightforward. It said it was above the law. Because components for nuclear weapons are produced at the plant and because it is a national defense facility, the DOE argued, it need not abide by waste laws that govern private industry. Indeed, it said all defense installations are exempt from hazardous-waste regulations because they are operated under provisions of the Atomic Energy Act. And that act, according to a government memorandum in support of its position, "is not aimed at the protection of human health and the environment from hazardous waste."

Not too surprisingly, then, the military did not want to have regulatory agencies examining its nuclear procedures. On the other hand, once high-level waste was ready for a repository, it wanted to place it in a commercial facility. It should be remembered that nuclear-weapons production and military waste are controlled not by the Department of Defense but by the DOE, which also would be responsible for a commercial repository.

It was this carefully drawn distinction between the merger of the two wastes that enabled Sen. James McClure, chairman of the Senate Energy Committee, to say during debate on waste legislation, "[W]e have to keep them [military and civilian waste] separate if we want to move a bill through Congress." Yet when McClure eventually shepherded his bill through the Senate, he did the opposite. He combined civilian and defense waste and gave the military everything it wanted. The act authorized the president, after considering "cost efficiency, health and safety, regulation, transportation, public acceptability, and national security" factors, to place high-level defense waste in a commercial repository.

So as not to attract undue attention, the defense-waste provision was not mentioned in the section of the act dealing with the repository. Rather, it was treated under the vague heading "Applicability." It set up a roundabout procedure in which the president must evaluate the use of the repository for defense waste "not later" than December 1984. "Unless the president finds that the development of a repository for the disposal of high-level radioactive waste resulting from atomic energy defense activities only is required," the bill stated, ". . . the Secretary [of Energy] shall proceed promptly with arrangement for the use of one or more of the repositories. . . ."

In the forword, or "Findings" section, the language suggests that the law applied solely to commercial high-level waste and used fuel rods. These phrases stand out: "Congress finds that . . . a national problem has been created by the accumulation of . . . spent fuel from nuclear reactors and radioactive waste from reprocessing of spent nuclear fuel; activities related to medical research, diagnosis and treatment. . . . Federal efforts during the past thirty years to devise a permanent solution to the problems of civilian radioactive waste disposal have not been adequate." Nowhere in the explanation of the bill's purpose is military waste mentioned. That the phrase "civilian radioactive waste" is stated so prominently gives the overwhelming, but mistaken, impression that the bill related only to commercial waste.

For the military, inclusion of its waste in the act offers a cheap alternative to its burial plans in the event they go awry. The pressure to find a final resting place for defense nuclear garbage is far greater than that on private industry. That's because the military has been churning out millions of cubic feet of high-level and transuranic waste since the 1940s and has yet to come up with a permanent storage system. It has already accumulated more than two hundred massive underground steel tanks holding radioactive liquid that must be solidified.

At the government's Savannah River plant, the DOE and its contractor, the Du Pont Company, are building the Defense Waste Processing Facility to convert that installation's 30 million gallons of liquid waste to a solid form. The $1 billion plant, according to a government report, will enable the United States to "demonstrate its ability to safely process radioactive waste for permanent disposal." When the project is completed, around the turn of the century, the government presumably will have demonstrated the feasibility of what it has been saying it could do since the early 1960s—turn radioactive liquid into a solid. Even when the facility is finished, there will remain the nettlesome question raised by France's Castaing commission as to whether a more advanced form of solidification should be employed before final burial. If that turns out to be the case, it will be too late for Savannah River's waste. Perhaps superior technology can then be applied at the Hanford Reservation, which has twice as much waste awaiting final treatment.

All that aside, once the government solidifies the waste of the Savannah River plant, it will have to place it somewhere. Its first choice is an experimental repository for defense waste that it is building near Carlsbad, New Mexico. The $1 billion project, known as the Waste Isolation Pilot Plant (WIPP)— technically a demonstration facility—is for the burial of transuranic waste piled up at the Idaho National Engineering Laboratory in Idaho Falls, Idaho, and at a number of other federal installations.

Transuranic waste is contaminated with plutonium and other long-lived radioactive substances. Although not as intensely radioactive as high-level waste, it is nonetheless lethal. A speck of plutonium will produce cancer or death if ingested and will remain hazardous for tens of thousands of years. The Ford Foundation once placed the threat in another context. Plutonium, the foundation said, is "1,000 times more toxic than . . . modern nerve gases." Although WIPP is earmarked for transuranic waste, the Department of Energy is authorized under a 1979 law to place a limited number of canisters of defense high-level waste there to monitor the effect on salt. It is hoped that Savannah River's solidified waste will be used for the experiment.

The WIPP site, twenty-five miles east of Carlsbad, covers nearly 19,000 acres. Plans call for 200 acres of rooms to be carved out of a 3,000-foot-thick salt formation, some 2,000 feet underground. The waste will be stored in steel drums and boxes. If the current timetable is met, some waste could be placed in the caverns as soon as 1987 or 1988. Even though construction is proceeding, there is no guarantee the facility will open on schedule. The possible delay is attributable in part to mounting opposition in New Mexico, which once welcomed the project as an economic boon.

The state's residents have become increasingly disenchanted with WIPP because of a rising concern over the suitability of the site and because of a series of federal policy switches that left them confused and apprehensive about Washington's ultimate intentions. About fifteen miles from the planned repository, portions of the salt formation appear to have inexplicably dissolved. Pressurized brine pockets have been found on the site itself. Both conditions raise the possibility that water will find its way into the storage caverns and carry off radioactivity. But it is politics more than geology that has caused the greatest anxiety—and with good reason.

When the United States government announced WIPP in 1975, it said that only military transuranic waste would be buried there. Once active planning got under way, federal officials—including members of Congress—began to expand the project without mentioning it to the people of New Mexico. An internal memorandum from the files of Congress's Joint Committee on Atomic Energy stated, "[Federal energy officials] confirmed that consideration is being given to using the Waste Isolation Pilot Plant as the first repository for commercial high-level wastes. . . . The Governor's committee has been receptive to having a high-level waste repository in the state; Congressman Lujan has maintained a neutral (wait-and-see) attitude. . . . Activities at the Carlsbad site appear to be proceeding satisfactorily within the schedule established for that site."

When the government decided to gradually let the public in on the secret, it first casually disclosed that it was looking at WIPP as a possible site for the storage of defense high-level waste. Next, the DOE recommended that WIPP be used as a "moderate scale demonstration of the capability for ultimate

Transuranic waste in temporary storage at the Idaho National Engineering Laboratory, Idaho Falls. *Philadelphia Inquirer / Nick Kelsh*

disposal of spent fuel in salt. . . . Up to 1,000 fuel assemblies
. . . would be involved." From a moderate-scale facility for
military transuranic waste, WIPP was evolving, without any
input from the state's residents, into a full-scale repository to
house the most intensely radioactive waste from defense as well
as from civilian nuclear programs. New Mexicans rebelled.
Congress subsequently rejected the proposal to allow a demonstration of commercial-fuel-rod burial, but did go along with a
request to place defense high-level waste there as a test.

The DOE's behavior further alienated New Mexico. The
agency assured the state's congressional delegation in 1978 that
it would have veto power over any federal repository, but that
authority was never granted. This turnabout was all the more
flagrant since the government had given a similar veto guarantee—in writing—to another state. Congress, in a 1979 law, also
instructed the DOE to negotiate an agreement with New Mexico spelling out the state's rights and authority in the WIPP
approval process. But federal energy officials refused to negotiate, forcing the state to file a lawsuit to compel them to do so.

The government has also fueled the suspicions and distrust
of New Mexico residents by talking as though WIPP's status
as a repository had already been confirmed. To be accurate, it
is what its name implies, a test facility. The congressional legislation authorizing WIPP described it as "a research and development facility to demonstrate the safe disposal of radioactive
waste resulting from the defense programs." Repeated public
comments of federal officials indicate, however, that the decision has already been made, raising questions about the seriousness and integrity of the testing program. In a report to a Senate
Armed Services subcommittee in March 1982, the DOE outlined this schedule: "The WIPP facility will dispose of defense
transuranic waste stored retrievably at the Idaho National Engineering Laboratory (INEL). By approximately 1990, all existing waste stored at INEL will have been removed to WIPP, and
the WIPP facility would be in a position to receive and dispose
of transuranic waste from other defense waste generating facilities."

While the military is counting on WIPP for the disposal of its high-level waste, it now will have the commercial repository as a backup. The DOE noted this option in a report on the Defense Waste Processing Facility at Savannah River: "The Nuclear Waste Policy Act of 1982 states that by 1987, a site for the first repository should be recommended, and that by 1998, the government [will] begin accepting waste for permanent disposal."

But there is another side to this coin. If defense waste may be placed in a commercial repository, then used fuel rods from utilities may be placed in WIPP, if no commercial repository is developed. A federal energy report in January 1977 allowed for just such a possibility. The report stated that WIPP is "being designed so it is not incompatible with the disposal of high level waste. This will permit optional use of the facility for commercial waste disposal should this be required in the future." The General Accounting Office echoed that view in a report released nine months later. The agency said the New Mexico site could "serve the needs of the commercial nuclear industry by becoming the first commercial waste repository." GAO said government officials told the agency that WIPP "may be able to handle all [defense] and commercial high-level and transuranic contaminated wastes through the year 2000."

Thus, if the defense high-level waste experiment at WIPP proves successful, there could be pressure to place used fuel rods there as well. Given the government's unreal world of nuclear-waste management, this possibility is not as unlikely as it may seem, especially not when one looks at how Congress dealt with the most crucial issue of all—a commercial repository.

6
The Search
for a Repository

PROSPECTIVE SITES

In shaping the Nuclear Waste Policy Act of 1982, Congress saved its most creative nuclear politics for a high-level-waste repository. The repository was, understandably, the most controversial matter to be decided. No state wants to become the home of lethal waste. Nevertheless, the soaring inventory of used fuel rods at power plants compelled Congress to confront the issue. The outcome was a bill that began by acknowledging past mistakes: "Federal efforts during the past thirty years to devise a permanent solution to the problems of civilian radioactive waste disposal have not been adequate." Next came a claim that the act once and for all established a "definite federal policy for the disposal of [high-level] waste and spent fuel." Those pronouncements were soon followed by a series of amendments that made a mockery of the lofty rhetoric.

The legislation came up at a critical juncture in the federal government's effort to provide underground storage. Over the preceding two decades, millions in tax dollars had been spent on the program. Federal officials or government contractors had produced a steady stream of reports on hypothetical repositories. They had traveled the country in search of favorable geological formations in areas of little earthquake activity where the waste could be isolated. On the basis of this research, the DOE and its contractor, the Battelle Memorial Institute of Columbus, Ohio, had identified eight prospective sites in six states—Louisiana, Mississippi, Nevada, Texas, Utah, and Washington.

Two of those states, Nevada and Utah, do not have any nuclear power plants in operation or in planning. Mississippi has one unit scheduled to start up in late 1984 or early 1985; three others are under construction, but their completion is uncertain. Washington has one operating unit; work on two others has been indefinitely delayed, and two have been canceled. Louisiana has three units under construction, only one of which is likely to generate electricity in the near future. Texas has four under construction, only two of which are likely to produce electricity soon.

Although the tentative repository locations are centered west of the Mississippi River, most of the used fuel rods are in power plants east of the Mississippi. Of the 38,713 assemblies in the storage pools of utility or reprocessing plants early in 1984, only 4,364, or 11 percent, were in five states west of the Mississippi—California, Iowa, Minnesota, Nebraska, and Oregon. Of the remaining 34,349 assemblies stored east of the Mississippi, 20,945, or 54 percent, were in just six states—Alabama, Connecticut, Illinois, Massachusetts, New York, and Pennsylvania.

This means that if the assemblies were shipped by truck to a repository in one of the targeted states, the nation's highways would become nuclear thoroughfares. Possibly, the assemblies could be transported by train rather than by truck, although many nuclear plants are not near existing rail lines. An atomic rail system also would require the marshaling of yards where individual cars would wait with their radioactive cargo while an entire train of fuel-rod carriers could be assembled. That would turn rail depots, most of which are in heavily populated areas, into radioactive-waste storage sites. So imagine, if you will, this scenario:

Used Fuel Assemblies
Stored at Nuclear Power Plants

State	Number of Assemblies	Percentage of Total	Cumulative Percentage
1. Illinois	5,240*	14.3	14.3
2. Alabama	3,901	10.6	24.9
3. New York	2,901*	7.9	32.8
4. Pennsylvania	2,833	7.7	40.5
5. Connecticut	2,150	5.9	46.4
6. Massachusetts	1,958	5.3	51.7
7. Minnesota	1,698	4.6	56.3
8. New Jersey	1,659	4.5	60.8
9. North Carolina	1,619	4.4	65.2
10. Florida	1,398	3.8	69.0
11. South Carolina	1,347	3.7	72.7
12. Georgia	1,284	3.5	76.2
13. Michigan	1,185	3.2	79.4
14. Nebraska	1,153	3.1	82.5
15. Vermont	1,082	2.9	85.4
16. Wisconsin	959	2.6	88.0
17. Maryland	868	2.4	90.4
18. Virginia	672	1.8	92.2
19. California	625	1.7	93.9
20. Maine	577	1.6	95.5
21. Iowa	576	1.6	97.1
22. Arkansas	484	1.3	98.4
23. Oregon	312	0.8	99.2
24. Ohio	140	0.4	99.6
25. Tennessee	130	0.4	100.0
Total	36,751*	100.0	

*The figures do not include used assemblies stored at closed reprocessing plants at Morris, Illinois, and West Valley, New York. These numbers are constantly changing as West Valley returns assemblies to power plants where they originated and as Morris accepts new assemblies. As of November 1983, there were 750 assemblies at West Valley and 1,212 assemblies at Morris, bringing the nationwide total to 38,713.

Source: Compiled from U.S. Nuclear Regulatory Commission records.

The above table shows the number of used fuel assemblies in storage pools at commercial nuclear power plants in twenty-five states as of April 1984. The table also lists each state's percentage of the national total and the cumulative percentage. Six states account for 51.7 percent of all the assemblies now held in temporary storage.

It is Monday, January 3, in the year 2000. During the day, tractor-trailers loaded with used fuel assemblies set out from power plants near Pittsfield, Massachusetts; Oswego, New York; Toms River, New Jersey; Annapolis, Maryland; Baxley, Georgia; New London, Connecticut; Moline, Illinois; Dothan, Alabama; Russellville, Arkansas; Newport News, Virginia; Fort Pierce, Florida; South Haven, Michigan; Sacramento, California; and several dozen or so other communities. Hauling half a ton of radioactive fuel rods, the trucks head for the nearest interstate highways—I-95, I-81, I-75, I-35, I-40—and proceed toward their common destination, a small town in Mississippi.

The next day, January 4, 2000, another truck convoy sets out from each of the power plants with a cargo of fuel rods, again heading for Mississippi. The scene is repeated on Wednesday, Thursday, and Friday. Meanwhile, as scores of trucks funnel into Mississippi from all directions, they converge near the tiny town of Richton, a cotton-farming and lumbering community about twenty miles east of Hattiesburg. Every hour, twenty-four hours a day, 365 days a year, the trucks roll past Richton and up to the gates of America's first repository for high-level radioactive wastes.

The storage facility covers three to four square miles of land. Buildings—including a waste-handling complex for lowering the assemblies into the ground, a sewage treatment plant, temporary storage depots, administrative offices, and other support structures—are grouped on about 400 acres. The repository itself, carved out of a salt dome 2,000 to 4,000 feet below the earth's surface, is spread over 2,000 acres. To help assure that radioactivity is contained underground, restrictions on how surface land is used—no drilling, for example—extend in a radius several miles beyond the buildings. The burial operation requires so much water that it must be pumped in at a rate of 500 to 1,400 gallons per minute.

As might be expected, the six states being considered as sites for the world's largest radioactive burial ground expressed opposition. When the waste policy act finally came up for debate in Congress, all had a special interest in its outcome, and the congressional delegations of all but one were prepared. John C. Stennis of Mississippi, a Democratic power in his thirty-fifth year in the Senate and chairman of its Armed Services Committee, complained of the tests already under way in his state. Two salt domes had been designated as worthy of more study. The prime contender was a formation near Richton. Responding to the pleas of constituents, who were reacting to published reports that the Richton salt dome was "number one" among possible sites, Stennis said he had personally inspected the area. The senator declared, "My investigation led me to question the Department of Energy's rationale for going into an established community like Richton, Mississippi, and tell the people that

An engineer's concept of a high-level waste repository. *U.S. Department of Energy*

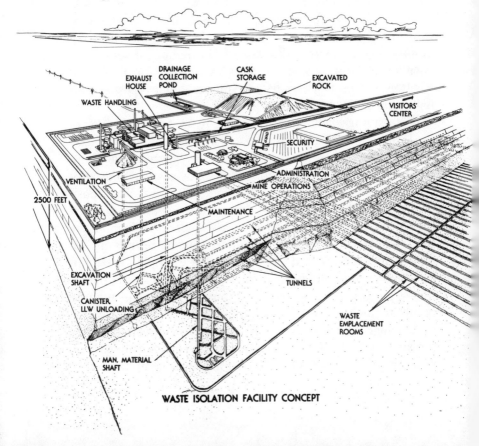

WASTE ISOLATION FACILITY CONCEPT

there was nothing to be afraid of, there was nothing to fear, that this was only a test, and if the Department of Energy were allowed to continue the work, everybody in the town would get rich. Or, as some said, 'It would be equivalent to the second coming.' "

Suggesting that the technology for the safe storage of high-level radioactive waste was still unproven, Stennis told his colleagues, "[I]t seems incredible to me that the work in Mississippi has progressed to the point it has. With the number of possibilities that exist in barren, uninhabited areas and with the number of possibilities in areas which have long been established as communities of nuclear workers, scientists and technicians, that we would create by legislating a program which would allow the further exploration of large, populated areas before we have adequately demonstrated that we indeed have the know-how to safely dispose of this waste."

The waste policy act subsequently passed by Congress directed the secretary of energy to prepare guidelines for the location of a repository. Those guidelines, according to the law, must disqualify any potential site situated "adjacent to an area one mile by one mile having a population of not less than 1,000 individuals." Conveniently, 1,200 people lived in a one-square-mile area in Richton. One of them was Senator Stennis's sister.

If any members of Congress thought that the 1,000-people-per-square-mile limitation was parochial, another Mississippian—Rep. Trent Lott, a Republican—had some advice. Remember, he said, that "this square-mile area could be a section of the city of Cleveland, Ohio, or a town within the state of Mississippi."

That prompted David D. Marriott, a Republican representative from Utah, to observe that the DOE had promised that no favoritism would be shown. Federal energy officials and others, Marriott said, had indicated "that every site will be evaluated fairly and evenly, that there is no hanky-panky going on, that no deals have been cut underneath the table, and that every site will be looked upon and we will then evaluate them based upon the criteria."

Marriott had more than a passing interest in the site-selection criteria. Another of the locations under study was a bedded salt formation in San Juan County in eastern Utah, between Moab and Monticello and bordering the Canyonlands National Park.* But the act also had a special provision that would discourage a repository there. It directed the secretary of energy, in drafting his guidelines, to consider a potential site's "proximity to components of the National Park System."

The key word in Representative Marriott's defense of the selection process was "evaluate." Although all sites might be evaluated fairly and evenly, some, such as the Richton salt dome, will not be chosen, thanks to special deals worked out with Congress or federal agencies. For example, take another of the eight potential repository locations, the Vacherie salt dome, about forty miles southeast of Shreveport, Louisiana.

Tests were conducted there just as they were at Richton. But even if the Vacherie dome is deemed safe for high-level radioactive waste, no repository will be built there. That's because Louisiana reached a private understanding in 1978 with the DOE that would permit it to bar such waste from the state. The agreement was little noticed at the time, because it was part of a pact dealing with the nation's Strategic Petroleum Reserve. Authorized by Congress in 1975, following the Arab oil embargo, the petroleum reserve was eventually to store one billion barrels of crude oil, largely in Louisiana salt domes. In exchange for the use of the salt caverns for oil storage, Louisiana officials extracted a guarantee from the DOE that the state would have final say on any nuclear-waste storage facility.

In February 1978, Edwin W. Edwards, the Democratic governor of Louisiana, and John O'Leary, deputy secretary of energy, signed a three-page "principles of understanding." The document listed ten items of agreement. Eight dealt with the

---

*Government reports over the years have referred to either eight or nine potential repository sites. The discrepancy comes from the counting of the Utah salt formation as one site in early reports and as two in later documents. The two locations are nearly adjacent and are situated in the same salt formation.

Strategic Petroleum Reserve. One called for the establishment of a DOE suboffice in New Orleans. Another involved radioactive waste. That provision stated, "All federal government studies relating to nuclear waste disposal in the Vacherie salt dome in Webster Parish and the Rayburn's salt dome in Bienville Parish will be subject to this stipulation: The Department of Energy will not construct any nuclear waste repository for long-term disposal in Louisiana if the state objects. Studies of possible areas in Louisiana as well as in other states would continue with some test drilling, which will always be preceded by complete discussions with state officials."

The agreement was signed on February 27, 1978, in the Old Executive Office Building in Washington, while Governor Edwards attended a conference on President Jimmy Carter's national energy plan. Shortly afterward, Edwards and O'Leary signed a second, slightly revised agreement to strengthen Louisiana's position. Because the phrase "for long-term disposal" might have been interpreted to mean that Louisiana would permit the interim storage of radioactive waste, those four words were deleted. The amended agreement stated flatly, "The Department of Energy will not construct any nuclear waste repository in Louisiana if the state objects." The change assured that none of Louisiana's inviting salt domes will "host" the nation's radioactive garbage.

Two years later, amid suggestions by some federal officials that the agreement should be ignored, Ronald Reagan rushed to the rescue. During the 1980 presidential campaign, Reagan assured Louisiana residents that if elected his administration would abide by the DOE commitment. "As long as the state lives up to its obligations," he said, "as president I will see to it that the federal government lives up to all its obligations which it has undertaken, including specifically the words that the government 'will not construct any nuclear waste repository in Louisiana if the state objects.' " Reagan added that "if the citizens of this country are to have confidence in its government, such agreements must be honored."

To date, then, the federal government has made this much

progress in choosing one of the eight potential sites for the country's first high-level radioactive waste garbage dump: The Richton salt dome in Mississippi will not be selected, because of a special deal worked out with Congress and incorporated into the Nuclear Waste Policy Act. The Vacherie salt dome in Louisiana will not be selected, because of a special deal worked out between the state and the Department of Energy. The bedded salt formation in Utah almost certainly will not be selected, because guidelines inserted in the Nuclear Waste Policy Act disqualify it. In addition, the Cypress salt dome in Mississippi will not be selected, because it is rated least desirable for technical reasons. It also is located in the DeSoto National Forest. That leaves four locations.

RICHLAND, WASHINGTON—Exploratory drilling was to start in 1984 on the federal government's Hanford Reservation near Richland to test the suitability of a basalt rock formation. Plutonium for weapons is produced at Hanford—the facility supplied the plutonium for the bomb dropped on Nagasaki —and one-third of all defense high-level radioactive waste is stored on the 570-square-mile installation. With a payroll of nearly $1 billion, Hanford provides employment for more than 12,000 people. Residents in the immediate area are staunchly pronuclear. They want the repository. The rest of the state opposes it.

The state's voters in 1980 overwhelmingly approved an initiative banning the further burial of low-level, nonmedical nuclear waste from out of state at the commercial burial ground adjoining the Hanford Reservation. Nuclear supporters, utilities, and the federal government challenged the initiative in federal court, which subsequently ruled the ban unconstitutional because it imposed restraints on interstate commerce and interfered in a field regulated by the United States government.

The state of Washington's attitude was best expressed by Sen. Slade Gorton, a Republican, during congressional debate on the waste policy act. "Throughout the discussion on high-level nuclear waste legislation during this Congress," Gorton said, "there has been a common misconception. That misconception is that the people of the state of Washington want a repository located in Washington state. To be fair, this is not the case. Were the disposal of nuclear waste in the state of Washington put to the people of the state of Washington, as a general proposition, the overwhelming majority would answer no."

In addition to popular opposition, serious technical questions about Hanford remain unanswered. Not the least of these involves the paths of underground streams that flow into the Columbia River as it cuts through the reservation. This is especially important since used fuel assemblies must be isolated from water for thousands of years. Failure to do so could contaminate rivers and drinking-water supplies. There is also concern about the suitability of the basalt. A National Academy of Sciences panel said that certain types of waste "would probably melt the adjacent rock material. Quite possibly the melting would not be sufficient to impair the integrity of the disposal site, but this kind of occurrence is not contemplated in current design for bedrock repositories and would need additional study."

These shortcomings notwithstanding, some nuclear-waste observers believe that Hanford's history could lead to its selection. They reason that because of mistakes in radioactive-waste handling that date from the 1940s and because of the large volume of defense waste now in storage, large chunks of the reservation already are among the most contaminated pieces of real estate on earth. Since the property, by the government's own accounts, will never be cleaned up—and therefore must be isolated from mankind forever—it is logical to place a repository there, even if the geology is not especially favorable.

BEATTY, NEVADA—Preliminary tests have been completed at the Nevada Test Site, sixty-five miles northwest of Las Vegas, on the suitability of a volcanic rock formation called tuff. As is the case in Washington, many Beatty area residents favor a repository at the 1,350-square-mile test site, while the rest of Nevada opposes it. Also like Washington, Nevada is seeking to restrict usage of a burial ground at Beatty for commercial low-level waste.

In Nevada, as in other states, opposition is bipartisan, as reflected in the state's four-year-old campaign to shut down Beatty's nuclear graveyard. The legal action was started by Gov. Robert List, a Republican, and continued by his successor, Gov. Richard Bryan, a Democrat. A spokesman for Governor Bryan summed up the dominant mood as follows: "The state's general attitude is Nevada's the dump site for everything that everybody else doesn't want, and it's a very kind of Western attitude, of we don't want to be the dump site for everything. . . . It's a blanket hostility." Nevada's governor has staked out an equally tough position toward a high-level-waste repository. "I am 100 percent against this continuing attempt to make Nevada a dump site for the nation's unwanted programs," Bryan said. "We will take advantage of all available avenues to see that this controversial program does not come within our borders."

There is another obstacle to burying millions of radioactive fuel rods at the Nevada Test Site: atomic bomb tests. Since 1950, more than six hundred nuclear weapons have been detonated at the desert range, above ground until 1962, below ground since then. Federal energy officials maintain that continued bomb tests below ground would have no effect on an underground repository. They say that, because the test site is near the California earthquake zone, the repository would have to be built to withstand earthquakes packing more force than the biggest bombs tested.

This claim lost some of its luster in February 1984. Following an underground nuclear explosion, a 9,000-square-foot section of the desert caved in unexpectedly. Technicians, their equipment, and trailers all dropped into a 30-foot-deep sinkhole. It was one of those accidents government experts had said could not happen, because the geology of the region would withstand the blast, which was equal to the force of a mild earthquake. Whatever the merits of the DOE's assurances about the safety of a repository, nuclear-defense officials would prefer that it be built elsewhere. They fear that weapons tests would be dragged into administrative proceedings concerning the repository, that secret bomb data would be disclosed, or that future tests might be tied up in litigation over radioactive waste.

HEREFORD and TULIA, TEXAS—Preliminary tests have been completed in two bedded salt formations in the Texas Panhandle, about six hundred miles northwest of Houston. One is a fat, crescent-shaped formation near Hereford, in Deaf Smith County, the other a large triangular formation near Tulia, in Swisher County. Ten bore holes have been drilled in the two counties, according to a spokeswoman for the Battelle Memorial Institute. Their purpose, she said, is "to obtain geologic and hydrologic information at various depths" and to "get a pattern of the geology, the strata of the rocks underneath, and of the flow of groundwater." She said that seismic measuring lines and "a micro-earthquake-detection network" had also been installed.

Of the eight prime candidates, Hereford and Tulia pro-

Nevada Test Site, a candidate for use as the high-level-waste repository. *U.S. Department of Energy*

voked the least opposition during debate on the waste policy act in 1982, on both the state and the national levels. Part of the reason may be geography. The counties are about 350 miles from the nearest major metropolitan center, Dallas, and are sparsely populated. With 9,700 residents, Swisher County averages 11 people per square mile. Deaf Smith, with 21,200 residents, averages 14 persons per square mile.

In any event, of the congressional delegations from the six potential repository states, the Texas contingent expressed the least concern during legislative debate. All that changed early in 1983, when the DOE formally advised Texas officials that their state had been selected. Residents of Deaf Smith and Swisher counties rallied against the project, charging that radioactive waste could contaminate the Ogallala aquifer, which supplies water for drinking and irrigation of rich farmlands in the two counties. As political opposition mounted, state legislators demanded that Congress enjoin the DOE from giving further consideration to Texas.

But Washington's bureaucratic machinery was grinding away. Nine days after Congress passed the waste policy act, the EPA issued proposed standards for the burial of high-level waste and used fuel rods. An obscure provision in the thousands of words of legal jargon pointed, by way of elimination, to Hereford and Tulia as appropriate locations: "Disposal systems shall not be located where there has been mining for resources, or where there is a reasonable potential for future exploration for scarce or easily accessible resources. Furthermore, disposal systems shall not be located where there is a significant concentration of any material which is not widely available from other sources. This requirement would discourage the use of geologic formations which are often associated with resources or mining activity. For example, the frequent mining of salt domes either for their relatively pure salt or for use as storage caverns would argue against locating a repository in this type of structure. However, this same concern would generally not apply to bedded salt deposits because they are much more common."

EPA's proposed standards would preclude the burial of

radioactive waste in Louisiana's salt domes—which already enjoy an exemption, courtesy of the DOE—but would permit it in Texas's bedded salt formations.* As 1983 gave way to 1984, events beyond the control of Texans seemed to be shaping the state's radioactive-waste destiny. Still, there was hope. Although Texas missed its chance to secure immunity in the waste policy act, as more-vigilant states did, all may not be lost.

Another catchall provision, a sort of kitchen-sink clause inserted in the act, may achieve the same result. It is called the "state veto provision," and it may turn out to be the biggest and the best of all the act's special-interest clauses. The ultimate escape mechanism for Texas or any other state that does not want to be the home of the world's largest radioactive garbage dump, it all but guarantees that a repository will not be built in any state where there is strong opposition. It provides that if a designated state files a formal objection with Congress, the repository can be built only if both the House and the Senate approve. Ordinarily, in matters of state and federal sovereignty, the law is heavily weighted on the side of the federal government. But under the veto clause, a state's disapproval is final unless both houses of Congress initiate action to override the objection—a difficult legislative task.

Like many other critical sections of the act, the veto clause was slipped in at the last minute, reversing what for years Congress had said would be the policy. Two years earlier, in December 1980, the waste policy bill passed by the House contained a "one-house sustain" provision. It provided that if a state objected to its selection, the facility would be built there anyway, unless either the House or the Senate voted to uphold the state's position. In other words, if Congress took no action —the easiest way out of any politically sensitive issue on Capitol Hill—the repository would be constructed regardless of a state's opposition.

Early in December 1982, when the House reaffirmed its version of the waste policy act, the bill still contained the one-

---

*The proposed EPA standards are expected to become final sometime in 1985.

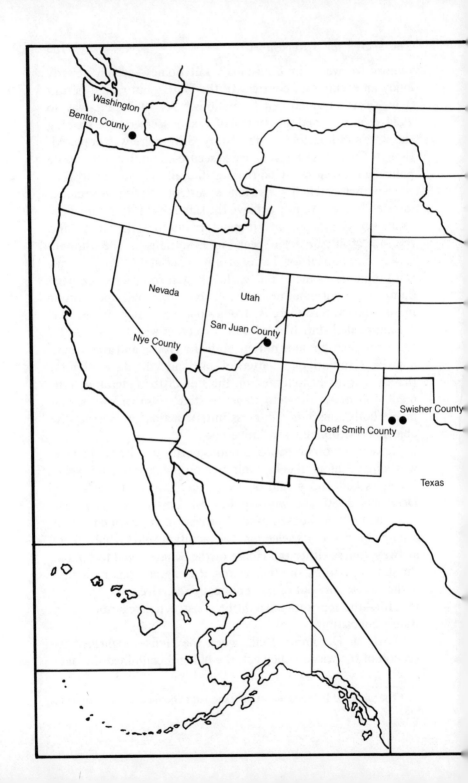

Webster-Bienville
Parishes ●

Louisiana

Mississippi

● Perry County
●

Prospective Sites for the Nation's First
High-Level Waste Repository.

house-sustain provision. But when it came up for final passage
in the Senate, on December 20, one of the seventeen unprinted
amendments substituted a two-house-veto for a one-house-sus-
tain approach. William Proxmire, the Democratic senator from
Wisconsin, introduced the amendment, saying that it was
"needed for insurance." Without his amendment, he said,
"once the president chooses a site and the state objects, the
objection means nothing unless one house of Congress votes to
uphold a state's objection. [That] would pit one state against the
forty-nine states, against DOE and against the president. Since
a state would have to live with a repository forever, it is outra-
geous that state objections are not given more weight."

Proxmire, who didn't mention that his home state of Wisconsin was targeted for further study as the site of a second
repository, asked his colleagues, "Would you want your state
to be stuck with dangerous nuclear waste which remains radioactive for thousands of years and have nothing to say about
it?" Agreeing with Proxmire's argument, the Senate passed the
amendment on a voice vote without debate. When the Senate
forwarded the bill to the House, with instructions to pass it or
defeat it without change, the House was forced to accept a
provision that was contrary to its previous measures, and one
the Senate itself had rejected.

Even lawmakers generally on opposing sides of nuclear-
power issues denounced the amendment. "If we are going to
have a two-house veto," declared Rep. Samuel S. Stratton, a
New York Democrat, "obviously no state is ever going to accept any repository, either interim or permanent. What we are
doing here is a charade because we are not going to get this kind
of a repository with this kind of legislation, and I think it is a
disgrace that we should allow one senator to do this." Rep.
Edward J. Markey, Democrat from Massachusetts, was equally
blunt. "As we pass this bill, what we are doing," Markey said,
"is we are guaranteeing that we will never see the day in which
a permanent repository is built."

In a way, the two-house veto recognizes what has been quietly understood, but seldom publicly admitted. A repository will not be built where it is not wanted. The former secretary of energy James R. Schlesinger told a congressional subcommittee in 1978, "[A]s a practical matter, I think we recognize that it would be inappropriate, or practically impossible, to site a permanent waste disposal facility in a state that was unwilling to take it."

Although one repository has proved impossible to construct for thirty years, the waste policy act calls for multiple repositories. The act directs federal energy officials to come up with five additional sites in coming years. After that list is pared to three, the president is to choose one by March 31, 1990, for the second facility. The DOE, for which the waste-repository program provides millions of dollars in staff salaries and contracts with private companies—the figure will swiftly swell to billions of dollars—is eagerly going along with the search. It has a practical reason to do so. A second repository is needed in part, the DOE says, "to provide an alternative location for disposal if operational problems develop at the first repository."

One of the proposed rock formations under study for the second facility is granite. A DOE spokesman explained, "There's a possibility that a site can be nominated in the East for the second repository, because there's a lot of granite around the Great Lakes and also running down the whole Atlantic seaboard from Maine just about down to Georgia. I think there's something like seventeen states that have granite formations, so we'll be looking at those in detail over the next few years."

Among the states to be surveyed more closely in the northeast are Connecticut, Maine, Massachusetts, New Hampshire, New Jersey, New York, Pennsylvania, Rhode Island, and Vermont. The department is also looking at five states in the Southeast (Georgia, Maryland, North Carolina, South Carolina, and Virginia) and three north central states (Michigan, Minnesota, and Wisconsin). Preliminary surveys have identified rock formations in each of the states deemed appropriate for further study.

In New Jersey, for example, four counties have potentially favorable geology—Hunterdon, Mercer, Morris, and Warren. In Pennsylvania, suitable rock formations have been found in nine counties in the eastern part of the state—Berks, Bucks, Chester, Delaware, Lancaster, Lehigh, Montgomery, Northampton, and Philadelphia. New York has nineteen counties with favorable rock formations—Bronx, Clinton, Dutchess, Essex, Franklin, Fulton, Hamilton, Herkimer, Jefferson, Lewis, Oneida, Orange, Putnam, Rockland, St. Lawrence, Saratoga, Warren, Washington, and Westchester.

The search along the densely populated East Coast for a high-level storage site perhaps best exemplifies the unreality of the federal government's nuclear-waste programs. If sparsely populated, politically conservative states like Nevada, Utah, and Mississippi heatedly oppose waste burial in their states, populous, politically powerful states like Massachusetts and New York would almost certainly oppose it even more vigorously.

Perhaps for that reason, the DOE has included in its waste-management strategy a fallback rock formation in another part of the country for a second repository. The department is studying the feasibility of argillaceous and sedimentary rocks other than salt in eight western states. They are Arizona, California, Idaho, Nevada, New Mexico, Oregon, Texas, and Utah. The DOE says it will designate "potentially acceptable sites for the second repository" by September 1985.

Congress's order to build several repositories has further eroded the government's already battered credibility. The General Accounting Office took federal energy planners to task on precisely that point after the Energy Research and Development Administration announced in 1976 that it was conducting a nationwide search for locations at which to build "up to six repositories." An ERDA representative said the first two repositories will begin "receiving waste in the middle of 1985. The next three facilities will start operation four years later [in 1989], with the remaining one following [in 1991]." GAO admonished in a September 1977 report, "Another aspect of the waste repository program which is not, in our opinion, based on realistic proposals, is the goal of building six repositories in the stated time period. This goal appears overly optimistic in estimating the time required to identify, study, design, construct and confirm the feasibility of the repositories. Such an unrealistic schedule could further decrease the public's confidence in the Energy Research and Development Administration's waste management program."

Here, then, is Congress's master plan to deal with high-level radioactive waste. The government will select sites at which to build two or more repositories where the used nuclear fuel assemblies will be buried permanently. The repositories will not be built in states with sufficient political influence to kill them. While the government prepares to build the repositories, it will also construct away-from-reactor facilities to store the assemblies temporarily, although there will be no need for them if the government really builds repositories. Simultaneously, the government will prepare plans to build monitored retrievable storage facilities from which the assemblies may be removed. But the most likely reason for removing the assemblies is to reprocess them and recover the plutonium for weapons, which federal law now prohibits. And finally, the government says it will allow utilities to ship their used fuel assemblies to temporary storage facilities only after they have exhausted all potential storage options on plant grounds. But most utilities have enough options for on-site storage that they would never need to ship assemblies to a temporary storage facility.

To sum up, the federal government will build repositories to bury the fuel assemblies permanently. It will build away-from-reactor facilities to store the assemblies temporarily. It will build monitored retrievable storage facilities to store the assemblies for a temporarily indefinite period. It will do some combination of the three. Or it will do nothing.

THE REAL SITES

It is that last option, nonaction, that is most likely to prevail. After all, the federal government has done little throughout the atomic age. It means that by default the utilities may store fuel assemblies at power plants until at least the middle of the twenty-first century. This will defer to future generations of lawmakers, utility executives, and taxpayers the responsibility for a solution.

Federal regulators have already opened the door to this eventuality. In the spring of 1983, the Nuclear Regulatory Commission took the first step to make it legal for nuclear power plants to continue to store assemblies at reactors for at least thirty years after the plants shut down. In a proposed rule issued in May, the NRC reversed a policy of three decades that provided that only a limited number of assemblies would be kept at a power plant and that all would be removed when it closed. Instead, the agency said, "The licensed storage of spent fuel for thirty years beyond the reactor operating license expiration either at or away from the reactor site is feasible, safe and would not result in a significant impact on the environment." The licenses of most reactors now operating will expire between 2000 and 2020. Under the NRC's proposal, the used fuel assemblies accumulated during the lifetime of one of these reactors —containing as many as half a million individual fuel rods— might stay at the plant until sometime between 2030 and 2050.

The NRC regulations were prompted by legal challenges to utility plans to rerack their storage pools. States and environmental groups, concerned about the threat posed by unlimited assembly storage at reactors, sought to block utility applications to expand their storage capacity. Lawsuits were filed in the late 1970s to prevent reracking at the Northern States Power Company's Prairie Island generating station in Goodhue County, Minnesota, and Vermont Yankee's nuclear plant in Windham County, Vermont. Both utilities had applied to the NRC for permission to expand pool storage. When the commission approved the applications, as it had done routinely in similar cases, opponents of the projects—the Minnesota Pollution Control Agency in Minnesota and the New England Coalition on Nuclear Pollution in Vermont—appealed the decision to the federal courts.

They argued that as a result of unsure government plans for

managing high-level radioactive waste, "the reactor sites might become long-term and possibility indefinite storage sites." Because of the uncertainty, they said, the NRC should be required to examine the safety and environmental implications of storing fuel assemblies at a power plant after it ceased operations. John W. Ferman, an official of the Minnesota Pollution Control Agency, explained his agency's concern as follows: "Reracking has the potential of converting the facility from a straight power plant to one where the possibility of very long-term spent [used] fuel disposal [exists], perhaps long after the time the plant is shut down. We call that the de facto repository. One of our concerns in that whole mess was that after a power plant has been shut down for the last time, the owner's interest in the plant begins to flag, and their attention would tend to go where they are making electricity. . . . We're not altogether aglow at the thought of NRC keeping good close tabs, for they're largely concerned with operating plants, too."

The NRC countered that, rather than have to go through similar proceedings each time a utility request for pool expansion was contested, it be permitted to issue a general nuclear-waste rule covering all power plants. The U.S. Circuit Court of Appeals in Washington agreed and sent the combined cases back to the NRC for it to implement "such procedure as it may deem appropriate."

Judge Edward A. Tamm, in a concurring opinion, said that the NRC should first establish whether it was "reasonably probable" that a repository would be opened before reactor operator licenses expired. If there was doubt, he said, the NRC should determine whether it was "reasonably probable" that the assemblies could be "stored safely on-site for an indefinite period." "Answers to these inquiries," Judge Tamm said, "are essential for adequate consideration of the safety and environmental standards."

The NRC played it safe and responded to both questions in its proposed rule in May 1983. The commission said "there is reasonable assurance that one or more mined geologic repositories for commercial high-level radioactive waste and spent fuel

Congested Storage Pools
at Nuclear Reactors

State:	Reactor	Nearest Town	Will Fill Authorized Capacity
Alabama	Browns Ferry 1, 2, & 3	Decatur	1985
Alabama	Farley 1	Columbia	1991
Alabama	Farley 2	Columbia	1994
Arkansas	Arkansas 1	Russellville	1998
Arkansas	Arkansas 2	Russellville	2003
California	Rancho Seco	Clay Station	1987
California	San Onofre 1, 2, & 3	San Clemente	1985
Connecticut	Millstone 1	Waterford	1991
Connecticut	Millstone 2	Waterford	1987
Connecticut	Haddam Neck	Haddam Neck	1994
Florida	Crystal River 3	Red Level	1997
Florida	St. Lucie 1 & 2	St. Lucie	1990
Florida	Turkey Point 3	Turkey Point	1987
Florida	Turkey Point 4	Turkey Point	1988
Georgia	Hatch 1 & 2	Baxley	1999
Illinois	Quad Cities 1 & 2	Cordova	2003
Illinois	Zion 1 & 2	Zion	1995
Illinois	Dresden 1	Morris	1990
Illinois	Dresden 2 & 3	Morris	1985
Iowa	Duane Arnold	Palo	1998
Maine	Maine Yankee	Wiscasset	1987
Maryland	Calvert Cliffs 1 & 2	Lusby	1991
Massachusetts	Pilgrim 1	Plymouth	1990
Massachusetts	Yankee-Rowe	Rowe	1988
Michigan	Palisades	South Haven	1988
Michigan	Big Rock Point	Charlevoix	1986
Michigan	Cook 1&2	Bridgman	1994
Minnesota	Monticello	Monticello	1991
Minnesota	Prairie Island 1&2	Red Wing	1988
Nebraska	Fort Calhoun	Fort Calhoun	1985
Nebraska	Cooper	Brownville	1996
New Jersey	Salem 1	Salem	1996
New Jersey	Salem 2	Salem	2000
New Jersey	Oyster Creek	Toms River	1987
New York	Indian Point 2	Buchanan	1984
New York	Indian Point 3	Buchanan	1993
New York	Fitzpatrick	Scriba	1991
New York	Nine Mile Point	Scriba	1990
New York	Ginna	Ontario	1992
North Carolina	Brunswick 1 & 2	Brunswick	1986
North Carolina	McGuire 1 & 2	Cornelius	1990
Ohio	Davis-Besse	Oak Harbor	1993

State:	Reactor	Nearest Town	Will Fill Authorized Capacity
Oregon	Trojan	Rainier	1990
Pennsylvania	Peach Bottom 2	Delta	1990
Pennsylvania	Peach Bottom 3	Delta	1991
Pennsylvania	Three Mile Island 1 & 2	Middletown	1986
Pennsylvania	Beaver Valley	Shippingport	1995
Pennsylvania	Susquehanna	Berwick	1997
South Carolina	Robinson 2	Hartsville	1985
South Carolina	Oconee 1, 2, & 3	Tamassee	1991
South Carolina	Summer 1	Winnsboro	2014
Tennessee	Sequoyah 1	Daisy	1993
Tennessee	Sequoyah 2	Daisy	1994
Vermont	Vermont Yankee	Vernon	1992
Virginia	Surry 1 & 2	Gravel Neck	1987
Virginia	North Anna 1	Mineral	1991
Virginia	North Anna 2	Mineral	1990
Wisconsin	Point Beach 1 & 2	Two Creeks	1995
Wisconsin	Kewaunee	Kewaunee	1991
Wisconsin	La Crosse	Genoa	1990

Source: U.S. Nuclear Regulatory Commission.

Electric utilities constructed storage pools at nuclear reactors to hold only a few years' worth of used fuel assemblies. Many utilities obtained more space by reracking, a process by which the assemblies are bunched closer together. The table shows the dates when commercial reactors will exhaust the space in which they are currently authorized to store assemblies. For a number of utilities, the dates can be extended through additional rerackings and possibly other techniques, such as rod consolidation, assuming the Nuclear Regulatory Commission approves.

will be available by the years 2007–2009. The commission also said that, just in case there are no repositories, "no significant environmental impacts will result from the storage of spent fuel for up to thirty years or more beyond the expiration of reactor operator licenses in on-site reactor facility storage pools or independent spent fuel installations located at reactor or away-from-reactor sites."

Once the NRC regulation becomes final, it will prevent anyone from questioning decisions by individual utilities to expand assembly storage. "A public interest group," an NRC spokesman said, "would not be able to raise this in an individual reactor licensing hearing." The lone NRC member who dissented from the rule, Victor Gilinsky, said that each power plant ought to be studied to determine whether assemblies could be stored there safely for an indefinite period. The rule, Gilinsky added, "puts off addressing the practical aspects of this problem for many years, and in some cases, decades."

If the used fuel assemblies stay where they are, it will take care of another troublesome waste worry of the utility industry —what to do with the reactors and other contaminated equipment that will remain radioactive for thousands of years. Government plans originally called for nuclear power plants to be dismantled immediately after they stopped generating electricity and for radioactive components to be carted away and buried. As with many other early government promises—reprocessing, waste-solidification facilities, permanent repositories— there is little likelihood that this one will be kept. Once again, the reason is miscalculation by scientists and engineers. They not only misjudged how radioactive a plant would become after thirty to forty years of operation but did not even recognize all the radioactive waste products that would build up. If a reactor was taken apart two years after it ceased generating electricity, a worker inadvertently exposed could receive a lethal dose of radiation in less than one minute from the accumulation of just one of several waste materials. And that would be after all the used fuel assemblies had been removed from the reactor.

Although small test reactors have been taken apart in the past, that work was little more than a laboratory experiment when compared with the dismantling of a large nuclear generating station. Even the Shippingport, Pennsylvania, reactor, the nation's first, which shut down in October 1982, and which the DOE expects to dismantle over the next several years, is less than one-fifteenth the size of today's commercial reactors. Perhaps equally significant, neither cost nor the volume of waste is a factor at Shippingport. That's because the taxpayer will foot the bill, whatever it may be, and because the waste will be deposited in a government-controlled burial ground.

With this in mind, the nuclear industry has hinted on occasion that it might be better, instead, to seal off reactor buildings —in effect, to entomb them. An official of the Atomic Industrial Forum, the nuclear-industry trade association, once told a House Science and Technology subcommittee that "because of costs, occupational radiation exposure and environmental considerations," it would be best to delay dismantling. If a power plant is allowed to sit for a century or so, radiation levels would fall off sharply, making the job easier and cheaper.

Although utilities would presumably have to continue to pay whatever expenses were involved in monitoring an entombed reactor, to guard against accidental radiation exposure to the public, the taxpayer might eventually pick up part of the tab. And that brings us to why it may be beneficial for utilities to allow fuel assemblies to remain at power plants for the next fifty to a hundred years—namely, another provision of the Nuclear Waste Policy Act of 1982, a special-interest clause that will ultimately free the utilities of any obligation to take care of their assemblies.

For the first time, the utility industry agreed to underwrite the cost of developing storage facilities, an expense that had previously been borne by the government. The act established a nuclear-waste fund that is financed through fees that individual utilities pay on the basis of the amount of electricity they generate with nuclear power. The levy, pegged at one mill per kilowatt hour, raised some $300 million in 1984. According to industry projections, the figure will increase gradually to about $600 million annually. By the year 2000, it is expected, utilities will have contributed more than $7 billion to the federal fund, with residential customers kicking in about $2.5 billion of that amount and business customers the rest. All these billions will go to finance the federal energy bureaucracy's quest for suitable sites and to build storage facilities, whether permanent or temporary.

But what happens in the year 2000 if no repository or storage center has been built? What happens if the federal government has frittered away billions of utility ratepayers' dollars and has nothing to show for it, just as it has done with billions of taxpayers' dollars for the last three decades? Perhaps foreseeing this eventuality, the utilities insisted on a provision in the waste policy act to protect their interests. In exchange for payments to the nuclear-waste fund, the secretary of energy, according to the law, will "dispose of high-level radioactive waste or spent nuclear fuel" beginning no later than January 1, 1998.

If no storage, either temporary or permanent, is available in 1998, how is the federal government to "dispose" of the used fuel assemblies? The most plausible answer is that they will stay exactly where they are, in reactor storage pools—but under new ownership. "They [the utilities] may be able to cook up a deal where they turn it over and leave it right on-site," says Russell Stanford, a waste specialist with the Edison Electric Institute, the electric-utility trade association.

In fact, it seems quite likely that the government will be obliged to do just that, for there appears to be little chance that a repository or monitored retrievable storage center will open in this century. Indeed, just one year after passage of the act, the DOE acknowledged that the repository's scheduled 1998 opening date would be missed by "two or three" years. Although many in Congress did not foresee the possibility of fuel rods' remaining at power plants under federal ownership, Andrea Dravo, a member of the House Interior and Insular Affairs subcommittee staff that helped draft the legislation, admitted, "[T]here is that kind of ambiguity in the statute. I suppose there would be an enormous fight about it, but there hasn't been any interpretation of the language to that extent."

So it is that the final legacy of the Nuclear Waste Policy Act of 1982 may be this: by the year 2000, a new generation of American taxpayers will be paying rent to the Consolidated Edison Company in New York, Commonwealth Edison Company in Chicago, Southern California Edison Company in Los Angeles, and other nuclear utilities to continue to store used fuel assemblies at their reactors.

7
Losing Track of Waste

FLAWED STATISTICS

"Low-level waste" is one of those deceptively reassuring terms that are the stock in trade of government and industry. After the first nuclear bombs were produced, the AEC lumped all radioactive by-products into two loosely defined categories. Liquid waste from the reprocessing of used fuel rods, intensely radioactive and lethal, was "high-level." All the rest was "low-level," and by implication harmless.

The distinction has allowed politicians, bureaucrats, and businessmen to obscure, and even to ignore, the potential hazard. In 1963, the AEC described low-level waste as "solids, liquids, and gases with radioactivity levels in concentrations so low as to present little or no problem of radiation safety protection. Very often, these are industrial wastes which are contaminated only slightly with radioactivity." In 1971, when Chem-Nuclear Systems Inc. was about to open a low-level burial ground at Barnwell, South Carolina, a company official assured area residents, "We are dealing in microcuries [millionths of a curie] of radioactive materials, most of which are short-lived. They have a short life of days or months." In 1977, the Federal Energy Administration, a predecessor of the DOE, offered this description: "Low-level wastes are those which contain limited concentrations or quantities of radioactivity and normally do not present significant environmental hazards."

In 1979, Mike McCormack, a Democratic congressman from Washington and a nuclear enthusiast known as Atom Mike on Capitol Hill, gave one of his periodic demonstrations during a House Science and Technology subcommittee hearing. To illustrate the insignificance of low-level waste, McCormack, had the following exchange with Gov. Dixy Lee Ray of Washington, herself a nuclear expert, who had once served as chairman of the AEC:

McCormack—"Governor Ray, I would like you to comment on a problem that keeps perplexing me. That is the problem of the double standards. We have a lot of double standards with respect to the nuclear industry, but I have brought in my Geiger counter, which I now have operating. It will make an occasional click for the audience.

"I have a radioactive substance in my hand I will hold up to it. That is reading about one millirem per hour, which is far higher than most of the bulk of a low-level waste that is being shipped around the country."

Ray—"Correct."

McCormack—"This is bought at the local hardware store in Washington, D.C., or Washington State, or anywhere else. It is a mantle for a Coleman gasoline lantern. Anybody can go down and buy one, or all you want of them. And they are far more radioactive than most of the low-level waste being shipped around the country."

Ray—"Yes, sir. The same thing can be said of smoke detectors. Smoke detectors, saving so many lives in private homes, are far more radioactive than most of the low-level waste."

Similarly, the Department of Energy, in a 1980 educational booklet, stated, "Low-level radioactive wastes are ordinary industrial and research wastes that have been contaminated in some way with a radioactive substance. These wastes contain very small amounts of radioactive elements. . . ."

Most low-level waste is less hazardous than used fuel rods

or other high-level waste, but the term does not describe its potential danger. While much of this waste is not injurious, if handled properly, some is deadly. Excerpts from two government documents, written more than a decade apart and not intended for public distribution, underscore the point.

A July 8, 1965, letter from Jon D. Anderson, general manager of the New York State Atomic and Space Development Authority, authorized the burial of waste with a radioactivity level of "10,000 rems per hour surface dose" at the commercial low-level dump at West Valley, New York. And on November 2, 1977, an NRC internal memorandum acknowledged that the operator of the low-level burial ground at Barnwell, South Carolina, "has handled waste ranging in intensity from five to 10,000 rems per hour." Anyone exposed for about three minutes to material emitting 10,000 rems per hour would be dead in a few weeks at most. West Valley and Barnwell are not exceptions. Waste with similarly high levels of radioactivity has also been dumped at other low-level graveyards. It will remain hazardous for hundreds of years.

Because the government can rightly say that some low-level waste is harmless, it has never bothered to keep an accurate count. It has no inventory of this waste. The government knows how many barrels of beer we produce in a year (194 million in 1982), how many cigarettes we manufacture (711 billion), how many pounds of peanuts we harvest (3.4 billion). But it cannot say with comparable accuracy how much low-level radioactive waste there is. This does not discourage it, though, from airily publishing waste statistics. The DOE released a fifty-eight-page report in the fall of 1981 showing that nuclear power plants had produced 1.4 million cubic feet of low-level waste the preceding year and that industries and institutions had generated another 1.3 million cubic feet. The document went on, "[C]ommercial low-level wastes are disposed of by shallow land burial at one of three commercial sites, which collectively received about 2.8 million cubic feet of low-level wastes in 1979 and 3.2 million cubic feet in 1980." (The figures included some government waste.) The report projected the annual waste production through the end of this century, putting it at 7.9 million cubic feet in the year 2000, up 193 percent from 2.7 million cubic feet in 1980. To add authenticity to its numbers, the DOE noted that its report was "prepared in consultation with the governors of the states, the Nuclear Regulatory Commission, the Environmental Protection Agency, the United States Geological Survey, and the United States Department of Transportation."

What is the problem with the statistics? Just this: no one measures how much low-level waste is generated, or what the level of its radioactivity is. The government merely records the volume and radioactivity of waste deposited at commercial and federal burial sites. It then assumes that the volume buried is the volume produced. That is as if the Department of Agriculture took the amount of wheat consumed or exported, which totaled 2.4 billion bushels in 1982, and announced that as the amount grown by farmers. To be accurate, 2.8 billion bushels of wheat were harvested—and 400 million of them were put in storage. When it comes to wheat and other items, the government gathers statistics on both the volume produced and the volume sold or disposed of. Not so with nuclear waste. As a result, federal agencies do not know how much radioactive garbage is turned out and then stored at unauthorized locations or dumped illegally, rather than shipped to licensed nuclear cemeteries.

Some state officials are suspicious of the statistics for other reasons. Joseph O. Ward, chief of the Radiological Health Branch of the Department of Health Services in California, questions the overall reliability of the government's numbers. "The data's been sort of bad anyway," he said, adding that "none of it ever seems to agree completely with what it is that's being shipped."

Individual states, which have few resources to track waste —yet are legally responsible for it—have attempted unsuccessfully to identify all waste produced within their borders. Milton Zukor, a nuclear-policy analyst with the Illinois Department of Nuclear Safety, said that Illinois once tried to obtain from the handlers of radioactive materials an accurate count of their waste volume. "For 1980, we did our own study by contacting people," he said, "but they don't know, really. The hospitals and users really don't have a good idea, [or] industrial users, of exactly how much they ship out. It seems strange."

William P. Dornsife, head of the Division of Nuclear Safety in the Pennsylvania Department of Environmental Resources, recalled another occasion when a research firm sought to conduct a survey of waste generators in each state. "Unfortunately," he said, "they didn't get a very good response. Less than 50 percent of the people they sent [survey] cards to did respond."

In another attempt to verify the data, a consulting firm working under a DOE contract collected statistics from low-level waste producers in Massachusetts for the years 1979–1981. The survey showed that Massachusetts businesses and institutions generated waste that contained 443,000 curies during the three years. Of that amount, 371,000 curies' worth was shipped to commercial burial grounds. But during the same period, the burial plots reported only 318,000 curies from Massachusetts—or 53,000 fewer than the state's generators said they shipped, and 125,000 fewer than they said they produced. Even this study was of limited value. It rested on a questionnaire sent to each known producer. It made no attempt at on-site verification.

The current state of low-level-waste accounting is most apparent in California's statistics for 1979–1981. During that period, the volume generated rose 40 percent, from 153,000 to 214,000 cubic feet. Yet the radioactivity in that waste plummeted 96 percent, from 83,000 to 3,000 curies, according to federal records analyzed by the authors. How is this possible? In three words, it is not.

No one, however, missed the curies in the first place. In theory, radioactive waste is the most closely monitored of all hazardous substances, its handling governed by federal and state regulations that run into millions of words. In practice, regulatory responsibility is split among so many different agencies that enforcement is fragmented and inconsistent, when there is any at all. No one knows how much low-level waste there is, where it is, or how radioactive it is. The primitive statistics defy explanation. Here is what regulators and statisticians had to say about California's disappearing radioactivity.

Leonard J. Arzt, a DOE spokesman, was puzzled by the contradictory numbers when they were pointed out to him. "It doesn't sound too logical," he said. "I don't have any way to explain that. . . . I don't know what the technicalities of it would be. It sounds a little strange." Arzt suggested that California authorities or someone at EG&G Idaho Inc., which collects low-level waste data for the federal government, might explain the phenomenon of soaring volume and plunging radioactivity.

Edward Jennrich, an EG&G Idaho official involved in compiling the statistics, was also perplexed. "We don't have an answer," Jennrich said after checking the company's records. He referred the authors to Joseph O. Ward at the California Department of Health Services, the state agency responsible for looking after radioactive materials. Ward was equally bewildered. He had this exchange with one of the authors:

Ward—"Oh, I don't have an answer for that. Golly, have you called EG&G in Idaho?"

Barlett—". . . They suggested you."

Ward—"I'm sorry I'm no help to you, I'm afraid. . . . That 83,000 to 3,000 [drop] astounds me. Quite frankly, I hadn't even noticed it. I wasn't tracking the stuff that closely, and so I don't know what caused that. But my curiosity is certainly piqued."

That no one could account for the 80,000-curie deficit— that no one had even detected it—flows from the casual attitude of federal and state governments toward low-level waste. It may well be that in time something will turn up to account for the missing California curies. Perhaps some radioactive waste is actually missing. Perhaps the curies disappeared in a bookkeeper's records or a computer—a nuclear-accounting error— rather than in the environment. Or maybe someone just couldn't count.

Nuclear-industry officials interviewed about irregularities

in other waste statistics said that curies are counted better today than they were in the past because of improved technology. For this reason, radioactivity was overstated in years gone by, they said, so it is only natural that today's figures are lower. Oddly, this theory seems to hold that low radiation readings should be accepted as the product of improved counting and waste management. High radiation readings, on the other hand, should be dismissed as mistakes, although the definition of a curie is the same now as it was half a century ago. In any event, none of this is to suggest that California's failure to look after its nuclear garbage is out of the ordinary. Quite the contrary. California is a radioactive barometer for the United States.

VANISHING CURIES

Despite obvious flaws in the data, it is still possible to draw some conclusions, solely on the basis of the waste that nuclear cemeteries reported receiving. An analysis of the statistics for the last two decades discloses a curious trend in the 1980s—a first in the atomic era. In 1981 and 1982, the nation recorded its first back-to-back yearly declines in low-level shipments to burial grounds. The figures suggest that as much as 1.4 million cubic feet of radioactive garbage disappeared. That is waste which, according to historical growth patterns, should have been buried, but was not.

If DOE projections are used, then more than 2 million cubic feet vanished in 1981 and 1982. From 1962 to 1980, the volume buried each year rose steadily, from 66,000 to 3.26 million cubic feet. Then it dropped 10 percent in 1981, to 2.94 million cubic feet, and fell an additional 9.5 percent in 1982, to 2.66 million cubic feet. The 1982 volume was actually 95,000 cubic feet below that buried four years earlier, in 1978. During the same years, however, electricity generated by nuclear plants rose from 276.4 billion to 282.8 billion kilowatt hours. Power plants account for more than half of all commercial low-level waste.

Some of the reduction may be due to compaction techniques designed to cut shipping and burial costs. A change in federal regulations also allowed medical institutions to hold some types of waste until it decayed to a harmless level, and then discard it in ordinary landfills. But it's highly unlikely that the entire decrease of 1.4 million cubic feet—or 2 million, as the case may be—is due to tighter packaging and reduced medical waste. What's more, preliminary data indicate that the amount buried fell again in 1983.

DOE officials are unable to interpret the shrinking numbers. They refer all questions to EG&G Idaho, which is a subsidiary of EG&G Inc., a company based in Wellesley, Massachusetts, whose annual revenue of nearly $1 billion is heavily dependent upon United States government nuclear programs. EG&G manages the Nevada Test Site, it supervises most nuclear-weapons tests, and it conducts research on nuclear warfare in space. It once worked on the government's abortive atomic rocket ship.

Asked why its figures show a continuing drop-off in low-level waste buried nationwide in the 1980s, an EG&G Idaho spokesman attributed the trend in part to compaction and increased on-site storage where the waste is produced. As to whether radioactive waste was being turned out in growing quantities but was not all being shipped to licensed burial grounds, the EG&G spokesman replied, "I guess that would be our—that's the basis we're going on now."

Neither compaction nor reduced medical waste would account for declining radioactivity. A physical substance can be compressed—but the radioactivity in that substance cannot be compressed. If three cubic feet containing ten curies are squeezed into one cubic foot, there are still ten curies in the smaller volume.

From 1980 to 1982, the radioactivity in low-level waste buried at commercial dumps averaged 342,000 curies a year. That was down 135,000 curies, or 28 percent, from the 477,000 curies in 1979's waste. When the decreases for the three years are totaled, the 1980–1982 decline amounts to 405,000 curies. The falloff came at a time when the curie output should have been going up because of growing nuclear power production, additional maintenance on aging reactors, and expanding use of radioactive materials by other industries. In fact, the curie output undoubtedly did rise.

The implication is that more than 400,000 curies are "lost." Like the California curies, moreover, they were not missed by anyone. No one knows whether they are iodine or cesium or strontium or plutonium or any other of the mostly man-made radioactive substances. This information would make a difference. Consider what two of these materials would do to someone who happened to come near them—keeping in mind that the effects do not take into account what would occur if the same materials were consumed in food or water.

If, say, 10,000 of the 400,000 or so missing curies were radioactive iodine 130, and you came upon that iodine, you would receive a lethal dose of radiation in three minutes. You would never notice the material, for 10,000 curies of radioactive iodine would be about 1/5,500 of one ounce. If the 10,000 curies were, say, cesium 137, you would receive a lethal dose of radiation in nine minutes. The cesium would be more noticeable, weighing a little over four ounces.

But iodine has a short half-life; every twelve hours it loses half its radioactivity. If you came across it forty days after it was produced, and if the decay process magically stopped at that moment, which it would not, you would thus have to stay around for over a century to receive a fatal dose of radiation. Cesium, by contrast, has a half-life of thirty years. If you came across it not forty days but ten years after it was produced, you would receive a lethal dose of radiation in eleven minutes.

Some of the missing curies are in waste that was discarded unlawfully. The General Accounting Office reported in March 1980 that "without a method to track waste from the point of generation to the point of disposal, it is highly probable that illegal dumping occurs." With rising transportation and burial costs, the GAO warned, "the incentive is growing for generators of low-level waste to illegally dump their waste."

In addition, an increasing amount of low-level waste is held in temporary storage across the United States, sometimes with

Low-Level Waste Production

(In Cubic Feet)

		1979	1980	1981	1982	Total
1	New York	338,026	257,192	247,940	235,792	1,078,950
2	South Carolina	285,655	278,627	237,134	252,283	1,053,699
3	Massachusetts	171,626	221,313	303,277	286,008	982,224
4	Illinois	238,652	287,456	268,210	178,971	973,289
5	Pennsylvania	241,018	273,401	194,474	212,873	921,766
6	North Carolina	187,305	326,054	165,340	156,335	835,034
7	California	153,333	216,439	213,685	190,943	774,400
8	New Jersey	106,225	195,322	144,046	126,530	572,123
9	Virginia	149,378	114,559	138,678	139,314	541,929
10	Alabama	129,673	108,767	98,915	97,184	434,539
11	Connecticut	140,197	111,769	112,546	64,695	429,207
12	Tennessee	39,940	94,430	106,013	104,989	345,372
13	Michigan	75,925	108,590	76,843	63,106	324,464
14	Florida	91,534	72,782	81,152	78,185	323,653
15	Texas	19,176	75,254	87,473	65,543	247,446
16	Georgia	44,531	30,547	94,218	70,063	239,359
17	Minnesota	51,594	70,699	55,055	61,694	239,042
18	Maryland	34,537	42,695	52,724	40,399	170,355
19	Oregon	43,048	50,499	31,288	35,243	160,078
20	Ohio	67,273	43,330	15,432	28,287	154,322
21	Nebraska	28,287	29,522	26,521	29,205	113,535
22	Washington	27,510	21,012	28,181	29,982	106,685
23	Iowa	33,937	31,571	20,200	18,434	104,142
24	Arkansas	9,358	8,864	55,302	29,628	103,152
25	Rhode Island	16,350	52,547	9,817	5,297	84,011
26	Wisconsin	17,198	22,672	9,535	12,890	62,295
27	Vermont	13,066	19,246	15,644	13,949	61,905
28	Nevada	141	33,584	16,350	4,661	54,736
29	Maine	14,691	15,256	15,785	8,122	53,854
30	Missouri	11,618	10,947	3,461	10,630	36,656
31	Kentucky	6,851	12,995	2,260	2,578	24,684
32	Utah	3,708	2,684	9,499	5,862	21,753
33	Colorado	7,946	3,567	3,531	2,260	17,304
34	Hawaii	2,931	1,801	7,946	2,154	14,832
35	Oklahoma	742	2,507	6,215	3,637	13,101
36	New Mexico	2,825	1,342	2,331	2,084	8,582
37	Distr. Columbia	1,165	2,472	0	3,990	7,627
38	Mississippi	2,401	1,201	3,461	0	7,063
39	Indiana	953	1,766	1,907	1,201	5,827
40	Delaware	4,238	71	0	1,342	5,651
41	New Hampshire	2,719	212	706	1,483	5,120
42	Arizona	1,907	1,730	706	106	4,449
43	Kansas	353	600	1,660	494	3,107

	1979	1980	1981	1982	Total
44 West Virginia	1,413	9	35	388	1,845
45 Louisiana	671	9	71	1,059	1,810
46 Montana	106	212	388	71	777
47 Idaho	247	9	35	0	291
48 North Dakota	71	141	0	0	212
49 Alaska	9	9	0	0	18
50 South Dakota	9	9	0	0	18
51 Wyoming	0	0	0	0	0
Total	2,822,067	3,258,292	2,965,990	2,679,944	11,726,293

Source: Compiled from U.S. Department of Energy records.

The table shows the amount of low-level waste produced in each state from 1979 to 1982 and the four-year totals. Because of rounding and the way government statistics are maintained, the figures may not be identical in all cases to those in other low-level waste tables.

the approval of regulatory agencies, sometimes without their knowledge. In 1980, Texas Health Department officials stumbled onto the fact that the Todd Shipyards Corporation had stockpiled 12,000 barrels of waste. The fifty-five-gallon drums, many in "deteriorated condition" and some containing plutonium and strontium, according to court records, were stacked up in a warehouse on Pelican Island in hurricane-prone Galveston Bay. Along with its facilities for building and repairing ships, Todd operated a radioactive-waste collection and processing center on the island. Electric utilities, medical institutions, and other waste generators sent their nuclear garbage to Todd's Research and Technical Division, where it was compacted and shipped to licensed atomic graveyards.

After Texas authorities began an investigation, Todd discovered an additional 4,800 barrels of waste on its property, bringing the total for the year to almost 17,000. A Todd official had an explanation for the newly discovered 4,800 barrels, which he spelled out in legal papers filed in Galveston County District Court. He said that 2,000 were an "administrative error," 1,500 held waste from a contamination accident and fire at the plant, and 1,300 "were an error in initial counting." How

Radioactivity in Low-Level Waste
(In Curies)

		1979	1980	1981	1982	Total
1	Massachusetts	138,146	126,203	53,942	84,655	402,946
2	Illinois	9,044	11,326	34,649	196,564	251,583
3	New York	78,961	63,406	71,878	29,164	243,409
4	California	83,281	32,002	3,271	18,070	136,624
5	Florida	88,345	2,970	2,520	2,794	96,629
6	Pennsylvania	11,837	20,798	9,279	15,033	56,947
7	Michigan	875	3,155	39,665	1,018	44,713
8	Alabama	9,543	6,801	6,889	11,598	34,831
9	South Carolina	2,784	3,503	16,742	11,176	34,205
10	North Carolina	4,504	8,048	7,663	5,450	25,665
11	Minnesota	13,315	886	943	10,126	25,270
12	Maryland	2,271	14,926	2,550	1,393	21,140
13	New Jersey	7,450	2,197	3,507	6,481	19,635
14	Virginia	9,314	793	4,231	1,249	15,587
15	Connecticut	2,764	3,056	2,813	6,843	15,476
16	Georgia	820	1,083	4,569	3,644	10,116
17	Iowa	1,216	5,741	1,063	1,273	9,293
18	Wisconsin	3,058	3,569	1,202	1,286	9,115
19	Arkansas	180	1,256	4,196	3,314	8,946
20	Maine	555	5,118	1,887	33	7,593
21	Ohio	5,632	140	128	427	6,327
22	Kentucky	37	5,320	107	24	5,488
23	Oregon	337	1,830	1,072	28	3,267
24	Nevada	62	1,368	1,817	1	3,248
25	Nebraska	140	1,869	600	593	3,202
26	Vermont	918	921	1,146	208	3,193
27	Indiana	1	2,446	5	2	2,454
28	Texas	410	717	1,012	257	2,396
29	Missouri	304	358	295	314	1,271
30	Washington	278	393	35	115	821
31	Distr. Columbia	333	126	0	162	621
32	Tennessee	56	85	127	332	600
33	Arizona	61	225	42	1	329
34	Oklahoma	266	1	1	20	288
35	Mississippi	54	155	1	0	210
36	Utah	9	2	3	104	118
37	Rhode Island	1	2	1	89	93
38	West Virginia	41	1	1	15	58
39	Hawaii	10	20	2	17	49
40	Colorado	25	8	5	3	41
41	Montana	32	2	1	0	35
42	Louisiana	1	3	1	10	15
43	New Mexico	1	13	1	0	15
44	Delaware	1	0	0	10	11

	1979	1980	1981	1982	Total
45 New Hampshire	3	3	3	2	11
46 Idaho	8	1	1	0	10
47 Kansas	3	1	1	0	5
48 Alaska	1	1	0	0	2
49 North Dakota	1	1	0	0	2
50 South Dakota	1	1	0	0	2
51 Wyoming	0	0	0	0	0
Total	477,290	332,850	279,867	413,898	1,503,905

Source: Compiled from U.S. Department of Energy records.

could such a "counting" error occur? The Todd executive explained that, too, in testimony during legal proceedings initiated by Texas to compel the company to send its nuclear garbage to some other state.

Assistant attorney general—"And it's just that somebody walked around going one, two, three, four, etc. and they missed it somehow?"

Todd executive—"With a number of that type I would, you know, that size, 1,300, I would say they must have missed some section of drums they thought they counted and didn't, something like that."

The inability of federal and state governments to track large volumes of radioactive waste is in sharp contrast to the way they respond when tiny quantities of usable radioactive substances go astray. These same agencies have launched hundreds of investigations to find a couple of curies, even a few thousandths of one curie, of nuclear materials that are not yet waste. They also have routinely imposed fines or other sanctions against businesses and institutions that have mishandled or lost radioactive substances used in medical testing and industrial processes. A random geographic sampling from the files of the Nuclear Regulatory Commission and state regulatory agencies tells the story.

CALIFORNIA. When a drilling company lost twenty curies of a radioactive material at the bottom of a 10,000-foot well, red iron oxide cement was pumped into the hole, plugs were installed at the 9,900-foot level, and a plaque warning about radiation was attached to the well casing.

FLORIDA. Police were notified and the news media alerted when a measuring gauge containing 1/17 of one curie was stolen from a construction site.

MARYLAND. Authorities mounted an investigation to determine how a company temporarily lost, and later recovered, a sealed container that held 1/200 of one curie.

MASSACHUSETTS. NRC health physicists joined state authorities in an effort to trace what happened to 1/5 of one curie of a liquid radioactive material that dripped from a truck along a state highway.

NEW YORK. Authorities conducted an investigation and subsequently compelled a university medical center to revise its procedures after 1/60 of one curie was vented into the atmosphere over a seven-day period.

PENNSYLVANIA. When a drilling company lost 1/40 of one curie of a radioactive material at the bottom of a 120-foot-deep hole in a coal seam at Acosta, in Somerset County, the well was cemented over, a plaque describing the radiation hazard was posted at the site, and the information was added to maps and deeds to comply with NRC guidelines.

TEXAS. Search teams scoured scrap yards and advised radiography companies to be on the lookout for a measuring gauge containing one curie that disappeared from a company.

There is no comparable accountability system for large quantities of waste, even though it, too, can cause cancer, birth defects, and death. Nor is there any pressure to devise one. A gauge that holds a fraction of one curie is a physical object that can be readily recognized and identified. If some unsuspecting person picks it up and suffers radiation injuries, the cause is immediately apparent. So are the legal consequences. But curies in waste dumped in the earth are invisible, next to impossible to trace to their origin. It is even more difficult to attribute to their presence a cancer that develops years later.

But when it comes to monitoring radioactive materials or waste, the federal government is very inconsistent. At the same time that it can misplace tens of thousands of curies and never notice, it can scour the countryside for a lost fraction of one curie; and while it is doing that, it can lose hundreds of pounds of enriched uranium and plutonium that can be used to make atomic bombs.

In Erwin, Tennessee, a nuclear-fuel fabrication plant run by Nuclear Fuel Services Inc., a Getty Oil Company subsidiary, is periodically closed as regulators and FBI agents attempt to find missing uranium. Nuclear Fuel Services was also the operator of the failed West Valley, New York, reprocessing plant. An internal NRC report, dated December 11, 1979, and originally classified "confidential," offered a sober assessment of uranium bookkeeping at Erwin.

During a four-year period, the Tennessee facility "has failed to establish an heavily enriched uranium accounting system which can consistently and confidently demonstrate account- ability for this sensitive material within acceptable limits of measurement error." This is not to say that government inves- tigators and company officials are unable to explain any of the uranium disappearances. They do know where some of it went. Because of an equipment failure, according to NRC records, and undetermined number of pounds went up the plant's smokestack. Radioactive particles rained over the surrounding area.

In addition, a random survey showed that the fifty-five- gallon barrels of waste the company shipped to burial grounds contained 20 percent more uranium than Nuclear Fuel Services had said. On still other occasions, the company shipped out barrels it labeled as empty when in fact they contained uranium, according to NRC records. Accounting was so haphazard that, following a joint FBI-NRC investigation in 1979, an NRC staff member concluded in a report, "Both the staff and the FBI have completed their investigations without being able to state con- clusively whether or not a theft has occurred at Nuclear Fuel Services."

Federal officials have been equally vague about the disap- pearance of enriched uranium or plutonium at other plants.

Back in the mid-1960s, nearly 400 pounds of enriched uranium vanished from the Nuclear Materials & Equipment Corporation, near the western Pennsylvania town of Apollo. CIA analysts publicly speculated years later that the uranium had been smuggled to Israel, where it was used to make that country's first nuclear weapons.

The United States government lost not only hundreds of pounds of uranium and plutonium but also scores of buildings contaminated with radioactive waste. During the 1950s and early 1960s, as many as 150 properties around the country, where radioactive materials had been handled in the early days of the atomic industry, were cleaned up and released for other purposes. Later, in the mid-1970s, the government found that it had not cleaned up some of them—which by then included public parks and factories—as much as it thought it had. Radiation levels in certain areas remained too high. In the meantime, the government had forgotten just where some of those sites were.

So it was with a plant in St. Louis where uranium ore was processed from 1945 to 1957 in buildings owned by the Mallinckrodt Chemical Works, now Mallinckrodt Inc. Between 1948 and 1952, some of the buildings were decontaminated and returned to Mallinckrodt by the government for unrestricted use —certified as radiation-free. A quarter-century later, in the summer of 1977, a survey by the Oak Ridge National Laboratory detected radiation levels above federal standards both inside and outside the buildings. It also found that the concentration of radium in a water sample exceeded federal guidelines and that there was excessive radium in the soil.

The St. Louis study was part of a nationwide program by the former Energy Research and Development Administration to locate properties once under federal control where waste had accumulated. James L. Liverman, then ERDA's assistant administrator for environment and safety, recounted the difficulty for a House Science and Technology subcommittee in June 1977: "One of the problems we found was that records indicating the degree of cleanup had been destroyed. In spite of searching through the federal record system and company record systems, it became totally impossible to locate records on about sixty or seventy of those sites."

At one point during its quest for radioactive properties, the agency distributed a press release asking citizens to notify the department whether they knew of buildings where nuclear materials had been handled in the past, and waste stored. The situation is much the same at the NRC, which is responsible for properties where private businesses are licensed to work with radioactive materials. Following an investigation completed in 1982, the General Accounting Office reported that the NRC's efforts to locate former sites and determine the adequacy of cleanup operations have been "hampered because of its inadequate records control system. The system does not allow NRC to locate all files, and the files located were, in many cases, incomplete and unclear, and did not contain evidence of cleanup action taken." The failure of the government's record keeping does not bode well for the future, when the number of properties contaminated with radioactive waste will be many times greater.

8
Burial-Ground States Revolt

THE FIRST DUMPS

In the beginning, the United States government had no difficulty in dealing with low-level radioactive waste. It simply packed the material into barrels and loaded them onto navy ships. The vessels headed out to sea. When they reached their appointed destinations, first off the California coast, later off the New Jersey coast and Massachusetts Bay, crewmen shoved the fifty-five-gallon drums overboard, where they sank more than 6,000 feet to the ocean floor. At that depth, the experts believed, the cleansing effect of the currents would safely disperse all radioactivity if the barrels should ever leak.

The practice began in 1946 and continued into the 1960s before concern mounted over the possible consequences of pollution. Such worry was well founded. An EPA study in the 1970s disclosed that as many as one-fourth of the 47,500 barrels jettisoned in the Pacific Ocean near the Farallon Islands, fifty miles west of San Francisco, had ruptured. The EPA found elevated levels of radioactivity in the seabed and marine life; in a report to the International Atomic Energy Agency, it said it was clearly evident that plutonium had been "released from the radioactive wastecontainers." Although some of the waste had been diluted, as had been promised, much of it remained on the ocean floor, where plant and animal life fed on it.

Scientists were divided as to the significance of the findings. Adhering to a long tradition of immediately dismissing most concerns over radioactive waste, industry scientists labeled the escaping radioactivity "inconsequential" and "trivial." Others offered a different view. W. Jackson Davis, professor of biology and environmental studies at the University of California at Santa Cruz, said the EPA studies "furnish the first concrete evidence that radioactivity from the dumpsite has entered the oceanic food chain." He added, "I hope the lesson of the Farallon incident is clear to all involved. If we put radioactivity into the ocean, it is going to return to us in the fish that we eat eventually."

Both sides were correct. No one was going to drop dead after eating fish caught at the underwater nuclear grave. On the other hand, a variety of sea life once free of radioactivity now was contaminated. More significant, the pollution resulted from

Naval crews dumping low-level waste at sea in 1957, a practice halted in 1970. *U.S. Department of Energy*

the dumping of a comparatively tiny quantity of radioactivity. Although government records were, as usual, very inadequate, the waste apparently contained no more than 100,000 curies. That works out to 0.0007 of 1 percent of the radioactivity in all commercial waste now awaiting burial.

The federal government's decision to end ocean dumping was based on economics and convenience rather than on health or environmental consequences.* During the 1940s and 1950s, most low-level waste came from the production of nuclear weapons. It either was buried at federal installations, such as the Savannah River plant or Hanford Reservation, or was dumped at sea, along with commercial waste. As the volume of commercial waste grew, industry objected to the cost of ocean dumping. The AEC, it argued, should permit the burial of waste on land, just as it did its own defense garbage.

To assist the fledgling atomic industry, the AEC announced in May 1960 that it would bury commercial radioactive waste, along with defense refuse, at two federal locations—the Oak Ridge National Laboratory in Oak Ridge, Tennessee, and the National Reactor Testing Station in Idaho Falls, Idaho. The commission emphasized that the plan was temporary, that eventually it wanted private enterprise to take over the burial of commercial low-level wastes. To that end, the commission decided that "regional disposal sites for permanent disposal of low-level packaged radioactive waste materials shall be established, as needed, on state or federal government-owned land."

The handful of companies that had been collecting nuclear junk, packaging it, and barging it out to sea seized the opportunity. The Nuclear Engineering Company of Pleasanton, California, acquired properties near Beatty, Nevada, and Maxey Flats, Kentucky, and quickly won AEC approval for the country's first privately managed low-level graveyards. The AEC guaranteed a captive market for the company, just as it did for Nuclear Fuel Services when the latter went into the reprocessing business. The commission announced in May 1962 that it

---

*See page 336 for detailed note.

would no longer accept industrial and institutional low-level waste at Oak Ridge or Idaho Falls. Henceforth, all waste would have to be sent to commercial cemeteries.

After Beatty opened in 1962, other corporate burial grounds followed. Maxey Flats and West Valley started up in 1963; Richland, Washington, in 1965; Sheffield, Illinois, in 1967; and Barnwell, South Carolina, in 1971. All came into existence without any overall planning or guidance from the federal government or from any other supervisory authority. Sites were selected and developed by private interests and licensed by the states or the AEC. The switch from sea to land burial proved an immediate success. The AEC reported in January 1964 that "now, principally because of economic considerations, more than 95 percent of the low-level wastes are buried on land."

Contrary to its 1960 policy statement, the AEC made no effort to set up regional burial grounds "as needed." Instead, they sprang up by happenstance. Little thought was given during the licensing process to the suitability or need for a facility in a particular location. Maxey Flats illustrates the point. From the time it opened, in 1963, until it closed, in 1977, about 4.7 million cubic feet of waste was buried. Of that figure, only 1 percent was generated in Kentucky.

The federal government promised, as it had with regard to reprocessing and high-level waste, that the technology for managing low-level garbage had been perfected. The commercial burial grounds would be modeled after the government's own nuclear cemeteries at a dozen defense installations. The waste would be packaged in steel drums or wooden boxes and placed in trenches up to fifty feet deep and several hundred feet long. When the burial pits were filled, a layer of earth would be spread over the containers.

Since there had never been any independent monitoring of government dumps, the public could only assume that all were successful. They were not. And before long, neither were the private dumps. By the mid-1970s, three of the six had experienced a common failure. Rainwater accumulated in closed

Low-level waste at Barnwell, South Carolina, in 1983. *Philadelphia Inquirer / Nick Kelsh*

trenches, eroded the earthen covers, and carried off radioactivity, contaminating neighboring properties. West Valley was the first to close, in 1975. Maxey Flats followed in 1977 and Sheffield in 1978.

The loss of half the nation's nuclear cemeteries came at a time of soaring waste production. When all six were open in 1975, some 1.4 million cubic feet of waste was buried. By 1978, the volume had jumped 60 percent, to 2.5 million cubic feet. The shutdown in Illinois, Kentucky, and New York left waste generators with little choice. They rerouted their shipments to the three remaining sites, creating political turmoil in those states, which began to see themselves, with some justification, becoming the nation's nuclear dumping grounds.

An analysis of DOE statistics shows that from 1979 to 1982, seven states accounted for 71 percent of the radioactive trash buried at Beatty, a hundred miles northwest of Las Vegas. Nevada was not one of them. Rather, the waste came from California (237,000 cubic feet), Pennsylvania (83,000 cubic feet), New Jersey (70,000 cubic feet), New York (59,000 cubic feet), Illinois (59,000 cubic feet), Nebraska (57,000 cubic feet), and Michigan (50,000 cubic feet).

Not only were the other forty-seven states carting all their unwanted waste to the three dump states but they were also careless in packaging and transporting it. Trucks that rumbled through Las Vegas dripped radioactivity along highways. A California shipper mixed long-lived uranium with gypsum, rather than the required concrete, and the shipment caught fire at Beatty, exposing ten persons to radiation. As Washington's Gov. Dixy Lee Ray summed up the situation in all three states, "What has happened there [at Richland], and with the other two sites, is that increasingly over the years we have been receiving more and more shipments coming from various places in the country that were improperly packaged, improperly handled on the way, arriving split open, spilling out, and various things of that sort."

So it was in July 1979 that Nevada's Gov. Robert F. List announced the temporary closing of Beatty. The shutdown was prompted when another truck hauling waste leaked radioactivity. In addition, the accident at Three Mile Island promised an unexpected surge in waste shipments, running into the tens of thousands of cubic feet. When List learned that Beatty might receive 700,000 gallons of contaminated water from the Pennsylvania plant, he told local newspaper reporters, "If it's liquid, the people responsible for it can drink it."

Although List reopened Beatty two weeks later, he began to pursue other legal options to close it permanently. Three months later, in October 1979, Governor Ray of Washington followed Nevada's lead and closed Hanford. That same month, after several barrels of radioactive waste were found some dis-

The chart shows the volume of commercial low-level waste produced annually and expected to be produced annually by 2020.

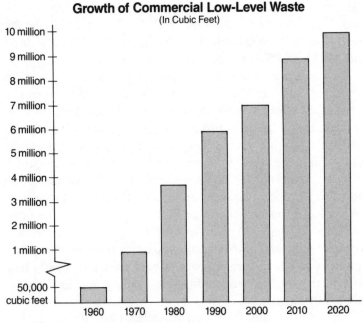

Growth of Commercial Low-Level Waste
(In Cubic Feet)

Source: Compiled from U.S. Department of Energy records.

tance from a burial trench at Beatty, Governor List ordered the Nevada dump closed once again. And still that same month, Gov. Richard Riley of South Carolina announced that though Barnwell would remain open, the volume of waste accepted for burial would be slashed by 50 percent over the next two years, from 2.4 to 1.2 million cubic feet.

These actions brought about the desired results. They focused public attention, for the first time, on the country's failure to develop a master plan for low-level waste. That only one dump was open, whereas six had been open just four years earlier, underscored the point. South Carolina's Riley told a House Science and Technology subcommittee in November 1979, "[The nation has] been guilty of gross negligence in the field of nuclear waste management. We have been willing to accept the advantages of nuclear energy, yet we have not had the wisdom and courage to come to grips with the problem of nuclear waste. . . . The states have, on the whole, been irresponsible, with the majority believing if they did nothing, someone —whether a few courageous states or the federal government —would come along and bail them out. The issue will not disappear nor will a few states carry the entire burden any longer."

As a result of the dump closings, waste began to back up in hospitals, research laboratories, industries, and power plants. Brokers, the atomic-trash haulers that collect waste from companies and institutions producing it and deliver it to burial grounds, were especially hard hit. Their warehouses, where they kept the waste before shipping it out, overflowed, as some began holding it longer than their licenses permitted. To protect themselves against possible future disruptions, brokers and utilities sought permission from the NRC to increase the volume of waste they could store temporarily. Such was the case of Applied Health Physics Inc., a broker in Bethel Park, Pennsylvania, twelve miles south of Pittsburgh.

The company had originally received a license to collect and store radioactive waste for a maximum of three months. Then it had to be transferred to a commercial burial ground. In the summer of 1980, the NRC discovered more than sixty barrels of waste in an open area, exposed to the elements, at the company's headquarters in an industrial park. Many of the fifty-five-gallon drums contained radioactive liquids and were deteriorating, according to NRC reports. Some had been in storage since October 1978, over a year beyond the permissible time limit. Robert G. Gallaghar, president of Applied Health Physics, blamed it all on the hospitals that had sealed the waste in the barrels. "These drums were illegally packaged and incorrectly described by these hospitals," he wrote to the NRC.

Applied Health Physics had shipped fifty-six barrels to the Barnwell burial ground in June 1979. All were labeled as containing solid waste. When they arrived, Barnwell inspectors found that two held radioactive liquid. All fifty-six were returned to Bethel Park because of improper packaging. Further inquiry, Gallaghar said, showed that sixteen hospitals at which the waste was picked up "had disposed of liquid wastes . . . and had described these drums as containing solids." Whatever the case, the NRC determined that continued storage of the barrels at Bethel Park "would present an unreasonable hazard to the health and safety of the public due to potential exposures to radioactive materials. . . ."

Furthermore, the NRC accused Applied Health Physics of engaging in "chronic non-compliance [that] indicates a careless disregard for the public health, safety and interest." In an order issued in December 1980, the commission directed the company to arrange for the "immediate transfer" of most waste in its possession and to accept no further shipments. At the same time, the NRC proposed a permanent ban on the company's collection of radioactive waste, which would effectively put it out of business.

Gallaghar advised the NRC in a letter dated January 27, 1981, that the company had implemented "corrective measures which we believe will prevent our being vulnerable to this situation again." Two months later, the commission, noting that the company's corrective measures would bring it "in compliance with commission requirements," lifted its previous order and allowed Applied Health Physics to resume operations. Among the proposed changes in the company's procedures was an increase in storage capacity at Bethel Park from 60 to 150 barrels.

CONGRESS REACTS TO A "CRISIS"

Even before Nevada, South Carolina, and Washington rebelled, low-level-waste planners had known that more dumps would be needed to take care of the projected growth in such garbage. No fewer than three separate studies came to essentially the same conclusion on how best to provide added burial capacity—namely, by expanding the federal role in the development and management of waste sites.

The House Government Operations Committee recommended in 1976 that Congress and the president consider legislation to "reassert federal jurisdiction and regulatory authority . . . over commercial land burial sites" to provide a comprehensive plan for centralized control, licensing, and long-term care. The next year, a Nuclear Regulatory Commission task force also called for greater federal involvement: "Federal control over the disposal of low-level waste should be increased by requiring joint federal/state site approval, NRC licensing, federal ownership of the land, and a federally administered perpetual care program."

Explaining why it thought the federal government, rather than the states, should take the lead, the task force said, "Waste disposal is a national problem, and the states have neither the resources nor responsibility to develop and implement a national low-level waste disposal program. The citizens of individual states should not bear the cost of major contingency actions or inadequacies in perpetual care funding for burial sites which serve national rather than state needs."

Early in 1978, a DOE task force came to the same conclusion. The panel recommended that the department take over the nation's commercial burial grounds and combine them with the defense dumps it already managed. By doing so, the depart-

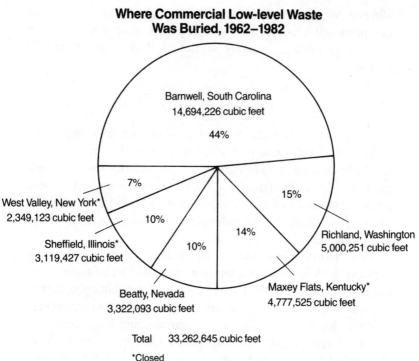

**Where Commercial Low-level Waste
Was Buried, 1962–1982**

Barnwell, South Carolina
14,694,226 cubic feet

44%

7%

West Valley, New York*
2,349,123 cubic feet

10%

15%

Sheffield, Illinois*
3,119,427 cubic feet

10%

14%

Richland, Washington
5,000,251 cubic feet

Beatty, Nevada
3,322,093 cubic feet

Maxey Flats, Kentucky*
4,777,525 cubic feet

Total   33,262,645 cubic feet

*Closed
Source: U.S. Department of Energy.

Low-level waste from power plants, industry, medical facilities, and educational and research organizations has been buried at six commercial dumps since 1962. Nearly one-half has been buried at the Barnwell, South Carolina, facility.

ment would have twenty sites that could be "managed as a single complex." The task force said that "such an approach would permit strengthening of technical/operating practices, the development of uniform criteria, the minimization of the number of additional sites required in the future . . . [and] the provision for long-term surveillance."

The notion that the DOE should assume responsibility for low-level waste and open its burial grounds for commercial use made a certain amount of sense. They were already established, the properties were owned by the United States government, and enough land was available for the interment of both commercial and military waste for years to come. Implicit in the studies was the idea that federal control would avoid the haphazard siting that had marked the early development of atomic graveyards. Continuing the existing patchwork regulatory scheme would inevitably lead, as the NRC study saw it, to an "undisciplined proliferation of low-level burial sites."

Although the federal approach would probably have pleased most states, it was vigorously opposed by Nevada, South Carolina, and Washington. The prospect of the national government's taking over nuclear dumps within their borders and deciding who could and could not bury waste in them, as well as how much, was politically unpalatable. The states feared that if they relinquished control, they would be compelled to continue burying most of the nation's radioactive waste. Since the DOE already operated defense low-level burial plots in all three states, that fear was very palpable.

With this in mind, Governors List of Nevada, Riley of South Carolina, and Ray of Washington formed a loose coalition to head off the drive for more federal authority. They countered with the suggestion that full responsibility be turned over to the states. This would replace the fractured system in which those states with laws comparable to the federal government's managed the waste, while the NRC looked after it in those without such laws. A report of the State Planning Council on Radioactive Waste, which Riley headed, outlined the concept as follows: "The State Planning Council recommends that the national policy of the United States on low-level radioactive waste shall be that every state is responsible for the disposal of low-level radioactive waste generated by nondefense-related activities within its boundaries."

In case there was any doubt about the seriousness of the dump states, Butler Derrick, a Democratic congressman from South Carolina whose district included Barnwell, introduced legislation patterned after that proposed by Governor Riley.

Derrick's bill, entitled the Low-Level Radioactive Waste Policy Act, made each state responsible for the waste it produced. A state could build its own dump or join with neighboring states to form a regional compact.

"It is my firm belief that the federal government should not acquire land or run low-level waste sites," Derrick said after introducing his legislation. "The solution should be left to the states and the states should be provided with the authority to form interstate compacts. . . . This approach would, as I envision it, result in the creation of approximately six or seven sites. It would insure that no single state would become the dumping ground for the rest of the nation's low-level radioactive wastes." The most significant feature of Derrick's bill was not the spirit of interstate cooperation that it was supposed to inspire but the authority it would confer on regional compacts, once organized, to bar waste from other regions.

To a dispassionate observer, the fifty states would hardly have seemed the ideal arena in which to settle acrimonious disputes over nuclear waste. During the years leading up to 1980, the issue had become increasingly contentious at both the state and the local level. Troubled by the possible environmental damage and health effects of radioactive pollution, state and local governments enacted laws or ordinances to restrict the burial, storage, or transportation of waste.

Alabama, Indiana, Louisiana, Maryland, Michigan, and Oregon banned the disposal of all radioactive wastes. Connecticut, Illinois, Montana, New Hampshire, South Dakota, Texas, Vermont, and West Virginia banned the disposal of high level waste only. Colorado, Connecticut, Kentucky, Louisiana, Maine, Minnesota, Mississippi, New Hampshire, and North Dakota required legislative approval before nuclear waste could be buried. Kansas passed a law prohibiting geological investigations of possible burial sites without the prior notification of the governor and legislature. Louisiana passed a law forbidding high-level waste from being transported into the state for any purpose. At the local level, counties, cities, and towns adopted ordinances that aimed to restrict waste transportation through their communities.

Nevertheless, many governors, especially those in the South and the West, found the appeal to states' rights irresistible. As support grew, the Carter administration, which had been pushing for more federal control, reversed course. Two years earlier, the DOE had urged a federal takeover of commercial dumps. Now it said the states should maintain responsibility. Worthington Bateman, deputy undersecretary of energy, told Congress in November 1979, "[W]e want to see the states solve the problem. We think it is a state problem." Joseph M. Hendrie, chairman of the NRC, also abandoned his former position, during an appearance on Capitol Hill. "There was a while a year or two ago, perhaps before," he said, "when I think I would have told you that I thought the federal government should step in and take over the low-level waste disposal responsibilities across the country. I have changed my mind on it. It seems to me the states could do a perfectly good job."

The proposed act received remarkably little congressional scrutiny. Ordinarily, waste legislation, because of its controversial nature, is subjected to long and vigorous debate. There are hearings on waste bills in every session, at which industry representatives, officials of the DOE, the NRC, and other federal agencies testify. But none were held specifically on Derrick's bill. Indeed, the only waste hearing at the time was a one-day session conducted by the House Science and Technology subcommittee in November 1979. And that was convened on the erroneous pretext that the nation's health-care system was jeopardized by a shortage of low-level burial grounds.

As the indefatigable "Atom Mike" McCormack explained, "We are indeed facing a national crisis, and the main problem is a medical one. It is hospitals, medical schools, and radiopharmaceutical manufacturers whose operations are most directly threatened. This situation is imperiling the health care of the nation."

Portraying low-level waste as largely a by-product of hospitals is a favorite tactic of nuclear supporters in and out of Congress. But such claims are misleading. From 1980 to 1982, some 56 percent of all commercial low-level waste was produced by nuclear power plants. An additional 29 percent was generated by industrial plants. Only 13 percent came from hospitals and research institutions. The remaining 2 percent came from other sources.

In some states, reactor waste constitutes the overwhelming percentage of the total. From 1979 through 1982, nuclear power plants accounted for 98 percent of Nebraska's low-level waste, 84 percent of Connecticut's, and 81 percent of Florida's. What's more, government projections put the percentage of low-level waste from power plants by 1990 at 63 to 68 percent.

Not only does medical waste make up a small amount of the overall volume but it is also much less radioactive than that produced by power plants. Most hospital waste decays to harmless levels in a matter of days, weeks, or months. Power-plant waste, by contrast, will remain hazardous for hundreds of years. Even so, both are classified as low level.

Given the difference in radioactivity and volume between hospital waste and other types, the medical community has little in common with industrial and utility producers. Some physicians and hospital administrators, along with federal and state officials, industry, and educators, have nevertheless sought to convey the opposite impression. After Governor Ray closed Richland, hospitals and research facilities in New England announced they were cutting down on the number of diagnostic tests using radioactive materials. The *Washington Post* reported that the dump closings threaten "to halt much of the nation's cancer research." Even Joseph Hendrie, the NRC chairman, got into the act, declaring that the lack of burial sites could force "substantial curtailment" of medical research. At the hearing conducted by the House Science and Technology subcommittee, Dr. Leonard M. Freeman, president of the Society of Nuclear Medicine, told lawmakers, "There is no question that nuclear medicine, which daily provides enormous benefits to tens of thousands of people, is in jeopardy. If the benefits of nuclear medicine are to continue uninterrupted, then, in fact, we must have means of disposing of low-level radiation waste. . . . The legislation and problems that this subcommittee is facing at this particular time are quite critical to the practice of medicine. I seriously doubt that Congress will stand by and watch this aspect of health care in the United States regress thirty years. The lives and health of millions of Americans are at stake and will be beneficially affected by passage of appropriate legislation to relieve the current problem."

While the dump closings did lead to a buildup of medical and all other waste, this was due largely to the unexpected nature of the shutdown, which did not allow sufficient time for the provision of other storage. If the situation turned critical, the Department of Energy could make its multiple dumps available for the comparatively small amounts of hospital waste, a remedy some lawmakers recommended. But the health-care community provided the ideal lobby. Electric-utility officials marching on Capitol Hill to press for the enactment of a low-level-waste bill would undoubtedly receive little sympathy. On the other hand, if hospital spokesmen suggested that people would be dying in the streets for lack of nuclear diagnostic tests if Congress failed to act, how could it possibly ignore the issue?

Robert Kurtter, deputy director for program development for the New York State legislature, thought the assertion that health care would be imperiled obscured the chief beneficiaries of Derrick's bill. "I have no doubt that if low-level waste was just a hospital waste problem we could solve it today," he said. "One should not fail to see behind the facade. The problem is a good solid utility reactor waste problem."

Although Congress did not take up Derrick's bill in the closing weeks of 1979, Governors List and Ray reopened their burial grounds, satisfied they had made their point with Washington. When lawmakers returned in January 1980, they were confronted both with Derrick's low-level measure and with the more important question of what to do with high-level waste. The Senate was the first to act. It combined low- and high-level wastes and in July 1980 passed the Nuclear Waste Policy Act.

Power Plant Waste as a Percentage
of All Low-Level Waste

	Utility Waste	All Low Level Waste	Power Plant Percentage
		(In Cubic Feet)	
1 Nebraska	27,808	28,384	98%
2 Alabama	106,135	108,635	98%
3 Arkansas	25,069	25,788	97%
4 Vermont	13,991	15,476	90%
5 Maine	12,080	13,464	90%
6 Wisconsin	13,651	15,574	88%
7 Michigan	70,341	81,116	87%
8 Georgia	51,657	59,840	86%
9 Connecticut	90,260	107,302	84%
10 Iowa	21,311	26,036	82%
11 Florida	65,923	80,913	81%
12 Virginia	98,558	135,482	73%
13 North Carolina	138,762	208,759	66%
14 New Jersey	92,180	143,031	64%
15 Pennsylvania	137,198	230,442	60%
16 Illinois	142,887	243,322	59%
17 Minnesota	30,673	59,761	51%
18 New York	134,861	269,738	50%
19 Massachusetts	114,347	245,556	47%
20 South Carolina	105,316	263,425	40%
21 Oregon	14,972	40,020	37%
22 Maryland	11,936	42,589	28%
23 Ohio	8,693	38,581	23%
24 California	43,340	193,600	22%
25 Tennessee	787	86,343	1%
Total	1,572,738	2,763,172	57%

Source: Compiled from U.S. Department of Energy records.

The tables show the volume and radioactivity of low-level waste generated by power plants in states with nuclear utilities, compared with the production of all such waste in those states. Low-level waste also is produced by industry, medical facilities and educational and research organizations. But power plants account for more than half in terms of volume. Similarly, in those states without large nuclear industries, power plants also account for more than half the radioactivity in low-level waste.

Radioactivity of Power Plant Waste as a
Percentage of All Low-Level Waste Radioactivity

	Utility Waste	All Low-Level Waste (In Curies)	Power Plant Percentage
1 Maine	1,935	1,898	102%
2 Vermont	809	798	101%
3 Georgia	2,545	2,529	101%
4 Virginia	3,544	3,897	91%
5 Illinois	56,881	62,896	90%
6 North Carolina	5,793	6,416	90%
7 Alabama	6,560	8,708	75%
8 Arkansas	1,619	2,237	72%
9 Connecticut	2,737	3,869	71%
10 Minnesota	4,469	6,318	71%
11 Nebraska	546	801	68%
12 Wisconsin	1,512	2,279	66%
13 New Jersey	2,448	4,909	50%
14 South Carolina	4,118	8,551	48%
15 Pennsylvania	6,731	14,237	47%
16 Michigan	5,149	11,178	46%
17 Oregon	361	817	44%
18 Iowa	956	2,323	41%
19 Florida	5,924	24,157	25%
20 New York	12,499	60,852	21%
21 Maryland	1,031	5,285	20%
22 Massachusetts	6,512	100,737	6%
23 California	1,199	34,156	4%
24 Tennessee	4	150	3%
25 Ohio	23	1,582	1%
Total	135,903	371,580	37%

Source: Compiled from U.S. Department of Energy records.

Government records show that power plants in three states—Maine, Vermont, and Georgia—turned out more curies than reported by the states as a whole, a physical impossibility. One explanation is that utility waste was in transit to a burial ground; therefore it had been counted by the utilities, but not burial ground operators. The figures are annual averages for the years 1979 to 1982.

The House approved its own version, which bore little resemblance to the Senate's, and the two chambers deadlocked on the issue. What happened next was a textbook study of how Congress enacts radioactive-waste legislation and how a special interest, in this case South Carolina, forges national policy to satisfy local political interests.

When it became clear early in December that the Senate and House would be unable to compromise on a high-level-waste bill, South Carolina mounted a powerful political offensive to salvage a low-level-waste bill. The plan called for a confusing parliamentary sleight of hand in which Derrick's bill would be substituted for the high-level-waste bill that everyone thought was dead.

Governor Riley quietly passed the word that he would shut down Barnwell if Congress failed to address the issue during the lame-duck session. The threat carried added weight since residents of Washington State had voted overwhelmingly in the November general election to close the Richland dump to all out-of-state, nonmedical waste. South Carolina's two senators —Strom Thurmond, a Republican, and Ernest F. Hollings, a Democrat—pushed for Senate action. But it was Butler Derrick, named the 1977 "National Conservationist of the Year" by the National Wildlife Federation and designated in 1980 as one of "Our Ten Best Friends in Congress" by *Outdoor Life* magazine, who led the charge. First, the forty-four-year-old lawyer, who had just been handily reelected to a fourth term, marshaled support in the House. Next, he took the extraordinary step of crossing to the other side of the Capitol, where he stationed himself outside the doors to the Senate floor and lobbied members of the upper chamber as they went in to vote.

Few lawmakers had been familiar with the high-level-waste bill that now would be carried over to 1981. Fewer still understood its substitute. William Proxmire, the Democratic senator from Wisconsin who is usually one of the Senate's more informed members, was typical. When the low-level bill came up for debate, he said he wanted to make certain that "neither Wisconsin nor any other state that had granite formations would be a likely storage site." Proxmire had confused low-level and high-level waste. Wisconsin, of course, was among the states the DOE was eyeing in its search for a possible repository for high-level waste. The granite formation had no connection with Derrick's low-level-waste bill.

Sen. James A. McClure, the Idaho Republican who had desperately sought enactment of a high-level-waste bill that year, added to the confusion. He repeated what had become the standard, if inaccurate, cliché that low-level waste consisted of "radioactive waste in hospitals [and] the radioactive elements that might be involved in independent experiments in laboratories at universities." He made no mention of the largest generator of such waste, electric utilities. McClure further obscured the bill's contents when he stated, incorrectly, "I wish to reemphasize that the bill does not require that each state is required or can be required to dispose of its commercial low-level wastes physically within the state." That was precisely what the bill required—by default rather than by explicit order. Any state that failed to join a compact would be obliged to bury its waste within its borders.

Over in the House, members were distracted by other considerations. When the bill came up, it was seven o'clock on a Saturday night and House members were eager to get back to what had been the most pressing issue of the day—a proposed 16 percent pay hike for themselves. The salary increase was part of an omnibus bill appropriating funds to operate the government. It contained a variety of legislative goodies, including a provision to make severance pay of some staff members tax-free. Whereas the House debated the merits of the pay raise bill for more than two hours, it rushed the low-level-waste bill through in ten minutes.

Thus, on December 13, 1980, the Low-Level Radioactive Waste Policy Act slipped quietly into law without dissent, or without much appreciation for what it said. The 535 members of the House and Senate, unable to reach a consensus on how to manage the nation's low-level waste, solved the problem by turning it over to the states, thereby requiring 7,000 lawmakers in fifty state legislatures to work out a plan among themselves.

Members of both chambers and both parties paid tribute to the work of the South Carolina congressional delegation that had made it all possible. "Without their tenacity and dedication," Senator McClure said, "this bill would not be before the Senate today. I salute them for their fine efforts." John D. Dingell, a longtime Democratic representative from Michigan, echoed, "I hope that the people of South Carolina recognize that passage of this bill is primarily a result of [Derrick's] personal efforts."

House and Senate leaders also agreed that the act would provide a mechanism for permanently dealing with low-level waste. Senator McClure said "this bill should provide the opportunity . . . to make meaningful gains in managing the nation's low-level wastes." Representative Dingell said the act "will enable the states to immediately and effectively address this problem by vesting them with the responsibility for providing capacity for the disposal of low-level radioactive waste generated within the state. . . ." And Rep. Tom Corcoran, an Illinois Republican, described the measure as providing "an excellent approach to the problem of low-level nuclear waste."

In time, these assessments would prove no more accurate than predictions in the 1950s of electricity too cheap to meter, forecasts in the 1960s of a profit-making reprocessing industry, and promises in the 1970s of underground repositories for high-level waste.

9
A Dump in Every State

REGIONAL CHAOS

It is hard to conceive of a more bewildering governmental maze than the one called for by the Low-Level Radioactive Waste Policy Act of 1980. On its surface, the act appeared simple enough. The law held each state responsible for the low-level waste it produced. Each state could set up a dump or join with neighboring states in a regional compact. The compact would then designate one state to bury all waste generated by its members and could refuse to accept waste from any nonmember states.

To implement this plan, the law set forth a series of convoluted procedures. First, each state had to decide which other states, if any, it wanted to team up with. Next, it had to appoint representatives to a multistate committee to develop a regional agreement. If the committee was able to draft one, it would then be submitted to each state legislature for ratification. But state lawmakers could not make substantive changes, a difficult restriction, given the politically sensitive nature of radioactive waste. If a legislature altered a measure, it had to be sent back to the bargaining table for concurrence by all other states involved. After three legislatures approved a tentative pact, it would then usually be submitted to Congress for confirmation. What would happen if Congress objected to the terms is not clear. Presumably, the document would go back to the states, where it would be renegotiated and sent through individual legislatures again. Nor did the act explain what would happen if Congress decided to take no action at all on a regional compact—an entirely plausible scenario, given the way lawmakers have responded to nuclear-waste legislation in the past.

To complicate matters further, the 1980 act was so poorly drafted that it gave the states almost no guidance on how to carry it out. It lacked a clear definition of the regulatory responsibilities of federal, state, and regional authorities over low-level waste, an oversight that soon led to growing confusion. "The act left so many questions unanswered that when the states first started sending out feelers, they weren't sure what the scope of these compact agreements would be," said one state official. "We're still haunted by that fact. If there had been one specific guide as to what was acceptable, then Congress should have said so."

One of the act's few precise directives set a January 1, 1986, deadline by which the fifty states had to come up with their master plan. Beginning on that date, a regional compact could bar waste shipments from any states that were not members. That authority is the crux of the legislation and the provision that has the greatest long-term impact. Large waste producers like California, Illinois, Massachusetts, New York, and Pennsylvania now send their atomic trash to burial grounds in Nevada, South Carolina, and Washington. If all goes according to schedule, those three states could refuse to accept waste from the outsiders after the 1986 cutoff date. By then, the large generating states must have their own burial grounds or access to other facilities.

Saddled with a tangled law, the states ventured forth in search of regional partners. Progress was slow. The single obstacle that stalled Congress so long, the acrimonious politics of radioactive waste, now runs through fifty state legislatures and fifty governors' mansions. At a meeting of Northeast compact negotiators in 1982, Rhode Island's representative, Dante Ionata, said the proposed agreement would have to be submitted to his legislature early in 1983, if there was any hope for seeing it enacted that year. "If we submit something like this close to the [March] filing deadline [for the state legislature]," said Ionata, "we would get killed. We must have this in by January or February if they are going to consider it this year." Ionata's observations proved correct. Not until March 1983 was the proposed compact introduced in the Rhode Island legislature, which did not approve it before that year's session adjourned.

Beyond traditional state rivalries and hostilities, the policy act introduced a new element of interstate tension. States that produce little waste are wary that states generating much waste might impose burial grounds on them. The large generators are quite often populous states, with little suitable land for the burial of radioactive waste. Thus, the act that Congress claimed would inaugurate an era of cooperation instead ignited political warfare, pitting state against state, region against region. The conflict is destined to burn ever brighter as the states struggle to meet the January 1, 1986, deadline.

Regional cooperation has been something of an anomaly itself. States, especially in the West, have formed interstate compacts in the past. But they involved less volatile issues, such as the allocation of water rights to rivers that pass through many states. Even so, it often took years to work out an agreement. A quarter of a century elapsed between the start of negotiations and the final approval of a four-state compact in the Southwest that spelled out the states' rights to water from the Red River.

But Congress gave the states only six years to organize on radioactive waste. "To think the states are now going to get together and do this real fast gives you another thing to think about," said Ed Pugh, an aide of Governor George Nigh of Oklahoma.

It is premature to speculate about the number of interstate alliances or burial grounds that might be set up. The only thing that can be said now is that Congress vastly underestimated the confusion, the number of regional alliances, and, most important, the total number of dumps that would result from the 1980 act. Lawmakers envisioned "six or seven sites" when they passed the bill. The DOE sent out guidelines in 1981 suggesting six possible regions. By 1983, it appeared that six would form. In early 1984 there were seven, and by the summer of 1984 there were eight. But many states had not yet joined a compact. Although it is thus impossible to say how many atomic burial grounds might be created, the total could easily rise to more than a dozen—about twice as many as Congress stipulated, and four times the present number.

The act's central flaws can be seen in the regions proposed so far. Congress took no account of wide variations in population and annual rainfall among different regions. It also ignored the risks of shallow land burial in wet climates, as evidenced by the failure of three commercial dumps in the 1970s. A look at two of the suggested compacts, Rocky Mountain and Northeast, brings out the illogic.

The Rocky Mountain compact includes four states— Colorado, Nevada, New Mexico, and Wyoming. The Northeast compact, as originally envisioned, included eleven—Connecticut, Delaware, Maine, Maryland, Massachusetts, New Hampshire, New Jersey, New York, Pennsylvania, Rhode Island, and Vermont.

If the Rocky Mountain compact selected Nevada for its burial ground and the Northeast compact chose Pennsylvania, here is what the two states would have to deal with: The four Rocky Mountain states produced an average of 20,000 cubic feet of low-level radioactive waste a year, or less than 1 percent of the nation's total volume in the years 1979–1982. The eleven Northeast states, on the other hand, produced 1.1 million cubic feet of radioactive garbage, or 38 percent of the total.

Under Congress's plan, Nevada—which has an average annual rainfall of nine inches and a population density of 7 persons per square mile—would bury less than 1 percent of the country's low-level waste. Pennsylvania, which has an average annual rainfall of forty-one inches and a population density of 264 persons per square mile—would bury 38 percent.

Of far greater significance than the volumes are the levels of radioactivity. The Rocky Mountain waste contained an average of 826 curies a year. The Northeast waste contained 234 times that level, or 193,000 curies. This means that arid Nevada would bury less than one-half of 1 percent of the radioactivity in all the nation's low-level nuclear garbage, while comparatively wet Pennsylvania would bury 51 percent.

States that generate little waste consider it only fitting that large producers like Pennsylvania should serve as regional burial grounds. After all, Pennsylvania ranked fifth among all states in total volume, and sixth in radioactivity. The states that turn out small quantities of waste are therefore banding together in compacts to exclude large producers, or are seeking guarantees that they will not have to provide burial sites.

One casualty of this attitude is California, which ranks seventh in volume and fourth in radioactivity. The Northwest compact—Alaska, Hawaii, Idaho, Montana, Oregon, Utah, and Washington—wanted no part of California. Those seven states produced an average of 76,000 cubic feet of radioactive trash a year, 3 percent of the national total, from 1979 to 1982. The radioactivity in that waste measured 1,100 curies, less than 1 percent of the nation's total. By comparison, California generated an average of 194,000 cubic feet of waste, more than two and one-half times as much as the seven Northwest states combined. The radioactivity in California's waste amounted to 34,-000 curies, thirty-one times more intense than that in the Northwest states.

For much the same reason, the Rocky Mountain compact also turned its back on the country's most populous state. California churned out an average of nine and one-half times more waste, with thirty-three times more radioactivity, than the four Rocky Mountain states. "California was considered by both regions," explained David W. Stevens, an aide to Gov. John Spellman of Washington, "but I think there was a feeling in both regions that the volume of waste California produced kind

States Burying Waste at Barnwell, South Carolina
(Figures in Cubic Feet)

1	South Carolina	993,339	27	Missouri	12,376
2	North Carolina	728,597	28	Washington	12,373
3	Pennsylvania	578,852	29	Mississippi	7,057
4	New York	564,641	30	Oklahoma	5,848
5	Virginia	481,401	31	Kentucky	5,046
6	Massachusetts	453,543	32	New Hampshire	4,616
7	Alabama	411,558	33	Delaware	4,309
8	Connecticut	374,625	34	Indiana	2,949
9	New Jersey	364,457	35	West Virginia	1,722
10	Illinois	355,360	36	Distr. Columbia	1,536
11	Tennessee	325,350	37	Louisiana	660
12	Florida	262,540	38	Kansas	626
13	Ohio	139,668	39	North Dakota	208
14	Michigan	139,018	40	Colorado	177
15	Georgia	119,118	41	Arizona	98
16	Iowa	93,878	42	Montana	71
17	Maryland	86,502	43	Utah	64
18	Rhode Island	72,906	44	New Mexico	28
19	California	52,260	45	South Dakota	17
20	Arkansas	51,805	46	Alaska	10
21	Wisconsin	43,152	47	Wyoming	0
22	Vermont	41,228	48	Nevada	4
23	Maine	39,677	49	Idaho	3
24	Nebraska	37,906	50	Hawaii	0
25	Minnesota	35,050	51	Oregon	0
26	Texas	18,700		Total	6,924,929

Source: Compiled from U.S. Department of Energy records.

States Burying Waste at Beatty, Nevada
(Figures in Cubic Feet)

1	California	237,430	27	Ohio	2,561
2	Pennsylvania	82,921	28	Distr. Columbia	2,101
3	New Jersey	69,705	29	Georgia	1,693
4	New York	59,190	30	Alabama	1,583
5	Illinois	58,656	31	Hawaii	1,488
6	Nebraska	56,921	32	South Carolina	1,393
7	Michigan	49,731	33	Indiana	1,050
8	Nevada	38,530	34	Kansas	709
9	North Carolina	29,345	35	Wisconsin	513
10	Minnesota	28,568	36	Oregon	505
11	Washington	23,371	37	Florida	364
12	Massachusetts	23,101	38	Arkansas	360
13	Texas	19,489	39	Alaska	8
14	Kentucky	13,692	40	Mississippi	6
15	Colorado	9,544	41	South Dakota	1
16	Rhode Island	9,251	42	Connecticut	0

#	State	Cubic Feet	#	State	Cubic Feet
17	Missouri	7,943	43	Delaware	0
18	Oklahoma	7,131	44	Idaho	0
19	Vermont	6,125	45	Louisiana	0
20	Tennessee	4,921	46	Montana	0
21	Utah	4,312	47	New Hampshire	0
22	New Mexico	3,868	48	North Dakota	0
23	Maine	3,546	49	Virginia	0
24	Maryland	3,335	50	West Virginia	0
25	Iowa	2,728	51	Wyoming	0
26	Arizona	2,613		Total	870,302

Source: Compiled from U.S. Department of Energy records.

States Burying Waste at Richland, Washington

(Figures in Cubic Feet)

#	State	Cubic Feet	#	State	Cubic Feet
1	Illinois	559,273	27	Vermont	14,552
2	Massachusetts	505,580	28	Hawaii	13,344
3	California	484,710	29	Ohio	12,093
4	New York	455,119	30	Maine	10,631
5	Pennsylvania	259,983	31	Colorado	7,583
6	Texas	209,257	32	Iowa	7,536
7	Minnesota	175,424	33	Kentucky	5,946
8	Oregon	159,573	34	New Mexico	4,686
9	New Jersey	137,961	35	Distr. Columbia	3,990
10	Michigan	135,715	36	Rhode Island	1,854
11	Georgia	118,548	37	Indiana	1,828
12	Maryland	80,518	38	Kansas	1,772
13	North Carolina	77,092	39	Arizona	1,738
14	Washington	70,940	40	Delaware	1,342
15	Florida	60,749	41	Louisiana	1,150
16	Virginia	60,528	42	Montana	706
17	South Carolina	58,967	43	New Hampshire	504
18	Connecticut	54,582	44	Idaho	288
19	Arkansas	50,987	45	Oklahoma	123
20	Alabama	21,398	46	West Virginia	123
21	Nebraska	18,708	47	North Dakota	4
22	Wisconsin	18,630	48	Alaska	0
23	Utah	17,377	49	Mississippi	0
24	Missouri	16,337	50	South Dakota	0
25	Nevada	16,202	51	Wyoming	0
26	Tennessee	15,101		Total	3,931,052

Source: Compiled from U.S. Department of Energy records.

The three tables show the volume of waste buried by each of the states at the nation's three operating commercial burial grounds from 1979 to 1982. In each case, the vast bulk of the amount buried comes from only a few states. Ten states accounted for 77 percent of Barnwell's volume, 82 percent of Beatty's, and 78 percent of Richland's burials.

of skewed what was happening in the rest of the region. There was a feeling, presumably, that California could go its own."

But California, which steadfastly refused to open a radioactive dump, was not inclined to "go its own." In fact, California felt so strongly about its exclusion from the Rocky Mountain and Northwest compacts that it asked the federal government for special treatment in 1982. Phillip A. Greenberg, an aide to the then governor Jerry Brown, wrote the DOE, "Congress should be urged to give special consideration to such exlcuded states, since the Low-Level Radioactive Waste Policy Act did not envision this eventuality."

After a change in administrations, the realization set in that California could not look to the federal government or to Congress to solve the problem. Early in 1984, California negotiated a tentative agreement with Arizona for a Western Low-Level Waste Disposal Compact. The Arizona legislature ratified the compact in April, but California's legislature failed to approve it before adjourning. At year's end, California was eyeing four southern counties in the state as the most likely sites for a dump —Imperial, Inyo, Riverside, and San Bernardino. Whatever the choice, California says a facility could not be in operation before 1989—more than three years after the January 1986 deadline.

Large waste-producing states like California should be logical candidates for a regional facility. But officials in those states do not want the political liability any more than do those in the small states, as California demonstrated in its failure to reach an agreement on even a two-state compact with Arizona. The situation is similar in Illinois.

A Midwest compact covering ten states was negotiated in 1983. By the summer of 1984, seven states had approved the agreement—Indiana, Iowa, Michigan, Minnesota, Missouri, Wisconsin, and Ohio. An eighth, Illinois, ratified a version that was unacceptable to the others. Two remaining states, North Dakota and South Dakota, had taken no action. Although negotiators did not select a burial site, it was presumed all along that Illinois would provide the land. That's because it is centrally located, generates 51 percent of the region's low-level waste, and accounts for 71 percent of its radioactivity. But Illinois, fearful of the political consequences of being the Midwest's dumping ground, did not volunteer. The state also objected to certain provisions in the Midwest compact, one of which could have made Illinois the Midwest dump state for many generations, and another of which seemed to lawmakers to shift the ultimate financial liability for the dump solely to the host state. Because of these concerns, a state official hinted privately that if the state were designated by the other states as the regional burial ground, Illinois would "go it alone."

Illinois's refusal to step forward made other midwestern states edgy. Anxious they might be chosen, some hedged their bets. Wisconsin negotiated with states in both the proposed Midwest region, which stretches over the upper and central part of the country, and the Central States region, which nine states in the nation's midsection are eligible to join. By playing a waiting game, Wisconsin, ranked twenty-sixth in low-level waste produced from 1979 to 1982 and eighteenth in radioactivity, hoped to join whichever compact first selected a burial site.

"If it [a site] happens in the Central States, we would look at it," Mark Musolf, Wisconsin's former secretary of revenue and a member of the state's negotiating team, said in 1982. "That would offer some incentive for us to get in. If it happens in Illinois, that would look good for our involvement there. We are naturally hoping someone will come forward and be a host state volunteer. At least that will postpone the likely time we would have to deal with it."

Illinois's reluctance proved especially trying for the region's smallest waste generator, South Dakota. If the waste policy act was meant to bring order to the chaotic low-level-waste situation, then South Dakota demonstrates how it has had the opposite effect. Before Congress passed the law, nuclear waste was not an issue in the state. South Dakota produced only about 5 cubic feet a year, a minute quantity compared with Illinois's 243,000 cubic feet, Michigan's 81,000 cubic feet, and Minnesota's 60,000 cubic feet. It would take South Dakota 133 years, at current rates, to produce the amount of waste that Illinois turns out every twenty-four hours.

The act ended South Dakota's isolation. As urged by Congress, the state took part in negotiations with other states on the Midwest compact. Legislation to join it was introduced in the South Dakota legislature. When none of the larger midwestern states volunteered to establish a dump, concern mounted that South Dakota, which has fewer people per square mile than all but two other states—Alaska and Wyoming—and thus has vast stretches of open land, might be selected. State officials inadvertently fanned that anxiety when they disclosed in the summer of 1982 that the state was studying the pros and cons of becoming the Midwest's nuclear cemetery.

The event that most aroused fears, though, came when Chem-Nuclear Systems Inc., operator of the Barnwell, South Carolina, burial ground, disclosed that a large tract near the town of Edgemont, in southwestern South Dakota, was under consideration as a future low-level cemetery. Adjoining the village of Igloo, about sixty miles southwest of Mount Rushmore, the property was once used by the U.S. Army to store bombs. The remains of massive, bunkerlike, concrete structures dot the landscape. To be economically viable, Chem-Nuclear said, Edgemont would have to bury up to one million cubic feet of waste a year—the equivalent of one-third of the nation's annual output. That's more than twice the amount the midwestern region produces each year.

Chem-Nuclear promoted the Edgemont project as a potential economic boon to southwestern South Dakota, a severely depressed uranium-mining area.* Residents of the immediate area strongly supported the dump, but most South Dakotans bristled at the thought that their state was being promoted as a national nuclear graveyard. A volunteer citizens' group, the Nuclear Waste Vote Coalition, launched a campaign to require a vote of South Dakotans before the state could join a compact

---

*See page 336 for detailed note.

or build a low-level facility. The initiative drive attracted wide support from a variety of organizations, including the South Dakota League of Women Voters, the South Dakota Farmers Union, the South Dakota AFL-CIO, and the Catholic Rural Life Conference of the Sioux Falls Diocese. Chem-Nuclear sought to persuade South Dakotans to go along with the proposed dump, launching a major public-relations campaign, complete with the slogan "Why Not Edgemont."

South Dakota plunged into a period of confusion and unrest over nuclear waste. The state that generated almost no atomic garbage suddenly was awash in nuclear legislation. By early 1984, nine bills dealing with low-level waste had been introduced in the legislature. Two offered varying versions of a North Dakota–South Dakota compact. Another authorized membership in the the Rocky Mountain compact. Still another called for a joint legislature-citizen study committee. One bill, reportedly drafted by Chem-Nuclear, called for South Dakota to be the dump state, a provision later deleted by a legislative committee. Gov. William Janklow promised that the state would not become a "dumpsite," but he did not elaborate, and left the controversial issue with lawmakers to decide. South Dakotans decided to take no chances on the whims of state legislators. By a resounding margin of 62 to 38 percent, voters approved the nuclear-waste initiative in November's general election, thereby giving themselves authority to make future waste decisions. Voter approval will be required before a dump can be opened in South Dakota or the state can join a compact.

The confused midwestern picture became more clouded in June 1984 when Illinois suddenly bolted from the Midwest compact and negotiated one with neighboring Kentucky. Called the Central Midwest Interstate Compact, the two-state agreement called for Illinois to provide the disposal site so long as Kentucky generated less than 10 percent of the waste. At present, Kentucky produces less than 2 percent. The arrangement allowed Illinois to have its own site and protected it from having to accept waste from other large midwestern producers. With Illinois's defection, other states in the region eyed Michigan, the next-largest producer, as the logical site for the mid-western burial ground.

Because of the political and potential financial liabilities of becoming a regional dump, more and more states have considered "going it alone." Although the 1980 act does not bar independent state action, Congress intended to encourage a handful of nuclear cemeteries, geographically positioned to serve all regions. As the act states, "Low-level radioactive waste can be most safely and efficiently managed on a regional basis." Furthermore, while going it alone has a certain political appeal, the idea may be fraught with risks. The policy act was so vaguely worded that it is not clear whether a state can also constitute a "region," and thus exclude waste from outside its borders.

Texas, which wants to open its own dump and avoid regional entanglements, has been wrestling with this ambiguity. Texas officials felt that their state, the nation's fifteenth-largest waste producer, had a sufficient volume of it to justify its own burial ground. As other states began negotiations, the legislature created the Texas Low-Level Radioactive Waste Disposal Authority to build and operate a dump for Texas waste. The authority contracted for a "conceptual design" of a burial plot and began to evaluate possible sites. But if the 1980 act is found to deny individual states the same authority that regional compacts have, Texas could pay a price for its independence. Tom Blackburn, director of special projects for the Texas authority, described the dilemma as follows: "We would hate to develop a site with the intention it was only for Texas and then have a higher court determine that was not legal and that we would have to accept out of state waste."

Even if Texas sticks with its decision to go it alone, the task of picking a dump site will not be easy. By the end of 1984, the waste-disposal authority had narrowed the search to locations in three counties—Dimmit, McMullen, and Webb. Situated in southwest Texas, all three counties are sparsely populated, their combined population of 111,000 representing less than 1 percent of the state's total. Nonetheless, citizen opposition to a dump anywhere in the state was building. State legislators urged further research on waste-management technology, including the question whether the facility should be a conventional burial operation or an above-ground storage center. "We must do everything within our power to prevent a nuclear Love Canal in Texas," Gary Thompson, a Democratic representative from Abilene, told reporters in calling for additional studies.

Whatever the outcome in Texas, the current maneuvering among the fifty states to comply with the 1980 law appears likely to lead to the "undisciplined proliferation" of burial grounds that federal studies warned against in the 1970s.

For example, in the Rocky Mountain compact, Nevada, which oversees the region's lone dump at Beatty, insisted on a clause requiring another state to provide the regional burial ground within six years. If approved, the Rocky Mountain compact would allow Nevada to shut down Beatty, possibly as soon as 1989. Similarly, South Carolina, home of the Barnwell burial ground, secured a provision in the Southeast compact that made another state responsible for the region's waste by 1991. In regions without dumps, proposed compacts direct the regional plot to be rotated every few years among states. A Northeast negotiator defended the concept, saying it was only "fair that the states share the responsibility for the waste over time."

What may appear "fair" today could prove a disastrous financial and environmental liability tomorrow. Rotating burial sites would increase the number of nuclear cemeteries to be developed and taken care of for hundreds of years. Instead of a handful in a few states, there could be fifty such facilities. The odds of environmental contamination would rise, and the burden on future generations would become ever greater.

While encouraging more dumps, some in unsuitable locales, the act will have the ironic effect of virtually closing off two of the nation's three commercial cemeteries to all but a fraction of low-level producers. At Richland, the waste volume would decline by 95 percent if the Northwest compact is approved by Congress and waste is excluded from outside the region. The seven member states—Alaska, Hawaii, Idaho, Montana, Oregon, Utah, and Washington—generate only about 76,000 cubic feet of low-level waste a year. Richland now buries 1.4 million cubic feet of low-level waste from more than forty states.

Likewise, the Beatty dump would bury much less waste than it has in the past if a proposed Rocky Mountain compact is approved. Beatty could then accept waste from only four states—Colorado, Nevada, New Mexico, and Wyoming, which together generate just 20,000 cubic feet of waste a year. Thus, if both the Northwest and the Rocky Mountain compacts were in operation, the existing western sites would bury only 4 percent of the nation's waste, compared with the 54 percent interred in 1982.

Efforts to form compacts encountered the least resistance in regions with existing burial grounds—the Northwest (which has Richland), the Rocky Mountain (Beatty), and the Southeast (Barnwell). Yet even in one of those regions, the Southeast, there have been political complications.

Although eight southeastern states approved legislation to join the compact, South Carolina, which would allow other member states to use the Barnwell dump, attached special conditions to its membership. According to one of the stipulations, a new burial ground must be set up in another state by 1991. When it approved the compact, South Carolina sent a stiff warning to its neighbors. "If any member state refuses to accept its designation as a host state," the state law stipulated, "then South Carolina shall immediately withdraw from the pact." In other words, if the Southeast states should encounter snags in developing a new burial ground, the region might suddenly find itself without a place to put its low-level waste.

Perhaps the most serious obstacle facing the states in trying to make the regional concept work is that the intensity of the low-level-waste problem varies greatly among them. Although every state produces waste, the volume differs radically. Take the case of two southern states, Alabama and Mississippi. The two have roughly the same land area—51,000 square miles for Alabama to 47,000 for Mississippi. Alabama has 3.9 million residents to 2.5 million for Mississippi. But as generators of low-level waste, they can scarcely be compared. Alabama produces sixty-one times the waste Mississippi does—109,000 cubic feet as opposed to 1,800 cubic feet.

In the Middle West, the neighboring states of Ohio and Indiana offer a similar picture. Ohio has 41,000 square miles and 10.7 million residents; Indiana has 36,000 square miles and 5.5 million persons. But Ohio turns out twenty-six times more low-level waste than Indiana, 39,000 cubic feet to 1,500.

Although such contrasts can be found in virtually every region, the bulk of the nation's low-level waste is produced by only ten states—Alabama, California, Illinois, Massachusetts, New Jersey, New York, North Carolina, Pennsylvania, South Carolina, and Virginia. The ten accounted for 69 percent of the volume from 1979 to 1982.

Northeast Dumps—An Impossible Quest?

Of all the regions that attempted to form a compact, the Northeast has had the most difficulty. In the Northeast the fallacy of cooperation is most apparent. In the same region are Massachusetts and New Hampshire, states with very different interests to protect when they approached the bargaining table. Massachusetts generates more low-level commercial nuclear waste every forty-six hours than New Hampshire produces all year. The gap between the two is typical of the division between the region's large and small states. The small generators—Maine, Vermont, New Hampshire, Rhode Island, and Delaware—produce only 5 percent of the Northeast's waste. Pennsylvania, New York, Massachusetts, New Jersey, Connecticut, and Maryland churn out 95 percent of it.

This disparity led to some odd proposals during the two years in which negotiators drafted a proposed agreement. If one idea that circulated among them is any guide, science and geology may take a backseat to politics and chance in the way the region ultimately chooses its dumps. This proposal called for a lottery. As one negotiator described the plan, "The names

Average Annual Low-Level Waste Production

	Cubic feet	Cumulative Percentage		Cubic feet	Cumulative Percentage
1 New York	269,738	9%	27 Vermont	15,476	97%
2 South Carolina	263,425	18%	28 Nevada	13,684	98%
3 Massachusetts	245,556	26%	29 Maine	13,464	98%
4 Illinois	243,322	35%	30 Missouri	9,164	99%
5 Pennsylvania	230,442	43%	31 Kentucky	6,171	99%
6 North Carolina	208,759	50%	32 Utah	5,438	99%
7 California	193,600	56%	33 Colorado	4,326	99%
8 New Jersey	143,031	61%	34 Hawaii	3,708	99%
9 Virginia	135,482	66%	35 Oklahoma	3,275	99%
10 Alabama	108,635	69%	36 New Mexico	2,146	99%
11 Connecticut	107,302	73%	37 Distr. Columbia	1,907	99%
12 Tennessee	86,343	76%	38 Mississippi	1,766	99%
13 Michigan	81,116	79%	39 Indiana	1,457	99%
14 Florida	80,913	82%	40 Delaware	1,413	99%
15 Texas	61,862	84%	41 New Hampshire	1,280	99%
16 Georgia	59,840	86%	42 Arizona	1,112	99%
17 Minnesota	59,761	88%	43 Kansas	777	99%
18 Maryland	42,589	89%	44 West Virginia	461	99%
19 Oregon	40,020	91%	45 Louisiana	453	99%
20 Ohio	38,581	92%	46 Montana	194	99%
21 Nebraska	28,384	93%	47 Idaho	73	99%
22 Washington	26,671	94%	48 North Dakota	53	99%
23 Iowa	26,036	95%	49 Alaska	5	99%
24 Arkansas	25,788	96%	50 South Dakota	5	99%
25 Rhode Island	21,003	96%	51 Wyoming	0	100%
26 Wisconsin	15,574	97%	Total	2,931,573	

Source: Compiled from U.S. Department of Energy records.

Average Annual Radioactivity in Low-Level Waste

	Curies	Cumulative Percentage		Curies	Cumulative Percentage
1 Massachusetts	100,737	27%	27 Indiana	614	99%
2 Illinois	62,896	44%	28 Texas	599	99%
3 New York	60,852	60%	29 Missouri	318	99%
4 California	34,156	69%	30 Washington	205	99%
5 Florida	24,157	75%	31 Distr. Columbia	155	99%
6 Pennsylvania	14,237	79%	32 Tennessee	150	99%
7 Michigan	11,178	82%	33 Arizona	82	99%
8 Alabama	8,708	84%	34 Oklahoma	72	99%
9 South Carolina	8,551	87%	35 Mississippi	53	99%

10 North Carolina	6,416	88%	36 Utah	30	99%
11 Minnesota	6,318	90%	37 Rhode Island	23	99%
12 Maryland	5,285	91%	38 West Virginia	15	99%
13 New Jersey	4,909	93%	39 Hawaii	12	99%
14 Virginia	3,897	94%	40 Colorado	10	99%
15 Connecticut	3,869	95%	41 Montana	9	99%
16 Georgia	2,529	95%	42 Louisiana	4	99%
17 Iowa	2,323	96%	43 New Mexico	4	99%
18 Wisconsin	2,279	97%	44 Delaware	3	99%
19 Arkansas	2,237	97%	45 New Hampshire	3	99%
20 Maine	1,898	98%	46 Idaho	3	99%
21 Ohio	1,582	98%	47 Kansas	1	99%
22 Kentucky	1,372	99%	48 Alaska	1	99%
23 Oregon	817	99%	49 North Dakota	1	99%
24 Nevada	812	99%	50 South Dakota	1	99%
25 Nebraska	801	99%	51 Wyoming	0	100%
26 Vermont	798	99%	Total	375,976	

Source: Compiled from U.S. Department of Energy records.

These tables show the annual volume and radioactivity in low-level waste produced by each state. The figures are an average of yearly data from 1979 to 1982. Because waste production often fluctuates greatly, the four-year average was used to obtain a more accurate reading.

of the eleven states would all go in a hat. Someone would pull a name out of the hat and that would be the host state."

One of the more protracted controversies arose over a drive by small states to exempt them permanently from having to provide a burial ground. They sought a clause that a state generating less than 3 percent of the region's waste would never have a dump. That was opposed by some of the larger generating states. Assemblyman John Bennett, a member of the New Jersey delegation, explained why. "When it's all said and done," he said, "an exemption would lend credibility to the notion that a low-level site is not safe and someone doesn't want it. I believe that if it is properly done and enough money spent that it could be done properly. We should not exclude any state."

The small states failed to secure the exemption when a

tentative agreement was approved by delegates early in 1983 and some indicated they would not join the compact. Maine was among the reluctant. Its legislature passed a bill requiring legislative approval of low-level-waste facilities in the state, a move that would bar the state's governor, if he so desired, from issuing an executive order allowing Maine to join the Northeast compact. The state went on to explore a linkup with New Hampshire and Vermont in a New England compact.

But, as is typical of radioactive-waste politics, leaders in those states were divided on whether to join Maine. John Sununu, the governor of New Hampshire, favored the eleven-state Northeast pact, but Ednapearl F. Parr, a state representative who heads the House State-Federal Relations Committee, opposed it. "All the big states want to dump on Maine, New Hampshire, and Vermont," she said. "They think we are very sparsely settled and a bunch of country hicks. When people say it's less populated, to hell with them."

The breach between small and large waste producers will widen in the years ahead. By some date decades from now, if nuclear industry plans are carried out, the nation's commercial nuclear reactors will be dismantled and the equipment shipped off for burial in a low-level cemetery. The radioactivity from only one reactor will be twenty-three times greater than that found in all low-level waste buried in the United States in 1981. New York and Pennsylvania will have at least fifteen reactors to dispose of; Maine, New Hampshire, and Vermont will have two, possibly three.

The large states in the Northeast were equally disenchanted with the proposed compact, but their reasons were different from those of the small states. "I think the compact has fatal flaws from the standpoint of New York," said Robert Kurtter, a New York State legislative specialist on radioactive waste. "They have done an inadequate job of dealing with the catastrophic-accident–long-term-liability question. It seems to me if a state is going to be a host state for the region, and something should go wrong at the site that was serious enough to create a major expensive cleanup, the responsibility for that should be borne by all the compact states in the region. Right now if there is an accident and it goes beyond the stated insurance limits, it is the host state's responsibility. I can't see any incentive for a state to assume that risk unless everybody else in the region is going to be a party to it."

It was the failure to set aside funds for long-term care, it should be remembered, that was one of the misfortunes that befell commercial low-level-waste dumps in the past. At the Sheffield burial ground in Illinois, the company that managed the installation from 1967, when it opened, until 1978, when it closed, paid about $198,000 to Illinois to maintain the burial ground after operations ceased. Illinois allowed nine years to go by before it set up a special account for the money, during which about $115,000 in "perpetual-care" contributions flowed into the state's general fund and was spent for other purposes. In 1976, the state finally established such an account, which took in about $83,000. By the end of 1983, only about $38,000 remained. The cost of correcting off-site seepage of radioactivity could cost, according to one federal estimate, as much as $18 million. Illinois's perpetual-care fund, designed to finance repairs, surveillance, and maintenance for hundreds of years, thus has enough money to pay for about one day of work during a two-year cleanup at Sheffield.

But questions of long-term responsibility are by no means the only ones dividing large states. Pennsylvania and New York were unhappy with Massachusetts. The state's voters approved a referendum in November 1982 that sets up an involved process for establishing a radioactive-waste site. Many observers believe the mechanism could block any effort to open a dump in Massachusetts.

Dr. Walter H. Plosila, deputy secretary for technology and policy development in the Pennsylvania Department of Commerce, questioned whether Massachusetts could bargain in "good faith" with other northeastern states: "Massachusetts would have their cake and eat it too. It might sign on to the compact, but would know it would never have to host a site because of its elaborate internal processes of the public referendums."

All of this helped create the impression that the Northeast

may be unable to take care of its low-level waste. A negotiator for a midwestern state who spoke to a Northeast representative at a national conference on the compacts came away with the feeling the Northeast faces "insurmountable" obstacles. "I remember talking to one gentleman from an eastern state who shook his head and said, 'I'm not sure which way we're going or how we're going to get there,' " recalled Dan Drain, former director of environmental resources in Nebraska.

Although Northeast negotiators spoke confidently of establishing a burial ground, some were privately concerned over whether the ground of that populous, rainy region was a proper place for radioactive waste. "When you talk about a good site for shallow land burial, the East Coast just isn't it," said a staff member who helped the delegation draft the proposed compact. "The western states have a lot of open land, much of it on federal property, with little rainfall and no water table problems. It's just much better suited for shallow land burial than anything you could find in the East."

Joanne Buehler, an official of US Ecology, the company that manages the Richland and Beatty dumps, said a delegation of eastern negotiators inspected the company's two western burial grounds in 1982. "They look around at these arid sites, and they're beautiful," she said. "Geologically, hydrologically, they're absolutely gorgeous sites for this. You couldn't pick a better site than the two western sites we operate. And of course the capacity is there. And they [in the East] just don't understand why they should be having to go through this hassle when this is available."

Beatty, for example, is in the desert about a hundred miles from Las Vegas, the nearest city. It is underlain with thick layers of clay that would retard the downward flow of water, if there were any water to flow into trenches. Beatty receives only four inches of rain a year, making it one of the driest places in the United States. Most areas in the Northeast receive from thirty-five to forty-five inches a year. The water table at Beatty is 300 feet below the surface. The water table at the three commercial sites that were shut down in the 1970s after water saturated trenches was 32 feet at Maxey Flats, Kentucky, 10 feet at Sheffield, Illinois, and 8 feet at West Valley, New York.

The track record at those plots led an official of the EPA to tell Washington lawmakers that "it may be infeasible, using current waste types, containers and procedures, to use the technique of shallow land burial in humid climates."

At least one industry official, James L. Harvey, president of the SouthWest Nuclear Company, one of the nation's largest low-level-waste handlers, believes that shallow land burial of radioactive material is not appropriate in the eastern half of the nation. "I don't have too much of a problem with a shallow land site in a desert area," Harvey said. "The only place I have a problem, and I've had a lot of experience in this, is where you have heavy rainfall. It's a real bear to operate a burial site in those places. I personally feel the type of sites that exists now [shallow land burial] is not a feasible option in the East anymore. It just doesn't work. There is no way to keep the water out. If you don't have a vehicle for migration [radioactive seepage], you've got no problem with the stuff. But water is a vehicle for migration, and once you get on the eastern half of the United States you got lots of water everywhere."

In addition to technical problems, population densities in the Northeast make the task of setting up a low-level burial ground even more difficult. New Jersey has an average of 979 persons every square mile. In Montana the figure is 5 persons per square mile. In Massachusetts it is 733, versus 10 in New Mexico. In Connecticut it is 639, compared with 7 in Nevada; in Pennsylvania it is 264, compared with 24 in Arizona. As the magnitude of the task confronting the Northeast states has begun to be apparent to public officials, some concede they would have sought another solution in 1980 had they recognized the burden the policy act would impose. A staff member who worked closely with Northeast governors to develop a regional compact says, "If you ask me, now, off the record, I would much rather have seen the Congress go the other way— the way high-level waste is going—and make it a federal responsibility rather than giving it to the states."

No one knows, of course, how things will turn out in the Northeast or in any other region. Two possibilities stand out.

First, even if compact agreements are negotiated for every region, some states might balk at approving them. Indeed, this has already happened. If, by some miracle, compacts were negotiated by every state, they could still unravel if states failed to agree on locations for regional burial grounds.

Whatever the future holds, it seems certain that Congress will have to take another look at the compacts in the years ahead. But Congress has no desire to do so. That became evident after the proposed Northwest Interstate Compact on Low-Level Waste Management was submitted to Congress. The agreement, the first regional pact introduced in Congress, was negotiated by seven states early in 1981 and ratified by legislatures soon afterward. For more than three years, Congress has failed to act on it or on similar legislation covering the Central, Rocky Mountain, and Southeast areas.

"We're urging Congress to take quick action on these compacts when they come in," said David Stevens, the aide of Governor Spellman of Washington. "If you want a system in place, one of the ways would be to ratify the first compact. That's a clear signal to the other areas that they're going to have to do something."

Not only has Congress given no sign, it is indeed indicating that it intends to wait until most, if not all, compacts have been negotiated before it acts. And not without good reason. "I just don't see any Congressman voting for a compact that would shut off a burial site for his state," Stevens said. "I just don't see him voluntarily voting on such a measure. Then he's really created a political problem for himself."

What Stevens means is that lawmakers from New York or Pennsylvania, which now ship low-level waste to Barnwell, are not going to approve the Southeast compact, which would shut off Northeast waste, until their region has a burial ground or some other arrangement. Thus, if one region cannot resolve its conflicts, it could hold up all the compacts.

The turmoil among the large waste-producing states and

the inevitable coming fight over access to the existing burial grounds has been ignored by Congress. Periodic reports in the House and Senate give updates on the "compacting" process, as lawmakers call it. The rhetoric here, as in most instances when nuclear waste is involved, has little to do with reality. Congressmen and senators regularly praise the states for their efforts to comply with the act, which they portray as a far-sighted, creative piece of legislation.

When a bill to sanction the Rocky Mountain compact was introduced in October 1983, Sen. Alan K. Simpson, Republican of Wyoming, gave high marks to the states involved. "I do want to congratulate all of those within the Rocky Mountain region who worked so long and diligently to pull this compact together," he said. "With all of these pressures, these states have taken on their responsibilities in a responsible and timely fashion, and for that I would like to commend and congratulate them." Similarly, Sen. Mark O. Hatfield of Oregon, a Republican, lauded the Northwest states when their compact was reintroduced in Congress early in 1983. "This compact, which has gone through a great deal of discussion in the affected states, deserves to be ratified by Congress," Hatfield said. "It is a good-faith effort, in my opinion, in recognizing a serious problem, and working out a framework for these states to begin negotiating a suitable low-level radioactive waste disposal site."

Sen. Strom Thurmond, Republican of South Carolina, painted an idyllic picture in August 1983 of regional waste efforts. The states, Thurmond said, "responded promptly" to the policy act. "They have organized themselves into six regional groups: the Northeast, Southeast, Midwest, Central, Northwest, and Rocky Mountain regions. Compacts have been negotiated in each of the six regions, and most have been ratified by the various state legislatures. . . . " To Sen. Malcolm Wallop, a Wyoming Republican, the regional alliances attest to the worth of the federal system. "These compacts reaffirm the states rights and reinforce the role states will play in solving many of the problems which face us today," he told colleagues in October 1983.

Even though small states have isolated large states, and in some cases have denied them membership in a compact, the late Henry M. Jackson, the longtime Democratic senator from Washington, said in January 1983 that "it appears at this time that each state will be able to affiliate itself with one group of states in some region of the country for achieving disposal of low-level wastes generated within its borders. This regional approach is necessary because few states generate sufficient low-level waste to justify on an environmental or economic basis the opening of a separate site within each state for a disposal facility." Jackson said that no state should "end up being excluded from participation in a compact." He praised his home state for "dealing with the current national problem in an exemplary fashion." Among the ways in which Washington dealt with the question was to exclude California from the Northwest compact.

In one respect, the glowing accounts are accurate. For in regions like the Northwest, Rocky Mountain, and Southeast— which produce little waste or have a burial ground in place or both—the process is working. Although praised for banding together, states in those regions had a more powerful incentive than states in the Northeast. By doing so they took the first move toward excluding waste from large generators and preserving local burial grounds for the exclusive use of their immediate region, a step that could be of immeasurable benefit in the years ahead.

In the Northwest, for example, Richland has enough capacity to take care of the region's waste for eighty years, on the basis of the current rate at which it produces waste. The 100-acre burial ground takes up a small part of a 1,000-acre tract the federal government leases to Washington State. If the full 1,000 acres were given over for low-level burial, it could handle the Northwest's needs for more than a thousand years. Similarly, Beatty has enough land left to handle Rocky Mountain waste for eighty years.

Despite the fact that Congress has not yet approved any compact, Nevada and South Carolina are already limiting access to their dumps. When stringent new packaging regulations went into effect in Nevada in December 1980, the volume of waste buried at Beatty plunged 88 percent, falling from 450,000 cubic feet that year to 53,000 in 1982. At Barnwell, where South Carolina imposed a volume-reduction program in 1979, the amount buried between 1980 and 1982 fell 37 percent, from 1.9 million to 1.2 million cubic feet. The third dump, Richland, picked up some of the slack, as burials there rose from 876,000 cubic feet to 1.4 million during the same years. But the rerouting to Richland still took care of only about half the volume of the cutbacks at the other two sites.

The restrictions imposed by Nevada and South Carolina have upset officials in other states. Ron Kucera, the deputy director of Missouri's Department of Natural Resources, said that when Nevada, Washington, and South Carolina sought support from other states in 1980 for the policy act, they promised to keep their facilities open while other states tried to set up burial grounds of their own.

"Instead, access is being frustrated and reduced long before we get to the 1986 date," he said, referring to burial restrictions imposed by Nevada and South Carolina. "We don't think that's good faith. Our state is trying to make this work, and we're moving as fast as we can. I don't think this is what Congress contemplated when it passed the law, and it certainly wasn't what the rest of the states thought would happen, and if this is what is going to happen, maybe we just ought to look at federalizing the whole system."

For all the divisiveness that marked efforts to form a Northeast compact, the eleven states that drafted a proposed agreement were able to agree on one crucial point—to make no mention of a burial site. Negotiators intentionally avoided the subject. "It's bad enough siting one of these things when the state says yes," said Joanne Buehler, the US Ecology official.

In the Northeast, with its high rainfall, population densities, and concern over radioactive contamination, no state will eagerly face the political ramifications of attempting to set up a radioactive dump. "Siting is the worst battle in government

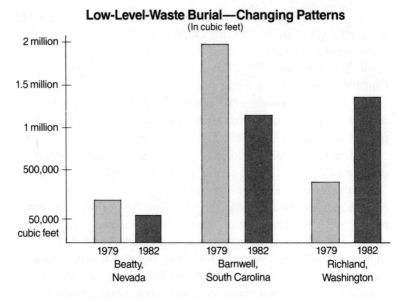

Low-Level-Waste Burial—Changing Patterns
(In cubic feet)

Source: Compiled from U.S. Department of Energy records.

This chart shows the dramatic change in the volume of low-level waste buried each year at the nation's three operating commercial burial plots from 1979 to 1982. The decline at Beatty and Barnwell came about because of strict inspections at Beatty and a volume-reduction plan at Barnwell. Much of the amount that had previously gone to those two sites was being buried at Richland by 1982.

today," said one observer of the Northeast talks. "The negotiators dealt with it by punting and saying we can't deal with this. We'll let the commission that is appointed at the end of this process decide on how to deal with it after everybody joins."

After the proposed Northeast compact was finally drafted, the region's states waited for one to volunteer as the dump state. Only if one willingly agreed to provide the facility, most observers believed, did the eleven-state Northeast compact have a chance to succeed. Most states looked to New York or Pennsylvania to volunteer.

New York thought that other states regarded it as the likely candidate. Centrally located within the region, New York was the largest generator of low-level waste among the eleven states from 1979 to 1982. Perhaps most to the point, it already had a commercial burial ground, albeit a failed one, at West Valley. Robert Kurtter, the New York State legislative official, said the compact, because it failed to mention a burial site, would be difficult to pass in New York. "I know what's going to happen if I were to take this bill to conference," he said in 1983. "Everybody is going to say, 'Okay, where is the site going to be?' And if I say, 'I don't know,' I'm liable to get lynched." A newsletter published in the same year by the state's Legislative Commission on Science and Technology also issued a warning. "No state has a current regional facility," it noted. "New York State is the only state which has operated a facility [at West Valley]. In terms of time to get into operation, New York is clearly ahead of the other states, none of which has even surveyed potential sites. If New York joins the compact and is designated as the original host state, there will be no reason for any other compact member to identify potential future sites. New York could find itself in the position of being redesignated by a two-thirds vote of the commission since it has a regional facility and no other state does. There is no protection against this eventuality in the proposed compact."

New York's anxiety was justified. A report by Congress's General Accounting Office in 1980 said that the state could "provide a vital service to its region and itself by agreeing to make the West Valley low-level waste burial ground available for use." Such suggestions from a federal agency contain a hint of tit for tat. The West Valley burial ground was established adjacent to the Nuclear Fuel Services commercial reprocessing plant that closed in 1972, leaving New York State with a potential cleanup bill so large that it had to go to Congress for help.

When Congress approved cleanup funds in 1980, John Dingell, a Democratic congressman from Michigan, suggested, "There is presently a critical shortage of low-level waste disposal sites, and the lack of such a facility in the Northeast, which is the largest generator of such waste, cannot be ignored. The enactment of this legislation should, therefore, provide a substantial incentive to the State of New York to consider the potential use of this site for meeting regional needs." It also abets New York's anxiety that, under a state-federal agreement, low-level waste from the cleanup of the defunct reprocessing venture is now being buried at West Valley.

Pennsylvania, too, worried that other states would designate it as the regional burial ground if it joined the Northeast compact. The state ranked third in waste production in the region from 1979 to 1982. But it was expected to become the largest producer as two new nuclear plants went on-line in 1984 and a third was scheduled to start up in 1985. Although Pennsylvania helped draft the Northeast compact, state officials were not enthusiastic about it. Subtle pressure from other states notwithstanding, Pennsylvania refused to volunteer. "Everybody is hoping somebody will volunteer and we are too," Thomas M. Gerusky, director of the state's Bureau of Radiation Protection, said in 1983.

Pennsylvania State University studied the Northeast under a Department of Energy contract in order to develop guidelines for the selection of a location, but did not make specific recommendations for a burial ground. If Pennsylvania were required to have a site, Gerusky said, "almost any county in Pennsylvania could accept the waste" under current Nuclear Regulatory Commission regulations.

As a practical matter, though, Gerusky said, "you sure couldn't put it in Philadelphia or Allegheny County [Pittsburgh] or a county that has a very high population density. You don't need much land. [But] you'd have to have it by a major highway. There are going to be trucks coming in and out of the site. There aren't that many areas one could look at away from major routes."

State officials said no work was under way to choose a site, but an earlier Penn State study, published in 1968, had identified "three potentially favorable" locations. Prepared by the university's Department of Geology and Geophysics for the state Department of Commerce, the 150-page report concluded that the three "suitable" areas were the following:

• Northwestern Pennsylvania, in Erie and Crawford counties, where a stratum of rock known as the Hiram Till consists of clay-rich tills offering a "desirable combination of conditions" for waste burial.

• Northeastern Pennsylvania, in the Bradford County region, where a stretch of land from Towanda to Athens, along the northern branch of the Susquehanna River, is "favorable for dispensing radioactive leachates in the subsurface."

• Southeastern Pennsylvania, where a path extending from "Gettysburg, Wellsville, and York Haven eastward to the Quakertown-Norristown-Doylestown region" is "a potentially favorable region for radioactive waste storage and disposal."

That the study found geological structures "suitable for waste storage and disposal" in southeastern Pennsylvania—including parts of Montgomery and Bucks counties—two of the most heavily populated areas of Pennsylvania, the nation's fourth-most-populous state, symbolizes the unreality that all too often characterizes much of the scientific community's attitude toward radioactive waste. Gerusky maintained that the Penn State study was out of date. New NRC regulations on land burial, he said, would have to be reviewed in selecting a burial site. Because the Penn State study "did not take all of these [regulations] into account," he added, it is "therefore invalid."

That, in capsule form, is the history of radioactive-waste management. Land once designated by scientists as perfectly suitable and safe for the burial of radioactive waste later turns out to be neither suitable nor safe.

By the spring of 1984, the fragile unity of the Northeast states began to crumble. In May, the New York State Energy Office released a study urging the state not to join the Northeast compact. "New York State should neither seek to renegotiate the specific provisions of the proposed eleven-state" compact, the report stated, "nor pursue any form of an eleven-state low-level radioactive waste compact." Instead, it recommended, New York should negotiate with one or more Northeast states to organize another compact to be submitted to the legislature in 1985.

The study also said the Department of Environmental Conservation should identify a site for a permanent burial ground in New York. Meanwhile, the report said, the state should store low-level waste from all producers except power plants in an above-ground facility at West Valley. This interim center could store waste from the state's nearly 400 medical, industrial, institutional, and academic producers. Electric utilities would keep their waste at the state's four nuclear power plants. Partly on the basis of the report, Gov. Mario Cuomo decided against joining the Northeast compact.

A month later, Pennsylvania also declined to join the eleven-state pact and decided to explore a new agreement with its neighbors. "Pennsylvania is prepared to do its share," Gov. Dick Thornburgh explained, ". . . but we are not prepared to accept sole responsibility for all the low-level radioactive waste produced in the Northeast." He said West Virginia and New York had expressed interest in teaming up with Pennsylvania. Ohio, a member of the Midwest compact, later called Pennsylvania's plan to accept waste from neighbors "an attractive option" and said it would reconsider its membership in the Midwest pact. Massachusetts, the second-largest producer, also decided against the eleven-state compact, in favor of developing its own site, possibly with neighboring states. Maine, New Hampshire, and Vermont likewise refused to join and were uncertain as to what they would do with their waste.

The increasingly muddled Northeast picture looked like this in the fall of 1984: New York might set up its own burial ground and take in a neighbor or two. New York and Pennsylvania might get together in a compact, with each establishing low-level-waste facilities. Pennsylvania and West Virginia might form a compact and exclude all other Northeast waste. Massachusetts might set up a dump with Rhode Island or some other small neighboring state. Maine, Vermont, and New Hampshire might form a compact, or the three might make separate deals with a large state—or they might go their own ways.

As for the Northeast compact, which was originally to have had eleven members, it was joined by only four states—New Jersey, Connecticut, Maryland, and Delaware. Of these, New Jersey was the most likely candidate for the regional site. The largest generator of the four, it is also centrally located within the scaled-down region. But establishing a low-level-waste site in the state would be an enormous political problem. New Jersey is the nation's most densely populated state, and its many toxic-waste dumps have in recent years ignited citizen concern about environmental contamination.

If there is anything positive in these chaotic machinations, it is that the states have finally faced a reality the federal government has been unable to recognize for forty years—that shallow land burial may not be the most appropriate method for dealing with low-level waste. New York is inclined toward above-ground storage. So, too, is Pennsylvania, whose secretary for policy and planning, Frank Wright, said flatly, "Shallow land burial [of waste] is unacceptable to Pennsylvania." Maine is studying above-ground storage at the Maine Yankee nuclear plant at Wiscasset. The Kentucky-Illinois compact perhaps best illustrates the change in thinking.

Because each had already had very bad experiences with burial grounds, Illinois and Kentucky were not about to embrace the concept again. Instead, the two-state agreement calls for "above-ground facilities and other disposal technologies providing greater and safer confinement." It permits land burial, but only in an enclosed engineered, "structurally enforced and solidified bunker."

The states' enthusiasm for above-ground or engineered storage is not shared by the federal government. Despite the failure rate for burial grounds in wet areas, the NRC is still pushing for a continuation of this practice. The commission is so wedded to shallow land burial that it has failed to issue regulations covering engineered or above-ground storage. The lack of regulations will, at best, further delay regional facilities or, at worst, force states to open burial grounds that experience indicates are doomed to fail.

The shift away from shallow land burial was summed up before the House Interior and Insular Affairs Committee on February 23, 1984, by Dr. Judith H. Johnsrud, speaking for a broad-based coalition known as the Network and Public Policy Group. "Many in the Northeast, having studied the history of shallow land burial, conclude that near-surface trenches, even those which conform to [current] Nuclear Regulatory Commission . . . standards, are not an adequate means of LLRW [low-level-radioactive-waste] isolation," she said. "They are a technology designed to fail. . . . Above ground engineered storage appears to offer the best existing means of isolating these wastes."

Although that type of storage would cost more in the beginning and pose a "certain vulnerability," Dr. Johnsrud said, it has distinct advantages over shallow land burial. "Onsite facilities at the locus of generation or use will minimize the transportation of these hazardous materials, a major consideration in the densely populated Northeast," she said. "Onsite facilities will retain the responsibility for proper control, as well as the costs of adequate surveillance, with those who produced the problem."

With the outlook for commercial burial increasingly muddled, electric utilities are girding for the probability that they will be forced to store low-level waste on-site for years. Until now, most have kept waste at power plants for no longer than a few months. As a rule, when they accumulate enough to fill a truck, they ship the material to a burial ground. Now, utilities are preparing to store waste up to five years.

Two utilities, after going through NRC licensing procedures, have erected specially designed low-level-waste-storage buildings next to their reactors. The Pennsylvania Power &

Light Company built a low-level-waste warehouse at its Susquehanna plant at Berwick, Pennsylvania. The company's first reactor began generating electricity in 1983, and the second unit started up in 1984. The Tennessee Valley Authority put up two storage buildings, one at its Browns Ferry plant at Decatur, Alabama, and another at its Sequoyah plant at Daisy, Tennessee. The two utilities are the only ones with specific licenses to store low-level waste, but they are by no means the only ones planning to do so. NRC regulations allow a utility to approach the matter in one of two ways. It may seek a special license, as TVA and Pennsylvania Power & Light did. Or it may pile up waste on-site under the authority of its operating license and merely advise the NRC later of its action and of the reason for it.

An NRC spokesman said that "it turns out that something on the order of two-thirds of all the utilities in the country have made some kind of change to accommodate more waste storage." The accommodations, he said, "may run anywhere from putting something in a back room to building a big facility, so there's a wide range of changes that have been made, depending upon the status of the utility."

An industry representative said that the power companies were reluctant to provide for the long-term storage of low-level waste but that they had little choice. "The last thing they want to do is store the damn stuff," he said. "They want to get rid of it. And the only reason they're doing it is a contingency, that if they can't get rid of it, they've got to [store] it." The upshot is that the nation's nuclear power plants, already ticketed to become de facto repositories for used fuel rods because of the failure of the national high-level-waste policy, could inherit the role as above-ground storage centers for low-level waste as well. Rather than the "six or seven sites," geographically positioned around the country, that the debate about low-level waste envisioned, the nation could easily have more than a hundred.

10
The Supersalesman
of Nuclear Waste

SPELLBINDER

Fred Beierle showed up in tiny Sheffield, Illinois, on a summer day in 1966, a salesman selling an idea. He proposed to convert an abandoned farm into a burial ground for low-level radioactive waste. Although there were skeptics among the townspeople, Beierle soon wore down their resistance. He organized publicity campaigns. He mobilized local business people in behalf of his project. It would, he said, create jobs in a county that was one of the most depressed in the state.

Perhaps more important, he allayed the fears of residents concerned about how radioactive the waste would be and what harm it would cause if anything went wrong. "The [radio]activity in a lot of cases is no more than the radium dial of your watch," he told citizens who turned out for a Bureau County zoning-board hearing.

As a further indication of his sincerity, Beierle assured the locals that he would be at the burial ground daily and would personally receive the largest dose of radiation that could be emitted. "In a year's time," he said, "I will absorb about the amount [of] two chest X-rays, and I will be there every day."

Having won the town over, he secured a permit to develop

the site, and within a year trucks carrying nuclear waste from around the country began to rumble over the back roads of Illinois. During the next ten years, thousands of fifty-five-gallon drums packed with radioactive waste were dumped into trenches twelve to twenty-six feet deep and covered with dirt. Just as the salesman had said, some of the drums contained no more radiation than the dial of a luminous watch. But others were loaded with lethal materials, such as plutonium in quantities sufficient to build atomic bombs as large as the one that fell on Nagasaki.

Today, the dump is closed. At least one radioactive substance, tritium, is seeping off the property and contaminating adjoining lands. Sheffield must now live with the nuclear cemetery for considerably longer than the 132 years the village has existed. There is little recourse except to wait and watch and monitor the radiation.

For Beierle, who sold Sheffield on the idea of the dump in the first place, the escaping radioactivity poses no problem at all. Soon after the first waste-disposal trucks rolled into Sheffield, he sold out and moved on.

The story of Fredrick P. Beierle, the supersalesman of low-level nuclear waste, is very much a part of the story of radioactive waste in the United States. Beierle set up two of the three commercial burial grounds operating today—in Richland, Washington, and in Barnwell, South Carolina. (The remaining dump, in Beatty, Nevada, was established by a company once headed by a business associate of Beierle.) Taken together, Richland and Barnwell account for 98 percent of the commercial nuclear waste buried annually.

Beierle's activities have made him a pivotal figure in the low-level-waste industry. But he has received little national publicity. He does not testify at congressional hearings delving into the problems of waste management. Repeated efforts by the authors to interview him in person or by telephone were unsuccessful. On one occassion, in November 1982, when a telephone call was placed to Beierle's Prosser, Washington, office in connection with a series of articles that was being prepared for publication in the *Philadelphia Inquirer,* a woman who identified herself as Mrs. Beierle answered and said her husband would not answer any questions. She explained, "We do not find that publicity with low-level radioactive waste ever comes out the way it is meant to, the way we talk to people, so our policy is no interviews. I am Mr. Beierle's wife. I have gone through all of these things personally. Newspapers per se have such a poor reputation with us that, you know, it is very difficult for me to even be nice to you on the telephone. You people twist the words, you leave out things, just so it comes out the way you want it to come out, not the way the people you are interviewing project it."

Indeed, it is likely that from Beierle's point of view, he has been doing this nation a major favor. The kind of nuclear trash he deals with is piling up at a great rate. It has to be put somewhere. If Beierle and other entrepreneurs don't find the sites, they might ask, who will? Not the federal government, that's for sure. It abandoned that responsibility years ago.

A onetime reactor operator from rural Washington State, Fred Beierle has gone a long way on persuasion and self-promotion. Operating out of Prosser, a small town in the agriculturally rich Yakima Valley, he has made a career out of wooing other small towns, quoting from Scripture and preaching the wonders of nuclear energy. To those who have observed Fred Beierle over the years, the effect has been little short of mesmerizing.

A businessman in a small Texas town where Beierle once tried to establish an atomic landfill says, "If he just walked in this door, and I knew nothing at all about him, I would think he was a preacher. When you talked to him for long, you were just made to feel he was a man of God, that he was standing there right at the foot of the cross."

A state regulatory official who has known Beierle for years says, "Fred really fools people. He's funny-looking, with freckles all over his face. He doesn't seem at first very impressive. But then he starts talking and you listen. Very few people can talk as well as Fred Beierle."

A Kansas man who has seen Beierle in action says, "One part of you says you ought to know better about some of the things he tries to tell you. But he's so convincing you find yourself believing him when you know you shouldn't."

Although Beierle approaches nuclear waste with an evangelical fervor, he is a man of many interests. He is both an inventor and a creationist, a person who eschews Darwin's theory of evolution, believing instead that the earth and all its life forms were created in much the way the Bible says. He has promoted a gasifier that, according to published accounts, runs on a secret material that converts cherry pits, cornstalks, wood chips, rubber tires, paper sacks, and chicken manure into synthetic gas. And he has adapted a pickup truck to run on hay, wood, weeds, and other waste products. To dramatize the truck's potential, Beierle and his brother once drove it from Los Angeles to New York.

The family business in rural Washington state, though, may be the best example of Beierle's knack for juggling different interests. In two small metal buildings on the outskirts of Prosser (pop. 3,000), The B & B Equipment Company has fabricated food-processing equipment and has repackaged liquid radioactive waste from power plants.

That Fred Beierle would become the nation's foremost salesman for nuclear cemeteries is perhaps understandable given his background. Beierle started his career at the sprawling Hanford works of the Atomic Energy Commission, in south central Washington. Covering an area equal to half of Rhode Island, Hanford dates from World War II, when it manufactured the plutonium for the atomic bomb dropped on Nagasaki.

Situated in a desolate area, more than a hundred miles from the nearest city of consequence (Spokane, pop. 175,000), Hanford is a world unto itself, fiercely proud of its role in atomic development. Nearby Pasco boasts a grocery store called Atomic Foods. The sports teams at neighboring Richland High School are called the Bombers. The school's symbol is a mushroom cloud.

It was in this decidedly pronuclear milieu that Fred Beierle (pronounced "buyerly"), born February 2, 1931, in remote Deer Lodge, Montana, broke into the business in 1954. Fresh from a tour of duty as a seaman in the U.S. Coast Guard, Beierle took a job as an assembly-line worker fabricating metal parts for the fuel elements of Hanford's nine reactors.

Within six months, Beierle had been promoted to reactor operator, a job that taught him how to start up, shut down, and refuel reactors. Most important for his future, it also taught him about handling the waste they churned out. At that time, most low-level liquid waste was discharged directly into the ground, on the theory that "natural environmental conditions," as the AEC's 1964 annual report put it, would diffuse the radioactivity

Fredrick P. Beierle.
Tri-City *(Wash.)* Herald / *Sue Taylor*

to "safe levels." This practice, like others in the waste business, was found to be a bad idea, and was later discontinued.

Beierle parlayed his experience at Hanford into a succession of jobs in the nuclear industry, according to records of state regulatory agencies. In a four-year period, he worked at plants in three states, "starting up," as he once described it, reactors. There were stints at the General Electric test reactor in San Jose, California; at the Hallam sodium reactor in Hallam, Nebraska; and at the AEC's experimental Elk River reactor near Minneapolis. Beierle compiled college credits toward a degree in mechanical engineering from Columbia Basin College, Pasco, Washington; San Jose City College and San Jose State College; and the University of Minnesota. Then, in 1962, a federal decision set the stage for his business.

This was the AEC's announcement that it intended to ban the burial of commercial waste at federal installations in order to encourage private development of nuclear cemeteries. Under this new arrangement, the task of determining where waste would be interred and managed, once a federal responsibility, would be given over to private enterprise. The decision went virtually unnoticed.

Unnoticed, that is, except by those who saw a way to get started in what was bound one day to grow into a booming business. Before the year was out, licenses to bury radioactive waste had been granted to the Nuclear Engineering Company for properties in Beatty, Nevada, and in Maxey Flats, Kentucky. To Beierle, then a shift supervisor at Elk River, the new government policy was an invitation to go into the nuclear-waste field. Along with two other men, one a professor of nuclear engineering at Purdue University and the other a health physicist from California, Beierle founded California Nuclear Inc. in April 1963.

The company was incorporated in California, had offices in Indiana, and established its first burial ground in Washington. Although California Nuclear proposed that it would provide a variety of services to the nuclear industry, a primary goal, as papers on file with the state of California spelled out, was to "own or lease, develop, and operate . . . burial grounds for radioactive wastes."

Of all the locations for which Beierle would summon up his superior powers of salesmanship, the site he selected for his first cemetery offered the least challenge. That was the property adjoining the Hanford works, the AEC reservation where Beierle had started out almost ten years earlier. Already committed to atomic development, people around Hanford had few anxieties about nuclear energy or its by-products.

It was not the public that had to be persuaded to buy the idea but rather state and federal officials whose help Beierle needed, for the United States government owned the land. After months of negotiations, California Nuclear worked out a deal by which the federal government leased the parcel to Washington State, which in turned subleased one hundred acres to California Nuclear.

Thus, at little cost to his company, Beierle managed to get control of land that would prove of inestimable value in years ahead. To help the company get started, the Small Business Administration provided a $147,000 loan, according to California Nuclear's records. And so, with a powerful assist from the federal government, which provided the policy, the land, and the working capital, Fred Beierle was on his way.

He was photographed with county officials when he received a building permit to begin work on what was to be called the Richland Burial Facility. At the start, the company would employ eight people, Beierle told a reporter, but he hoped employment would eventually rise to fifty. He suffered a temporary setback when a state court invalidated the company's lease for technical reasons, but a bill was shepherded through the Washington legislature that enabled California Nuclear to begin operations late in 1965.

ON THE ROAD

Even before the first barrels of radioactive waste were buried at Richland, Beierle was on the lookout for a second site. He settled on rolling farmland three miles southwest of Sheffield, Illinois, a town of 1,000 about 125 miles west of Chicago. Sheffield was ideal for Beierle's purposes. It was strategically located in north central Illinois, only a few miles from Commonwealth Edison Company's Dresden nuclear power station, the nation's first full-scale commercial reactor, and within close range of six other projected nuclear plants, which would soon make Illinois the foremost state in the generation of electricity by atomic power.

The property was in a sparsely populated region where Beierle was not likely to encounter much opposition. He intended to purchase the land, then deed the burial ground to the state. Federal policy encouraged the private development of dumps, but it required that the land be owned by either the federal or the state government.

Beierle moved his wife, Vesta, and the children to Sheffield. He opened an office on Main Street. He joined civic clubs. His wife played bridge with other housewives. He mingled with village leaders and extolled the economic benefits of radioactive-waste burial grounds. "He moved right in like he was here to stay," recalled Jay Langford, the owner of the town's only pharmacy.

Beierle took an option on a sixty-six-acre farm in July 1966 and sought to get the zoning changed from agricultural to light industrial. At a public hearing on July 29, 1966, he told townspeople of his plans for the Sheffield Nuclear Waste Facility. According to a transcript of the meeting found in records of the Bureau County Zoning Board of Appeals, Beierle said the property was "the best possible site in the State of Illinois as far as the geology and the hydrology is concerned." The radioactive particles, he assured residents, would remain in the burial ground, where "the soil in fact acts as a water softener, so this radioactive material can die away and present no hazard because it is contained within that soil. . . ."

When one resident asked whether cattle could graze on the burial ground after it was filled with nuclear trash, Beierle replied, "It is possible." Noting that radioactivity levels in the waste to be buried would be quite low, Beierle declared, "The material we handle is sweeping compound, glassware, rags, clothing, contaminated tools and even chairs. In some cases the rubbish material we put in the drums and bury is less than the radium of an alarm clock."

Years later, after learning that thirty-four pounds of plutonium and seventy pounds of enriched uranium were buried at Sheffield, residents bitterly recalled Beierle's assurances. Both materials are lethal; neither could be buried under regulations that now govern so-called low-level graveyards like Sheffield. Ironically, Sheffield also turned out to be the burial plot for a nuclear reactor that Beierle himself helped start up before he entered the business. About 47,000 cubic feet of debris from the Elk River test reactor was dumped into Sheffield's trenches in the early 1970s.

The only opposition at the 1966 rezoning hearing came from a United Mine Workers representative who arrived from Washington, D.C. The union official spoke against the project because the nuclear industry threatened to take jobs away from mine workers by reducing the demand for coal. With no local resistance, the zoning board unanimously approved Beierle's rezoning request.

Three weeks later, California Nuclear applied to the AEC for a burial license at Sheffield. The company submitted voluminous documents to support its claim that it possessed the necessary expertise. Beierle, whom it described as a man of long experience in the field, would be the company's resident manager. "Mr. Beierle," the application stated, "is now living at Sheffield. . . . All burial operations will be under the direct personal observation of Mr. Fredrick P. Beierle . . . ."

The company also contended that the property was ideal for nuclear-waste burial. A geological report of the company's private consultant said that Sheffield was "adequate on nearly all counts." California Nuclear assured the AEC that "no increase in the natural radioactivity will be measured outside the Sheffield Nuclear Center due to the burial of radioactive wastes."

Although Sheffield received substantial rainfall, which led to major fluctuations in the area water table, no government agency seriously questioned California Nuclear's optimistic as-

States Producing the Most Radioactivity
in Low-Level Waste

		curies	cubic feet	cubic feet of waste per curie
1	Indiana	2,454	5,827	2
2	Massachusetts	402,946	982,224	2
3	Florida	96,629	323,653	3
4	Illinois	251,583	973,289	4
5	New York	243,409	1,078,950	4
6	Kentucky	5,488	24,684	4
7	California	136,624	774,400	6
8	Wisconsin	9,115	62,295	7
9	Maine	7,593	53,854	7
10	Michigan	44,713	324,464	7
11	Maryland	21,140	170,355	8
12	Alaska	2	18	9
13	South Dakota	2	18	9
14	Minnesota	25,270	239,042	9
15	Iowa	9,293	104,142	11
16	Arkansas	8,946	103,152	12
17	Distr. Columbia	621	7,627	12
18	Alabama	34,831	434,539	12
19	Arizona	329	4,449	14
20	Pennsylvania	56,947	921,766	16
21	Nevada	3,248	54,736	17
22	Vermont	3,193	61,905	19
23	Montana	35	777	22
24	Georgia	10,116	239,359	24
25	Ohio	6,327	154,322	24
26	Connecticut	15,476	429,207	28
27	Missouri	1,271	36,656	29
28	Idaho	10	291	29
29	New Jersey	19,635	572,123	29
30	South Carolina	34,205	1,053,699	31
31	West Virginia	58	1,845	32
32	North Carolina	25,665	835,034	33
33	Mississippi	210	7,063	34
34	Virginia	15,587	541,929	35
35	Nebraska	3,202	113,535	35
36	Oklahoma	288	13,101	45
37	Oregon	3,267	160,078	49
38	Texas	2,396	247,446	103
39	North Dakota	2	212	106
40	Louisiana	15	1,810	121
41	Washington	821	106,685	130
42	Utah	118	21,753	184
43	Hawaii	49	14,832	303

	curies	cubic feet	cubic feet of waste per curie
44 Colorado	41	17,304	422
45 New Hampshire	11	5,120	465
46 Delaware	11	5,651	514
47 New Mexico	15	8,582	572
48 Tennessee	600	345,372	576
49 Kansas	5	3,107	621
50 Rhode Island	93	84,011	903
51 Wyoming	0	0	0
National average	1,503,905	6,498,299	8

Source: Compiled from U.S. Department of Energy records.

Depending on the source of low-level waste, the amount of radioactivity in it varies considerably. The table ranks the states by the level of radioactivity, or curies, in the waste produced. For example, there is one curie in every four cubic feet of waste generated in New York. But there is one curie in 103 cubic feet of waste turned out in Texas. A state may generate a substantial volume of waste with comparatively little radioactivity, such as Washington, or a relatively small volume with high radioactivity, such as Indiana. The figures are annual averages for the years 1979 to 1982.

sessment of the geology. The Illinois State Geological Survey said that Sheffield was a "far superior" location, compared with others in the state, and possessed the "appropriate geological and hydrological factors." The U.S. Geological Survey said that company data indicated that conditions "appear to be suitable for burial of low-level solid radioactive wastes." The AEC expressed concern about the "inadequacy" of some data, but after California Nuclear drilled a few more test wells, the federal agency was satisfied. On July 13, 1967, it gave the company permission to begin burials.

Within a year, California Nuclear and Fred Beierle, the man who told Sheffielders that he would be at the cemetery "every day," were gone. The business was sold to the Nuclear Engineering Company, which then had owned and operated the Beatty and Maxey Flats dumps. California Nuclear's licenses for Sheffield and Richland were transferred to the new owner.

But that was not the end of the Sheffield story. In 1976,

States Producing the Most Radioactivity
in Power-Plant Waste

	Curies	Cubic Feet	Cubic Feet of Waste Per Curie
1 Illinois	227,525	571,550	3
2 Maine	7,740	48,320	6
3 Minnesota	17,876	122,693	7
4 Wisconsin	6,049	54,602	9
5 New York	49,995	539,445	11
6 Florida	23,696	263,692	11
7 Maryland	4,123	47,744	12
8 Michigan	20,596	281,362	14
9 Arkansas	6,474	100,275	15
10 Alabama	26,240	424,541	16
11 Vermont	3,237	55,964	17
12 Massachusetts	26,046	457,388	18
13 Georgia	10,180	206,628	20
14 Pennsylvania	26,922	548,794	20
15 Iowa	3,823	85,244	22
16 North Carolina	23,173	555,050	24
17 South Carolina	16,470	421,265	26
18 Virginia	14,175	394,232	28
19 Connecticut	10,949	361,042	33
20 California	4,796	173,359	36
21 New Jersey	9,792	368,722	38
22 Oregon	1,444	59,886	41
23 Nebraska	2,183	111,231	51
24 Tennessee	20	3,150	157
25 Ohio	92	34,774	378

Source: Compiled from U.S. Department of Energy records.

All nuclear power plants produce substantial volumes of low-level waste. But the amount of radioactivity in that waste varies considerably from state to state. There is one curie in every 3 cubic feet of power plant waste in Illinois, but one curie in every 36 cubic feet of power plant waste in California. The radioactivity and volume figures are the totals for the years 1979 to 1982.

Illinois health inspectors discovered that water was seeping into closed trenches and carrying off radioactive tritium. The Illinois Department of Public Health was disturbed. Up to then, Sheffield's trenches had been considered "impermeable" because the waste was buried in clay. "If tritium could migrate," a state legislative report warned, "so could other contaminates."

Nevertheless, the health department did not acknowledge to the public that the burial ground might be geologically unsuitable. In a letter to a Sheffield resident in 1977, Dr. Allen N. Koplin, the department's acting director, said, "The soils at the site are highly impervious to water . . . the time required for the waste to migrate from the point where it is buried to the site boundary will be long enough for the radioactivity to decay away."

That assessment proved far too sanguine. By late 1978, tritium leakage was more pronounced. A Bureau County judge determined in March 1979 that "radioactive contamination has reached, or is about to reach one site boundary." Early in 1982, tritium showed up for the first time in monitoring wells outside the graveyard. This prompted renewed court action against Nuclear Engineering, which by then had changed its name to US Ecology, and led to the drilling of more test wells.

Additional tests in 1983 turned up more evidence that radioactivity was leaking out of the burial plot. According to court papers filed by the Illinois attorney general, tritium had "migrated at least 700 feet away from the site boundary through at least one relatively narrow geologic pathway consisting of coarse, sandy soil extending away from the site in a northeasterly direction toward a strip mine pond." Although Sheffield was shut down in 1978, when the existing twenty-acre burial ground was filled to capacity, the leaks go on.

Just what, if anything, can be done is the subject of considerable debate. A Nuclear Regulatory Commission study commissioned in 1980 offered a variety of bizarre remedies, ranging from the dropping of forty-ton weights on defective trenches to the dynamiting of portions of the burial ground.

The Illinois attorney general's office, for its part, came up with more-conventional solutions: constructing a barrier wall to prevent further leakage; shoring up the trenches and pumping out those that contain water; constructing a facility to capture and treat all escaping radioactive material; and digging up defective trenches to remove contaminated material. If none of these suggestions are approved, the attorney general's office has a fallback position: it would seek a court order forcing US Ecology to purchase more land to the north and east as a buffer to absorb the steadily moving tritium. In other words, Illinois would create a second nuclear-waste site to trap the radioactive runoff of the first.

Thus, the nuclear burial ground that Beierle opened at Sheffield is likely to be the subject of legal wrangling between Illinois, private landowners, and US Ecology for years.

When Sheffield and Richland were sold to Nuclear Engineering, in 1968, Beierle joined the new owner as manager of sales and promotion, but the association lasted less than six months. By the end of 1968, Beierle was on the road again, in search of another burial ground. His attention soon focused on South Carolina, which, like Washington State, looked favorably on atomic development. South Carolina was the home of the Savannah River plant, the huge AEC installation that manufactures plutonium for nuclear bombs.

Beierle's new company was first called Intercontinental Nuclear Inc.; a few months later the name was changed to Chem-Nuclear Services Inc., with offices in Richland, Washington, and in Rockville, Maryland. On November 4, 1968, Intercontinental filed a proposal with South Carolina to build and manage a radioactive-waste burial ground. Though no site was mentioned, the company said it intended to work with state officials to locate one. Beierle was identified as its general manager.

The directors included Dr. Robert E. Bergstrom and Dr. Walton A. Rodger. Bergstrom was head of the groundwater section of the Illinois State Geological Survey. Rodger, the application stated, had been general manager for the "construction, start-up, licensing, and operation of the world's first privately-owned nuclear fuel reprocessing plant," at West Valley, New York. Other directors were from Beierle's home state of Washington. Among them were the owner of a drive-in restaurant in Longview, a wheat rancher in Lind, and an ap-

ple orchardist in Moses Lake. The company's assets totaled
$150,138.

Working closely with state officials, Beierle soon settled on
a 200-acre tract near the Savannah River plant, outside the
small town of Barnwell, South Carolina. In June of 1969, he
unveiled his proposal for the property, but Barnwell residents
were given little indication that it was destined to become a
graveyard for much of the East Coast's low-level radioactive
waste. Instead, they read the following account in the *Barnwell
People-Sentinel:*

"Chem-Nuclear Services Inc. announced today that it will
build and operate a facility near Barnwell to provide pollution
control services to the chemical industry.

"Fred Beierle, president of the Richland, Wash., firm, said
Chem-Nuclear hopes to eventually expand the operation to
provide burial facilities, materials packaging and other services
to the chemical and nuclear industries.

"Beierle said the initial operations would center primarily
around the receipt and above-ground storage of materials from
chemical plants."

The new entity, Beierle continued, was to "make available
to the chemical industry in this region the safe techniques and
procedures for pollution control that have been applied so successfully for a number of years in the nuclear field." Beierle
praised state officials and legislators for their help. "I know of
no state where it is such a pleasure to do business," he said.

For a time, Beierle's new company did indeed engage in the
chemical business. But on April 13, 1971, South Carolina
granted Chem-Nuclear permission to bury radioactive waste on
the property. By then, Beierle had moved on. As soon as the
property was selected and the regulatory process under way, he
and his partners sold their interest to a company called the
Great Columbia Corporation, which soon changed its name to
Chem-Nuclear Systems Inc. For several years afterward,
Beierle was a director of that publicly held corporation, which
emerged as one of the largest handlers of nuclear waste and
which has managed the Barnwell burial ground ever since.

Between attempts at setting up nuclear cemeteries, Beierle

returned to Washington State. Nestled at the foot of the pictur-
esque Horse Heaven Hills, Prosser—"A Pleasant Place With
Pleasant People," as a road sign on the edge of town puts it—
is home ground for an extensive clan of Beierle's relatives:
brothers, cousins, nieces, nephews, daughters, and grandchil-
dren.

It is also the home of the family business, B & B Equipment.
The company's officers include Beierle, his wife, Vesta, his
brother, Lenard, and Lenard's wife, Pat, according to state
corporation records, and it has provided employment for other
family members over the years. Beierle's father was the company's night watchman, living in a trailer adjoining the property until his death in 1981.

Papers on file with the state describe the company's business
as the "fabrication of potato-processing equipment." And that
is the type of work with which many local business people
associate the company. "B & B manufactures agricultural
equipment," said Richard Gay, publisher of the *Prosser Record
Bulletin.* "Farmers need all kinds of specialized equipment."

B & B has also repackaged radioactive waste—on the same
property where it has manufactured food-processing equipment. The waste repackaging has been done for electric utilities
with nuclear generating plants. It consists of solidifying liquid
low-level nuclear waste so that it can be shipped to a commercial burial ground. Regulations prohibit the burial of liquid
nuclear waste. To do the job, B & B was issued a radioactive-
materials license by Washington State. More recently, work
was performed there under a similar license held by the South-
West Nuclear Company of Pleasanton, California, headed by a
business partner of Beierle's, James L. Harvey. Beierle once was
president of SouthWest.

On an inspection trip to B & B in September 1979, when
one of the waste-solidification jobs was in progress, an inspector
for the state Department of Social and Health Services observed
violations of radiation-protection regulations. Beierle, his two
sons, and other B & B workers were draining liquid from twelve
containers of radioactive waste. The drums had originally been
shipped to Beatty, Nevada, by the Consumers Power Company

from its Palisades nuclear plant, near South Haven, Michigan. When the drums arrived in Nevada, inspectors noticed fluid leaking from four containers and refused to accept them. The containers were taken to SouthWest Nuclear's warehouse in Pleasanton, then trucked to B & B in Prosser, where the liquid was to be solidified.

During the work, in which fifty-seven gallons of radioactive fluid were removed, the inspector observed what he described in his report as a somewhat "lax attitude" toward the decontamination process. Although workers took off their gloves to enjoy soft drinks, they were still clothed in the "overalls and booties" they had worn while extracting the radioactive liquid. The company official who was monitoring radiation levels walked in and out of the restricted area "without checking himself for contamination," the inspection report noted. Moreover, B & B did not use all the required radiation instruments. SouthWest Nuclear was cited for violations on March 3, 1980. When the company told the state that it had implemented "corrective" measures, no further action was taken.

The Beierle family business, B & B Equipment, Prosser, Washington.
Philadelphia Inquirer / Nick Kelsh

DUMPS AND DINOSAURS

After South Carolina, Fred Beierle put down roots in a different part of rural American in an effort to set up yet another nuclear burial ground. This time it was in Texas, in the dirt-poor county of Delta, about seventy-five miles northeast of Dallas. Spliced into land between the north and south forks of the Sulphur River, Delta County's population had been declining for more than half a century and was down to 4,500 when Beierle arrived in the summer of 1975. To help bankroll his new endeavor, Beierle teamed up with a group of Dallas promoters who were principals in a business called the Enntex Oil & Gas Company. Together they formed the SouthWest Nuclear Company, with the oil company's officers as directors.

Beierle brought his family with him and moved quickly to establish himself as part of the community. He opened accounts at two banks in Cooper, the county seat. He purchased furniture from a local merchant. He opened an office a few doors from the Cooper town square. He and his family attended services at the First Baptist Church. And he bought a new pickup truck. "Everybody here has a pickup truck," said Grace Swenson, a local homemaker, who opposed Beierle's planned dump. "You do everything in your pickup truck. You hunt, you go to church in it. Even the young boys use them on their dates. He did try to fit in."

For his next burial ground, Beierle chose a 268-acre tract of rolling land in eastern Delta County. On this farmed-out parcel, he said in an interview in a local newspaper, he would bury both chemical and "low-grade" radioactive wastes. After taking an option on the land, Beierle put to work his well-honed techniques to win over the county.

He paid a courtesy call on county commissioners. He made the rounds of leading businesses and the chamber of commerce. As one person recalled, he said that he was "going to employ quite a few people at good salaries, and that this would help our economy." He appeared on the "Delta County Hour," a radio program broadcast from Paris, Texas, thirty miles to the north.

He bought space in the local weekly newspaper to publish a column entitled "Nuclear News."

"I dare say that if our present environmentally conscious society had been around when initial studies and bomb experiments were being conducted," Beierle wrote in one column, "I sometimes wonder if we would have ever exploded the first device and hence be unable to enjoy the immeasurable nuclear benefits we have today." In another column, he sought to point out the benefits of nuclear energy:

"You all remember the news release about the first atomic bomb which was exploded over Japan and literally wiped out a whole city. Unfortunately this image is still with us today and many people envision the mushroom cloud whenever the word nuclear or atomic is mentioned. There are, however, a lot of benefits we enjoy from nuclear energy, but today I want to share with you some proposed work that will be done by using atomic bombs.

"For those of you who may be familiar with the use of dynamite to dig trenches . . . the same result can be obtained by arranging nuclear devices in a row then exploding them in the right manner. You can dig a very large canal, big enough to float ships over a great distance and through mountainous terrain, in a matter of minutes at relatively low cost."

As for his project to "incarcerate" waste, Beierle wrote that "residue from various sources will be reclaimed for resale or placed in a geological environment that will contain the material for an indefinite time or until future technology will permit reclamation or reuse."

If Beierle's plan sounded inviting to some Delta Countians, it was a call to arms for others. For once, he encountered spirited opposition, at least in part because of growing skepticism across the country over government and industry claims about the safety of radioactive-waste practices. A group calling itself Concerned Citizens for Delta County circulated petitions opposing SouthWest Nuclear's proposal. The group bought space in the local newspaper to rebut Beierle's assertions about nuclear safety. The controversy even found its way into the pulpit, when one minister denounced a Beierle opponent for allegedly slandering "this fine Christian man." Almost overnight, Delta County found itself deeply divided.

"It was a tooth and toenails battle," recalled Hiram Clark, Jr., a county commissioner. "He [Beierle] is a real cool operator. He would be what I would describe as a supersalesman. He had a package to sell, and he almost sold it."

Indeed, although more than half the county's registered voters eventually signed petitions opposing the burial ground and although county commissioners went on record against it, Beierle might still have prevailed and secured a state permit had another event not sealed the project's fate. On November 20, 1975, the Texas attorney general filed a civil complaint in Dallas accusing Enntex Oil & Gas of selling unregistered securities. The state contended that Enntex and its officers had "employed schemes or artifices to defraud or obtain money by means of false pretenses." Three of those officers were also incorporators of SouthWest Nuclear.

When word of the lawsuit reached Delta County, it was enough to finish off Beierle's once-grand design for a nuclear-waste burial ground there. Although Beierle was not involved in the lawsuit, the fact that his business partners in SouthWest Nuclear were accused of securities violations damaged Beierle's campaign to secure public acceptance of the dump proposal, and he formally abandoned his plans in March 1976.

But Beierle did not give up on Texas. He still had hopes of persuading one of the rural counties in the northeast section of the state to provide him land for a nuclear graveyard. A month after he closed SouthWest Nuclear's office in Cooper, Beierle opened a religious book store called Thee Book and Bible Store in nearby Commerce, and from that base he continued the search.

It looked for a while as if he might end up in Lamar County, which borders Delta on the north. Beierle held a series of meetings with local business leaders and politicians in April 1976. He escorted the group to South Carolina to look at the Barnwell burial ground, which prompted one county official to say at the time, "[I] didn't see anything with my own two eyes I was concerned about."

But opposition quickly arose in Lamar County as well, leading the county commissioners to unanimously oppose Beierle's endeavor. And when rumors circulated that Beierle was eyeing nearby Fannin County, the commissioners there also voiced their opposition. For one of the few times in his life, Fred Beierle's ability to sell had failed him.

The Texas period was not a complete loss for Beierle. It brought him close to a meandering, muddy stream known as the Paluxy River, sixty miles southwest of Fort Worth. Winding through flat, uninspiring terrain, the Paluxy is not high on the list of America's most scenic rivers. To Beierle, it had another appeal.

The river has periodically yielded curious fossils—huge tracks thought to have been made by dinosaurs, as well as indentations that resemble human footprints. As a result, the Paluxy has become a mecca for archaeological expeditions by fundamentalist religious groups that see in the tracks hard evidence to refute the theory of evolution. If the tracks had indeed been made by dinosaurs and humans at the same time, they would cast doubt on evolutionary theory, which holds that dinosaurs evolved and died out millions of years before man appeared on earth.

Beierle finds evidence in the Bible to support his creationist beliefs. From the Book of Job, he once cited a reference to a "leviathan," who, "when he raiseth up himself, the mighty are afraid." Beierle wrote, "Here it appears that God is describing a large swimming dinosaur, perhaps a plesiosaur. If these were dinosaurs, they may have either survived the Noahian flood or been transported by Noah aboard the ark. In any event, they appear to have become extinct, except perhaps for the Loch Ness monster which some believe to be a living plesiosaur."

The Valley of the Paluxy, with its rich fossil lore, was thus a logical region for him to explore. During a lull in the Delta

County battle in 1976, Beierle led his first expedition. He rented a backhoe and enlisted family members to help him dig along the riverbank. Beierle later wrote and published a book about his Paluxy experiences entitled *Man, Dinosaur and History,* which was distributed by the Bible-Science Association of Minneapolis. In it, Beierle described as follows the method he and his family used in the search for fossil tracks:

"We spent the . . . afternoon wallowing in the Paluxy River. The procedure was to form a human chain with everone getting into a crawling position, touching hands and searching the riverbed. With five individuals, we could reach halfway across the river. Then everyone got down and began to half crawl and half swim, searching with their fingertips into the various crevices and holes to find the places where [another] track had been excavated; this in turn would locate the general area wherein the tracks could be found."

Although Beierle did not discover human prints on that outing, he and his family returned the following two summers for additional digs. During a dry spell in the summer of 1978, a discovery was made. "Trusting in the Lord," he later wrote, "we began to dig and bail water with shovels, jars and a chocolate milk carton. The water bailing was necessary because here the strata dipped down, and until this year the area had always been covered with three to four feet of water. After about an hour of very tiring and frustrating work over rough but level strata, my wife Vesta thought she had discovered a probable impression. We all began to remove the surrounding sand and loose rock. We then built a dam to hold back the water and bailed out the hole. Sure enough, it was a man track."

Beierle did not doubt that many of the indentations in the river bed had been made by humans. He wrote, "Fossil evidence around the world dictates that giants from the plant and animal kingdom once existed on earth. Newly found geological evidence appears not only to substantiate the presence of such giants, including the dinosaur, but also the concurrent presence of giant humans."

NEXT STOP: LOUISIANA

With his hopes for a nuclear-waste dump in Texas dashed, Beierle began to scout for a location in another state. He was backed again by the interests that had bankrolled him in Texas, including the oilmen who had been accused of selling unregistered oil and gas securities in the Enntex case. In the wake of the attorney general's complaint, Enntex was dissolved. Some of its officers founded a new company called the Spindletop Oil & Gas Company, operating out of Enntex's former Dallas offices.

Late in 1976, Beierle teamed up with Spindletop to establish a hazardous-waste burial ground, this time in Louisiana. Court records show he received a $47,000 advance from the company. Once in Louisiana, Beierle lined up powerful political support, retaining the law firm of Nolan Edwards, a brother of Edwin W. Edwards, the governor of Louisiana, to help form a Louisiana corporation. On January 28, 1977, Beierle organized Southwest Environmental Company (SWECO), listing himself and an attorney in Edwards's Crowley, Louisiana, law firm as registered agents.

To help find a piece of land, Beierle called on another brother of the governor, Marion D. Edwards, who owned a real-estate company in Crowley. They decided on a 383-acre tract near the town of Livingston (pop. 1,500), about twenty-five miles east of Baton Rouge, the state capital. Beierle opened an office and had stationery printed carrying the SWECO slogan, "Preserving Our Bountiful Heritage Through Sound Environmental Practices."

With Marion Edwards at his side, he appeared early in 1977 before the Livingston Parish police jury, the Louisiana equivalent of a county council, and outlined his proposal for a chemical-waste installation a mile south of town. Beierle said the project would create jobs and bring business to the parish. Whether his proposal for a chemical dump was a step toward the ultimate burial of nuclear waste is not clear. In South Carolina, Beierle had at first talked about a chemical-waste facility at a site near Barnwell that later was licensed for the burial of low-level radioactive waste.

Nick Erdey, the mayor of Livingston at the time, described in an interview how Beierle secured the support of parish officials. "The police jury met on a Saturday morning," He recalled. "I don't think they knew what the meeting was about until they got there. At the time, Marion Edwards was the brother of the governor and in a position to influence the police jury. And he gave them a real good snow job. The people of Livingston were entitled to a hearing, but by the time they found out about the meeting two weeks had gone by and it was too late."

After the meeting with Beierle and Edwards, Livingston Parish officials sent a letter to the Louisiana Department of Health and Human Resources saying they did not object to SWECO's project. The letter was not an official endorsement but an indication to state officials that the project was not locally opposed. It helped pave the way for state approval in February 1977, and Beierle purchased the land the next month for $596,960, according to Livingston Parish records. Erdey, the former mayor, recalled Beierle's next moves as follows:

"He started attending the local church. He gave the impression he wanted to be part of the community. He invited me to take a tour of the plant [burial site.] They had one hole dug with some barrels in it. He told us how they were going to put a layer of topsoil over it and then plant trees. Make it look just like it used to. He said they were going to reserve the part of the property next to Interstate 12 and Highway 63 for residential development. He painted quite a picture. If you came by that place today, you would ask yourself who would ever want to live next to that dump."

Rather than provide an economic stimulus for Livingston, Beierle's dump created a civic liability. It was built on land that sloped gently toward streams that flowed into Lake Pontchartrain, which borders the northern city limits of New Orleans farther south. The area is one of the nation's wettest, receiving an average of sixty inches of rain a year. Later studies showed that the water table under Beierle's toxic-waste dump was only five to six feet from the surface in some places. The study also disclosed the existence of sand layers running through the property only a few feet from the bottoms of burial pits, meaning that there was a pathway along which contaminates could be carried off to groundwater supplies.

Problems plagued the SWECO dump almost from its opening. Less than two months after burials began, in August 1977, a Louisiana State official found violations during a routine inspection. A state health officer formally reprimanded Beierle by letter on September 27, 1977: "It was reported that rainwater contaminated with various industrial wastes was pumped from a pit containing wastes onto the surface of the ground, from which point it entered surface drainage which ultimately led to Bayou Coyell and the Amite River."

Although the "magnitude of the contamination" is not clear, the letter went on, "the handling of potentially contaminated rainwater in such manner that it can escape from your site constitutes a hazard to public health and the environment and is contrary to your company's operational plan. . . ." The Louisiana Stream Control Commission cited SWECO for water violations on October 12, 1977, and ordered the company to make a full report outlining steps to correct the runoff. Beierle, in a letter to state officials, blamed workers who exercised "poor judgment" for pumping the toxic wastes onto the earth and said they had not received "adequate instruction."

In May 1978, a state health inspector discovered liquid in another pit and ordered it removed. There were also an increasing number of complaints from residents alleging improper burial practices and environmental pollution. On one occasion, according to published reports, a diver whose truck had just pulled out of the dump oozing blue sludge told a deputy sheriff that he was carrying a load of radioactive waste.

Even with its flaws, the Livingston dump was a valuable property, and Beierle and his Dallas partners were soon embroiled in a behind-the-scenes battle over ownership of Southwest Environmental's stock. Whoever controlled the stock would get the lion's share of ever-greater revenues as the volume of waste buried increased.

Spindletop contended that it was entitled to two-thirds of the shares and Beierle to one-third. Beierle countered, according to a court action later filed by Spindletop, by trying to transfer SWECO's stock to "certain third parties, including his brother, Lenard Beierle, and his cousin, Zeke Beierle." Spindletop sought a court order to bar distribution of SWECO's stock in a lawsuit filed in the U.S. District Court in Dallas. The warring forces patched up their feud early in 1978 when they found a buyer for the Livingston dump.

The purchaser was Browning-Ferris Industries Inc., the nation's largest hazardous-waste handler, then managing more than sixty landfills. On May 19, 1978, Browning-Ferris bought the Livingston property for $1.1 million, according to records on file with Livingston Parish. The sale agreement provided that Beierle and Spindletop would receive royalties from Browning-Ferris on the gross revenue generated by future chemical-waste burials. Subsequent court papers showed that the royalties would soon exceed $100,000 a year.

The Livingston dumps assorted failings—especially that of water flowing out of toxic-waste pits following heavy rains—continued after Browning-Ferris acquired the business. Inspectors from the Louisiana Stream Control Commission found "contaminated water outside the waste disposal pits" in October 1978. Browning-Ferris eventually paid a $50,000 fine for violations both at Livingston and at another property the company maintained in Louisiana, according to officials of the state Department of Natural Resources.

Livingston was the subject of a lengthy and controversial licensing proceeding in 1982, as Browning-Ferris sought state approval to keep on managing the facility. After months of hearings and deliberations, the state Environmental Control Commission voted thhree to two to allow the company to keep the dump open, but only if extensive changes were made, including the construction of an earth levee to try to hold down the off-site flow of rainwater. The company subsequently said it would install polyethylene liners in burial pits and place an inflatable dome over open pits to keep out water.

In 1981, in a lawsuit filed in the U.S. District Court in Dallas, Browning-Ferris contended that the "land farm" Beierle had established was "improperly constructed and could not be brought in compliance with generally accepted land farming principles." After taking over, Browning-Ferris said, it found that several of the pits were "leaking" hazardous wastes. The company demanded that SWECO "repair the leaking cells," but Beierle and his Dallas partners refused to do so, forcing Browning-Ferris to pay for the work.

To the people of Prosser, Washington, Beierle is a curiosity, a charming, engaging figure and imaginative inventor. "Fred's a dreamer," said one businessman. "But I guess it's the dreamers who make the discoveries. They don't always succeed, but sometimes they hit the jackpot."

In recent years, Beierle has been promoting a gasifier that converts agricultural wastes, refuse, and other materials into synthetic gas. The gasifier and the chemical process producing the conversion are the brainchild of Dr. Donald E. Chittick, a former professor of chemistry at George Fox College in Newberg, Oregon. He and Beierle were brought together at a convention of creationists in Minneapolis.

Chittick, according to published reports, believes that oil, coal, and other hydrocarbons were created by a catalyst in the earth that was present at the time of Noah's Flood. After Chittick discovered what he felt was the catalyst, he and Beierle formed a company in 1979 called Pyrenco Inc. to promote and develop the gasifier.

For his part, Beierle is marketing the gasifier with the same zeal he brought to nuclear waste. "Every time you talk to him about the work he is doing in energy," said a Beierle observer in Prosser, "he always manages to link it up with the Lord. To Fred you can't talk about one without mentioning the other."

Beierle eagerly shows off the gasifier to interested parties, saying that it runs a generator that gives him excess electricity to sell back to the local power company. The utility district said that it did purchase power from Beierle's generator, but only rarely. A utility spokesman noted that the generator usually ran only when Beierle was showing it to a vistor. The reason for the infrequent operation, the spokesman said, is that it costs Beierle more to generate a kilowatt-hour of electricity than the utility pays him.

So far, Beierle has managed to get the gasifier placed in a U.S. Forest Service greenhouse at Carson, Washington, for an experimental test run. He was negotiating a contract with a rural Michigan county to build a three-megawatt electric generating plant fueled by scrap wood. The power plant is intended to serve as a focal point of an industrial-development project in the county. Money would come from the U.S. Department of Housing and Urban Development, from the state of Michigan, and from industrial revenue bonds.

Does this mean that Fred Beierle, America's salesman of nuclear burial grounds, has moved on to another calling? Not quite. For as Beierle traveled about the country preaching the benefits of his new gasifier, he was also waiting. He had found a site for another nuclear graveyard and had applied to another state government for a permit to bury radioactive waste. If approval is granted, it could lead to Beierle's most lucrative venture of all.

11
America's Favorite Dump Site

THE ATTRACTION OF LYONS

With its well-tended frame houses, red-brick streets, and stores ringing a courthouse square, the central Kansas town of Lyons has an All-American look. In Lyons, where the price of wheat overshadows world events, radioactive waste is a topic that should be of scant concern to the 4,000 residents. After all, Kansas ranks forty-third among states producing low-level radioactive waste. And it has yet to generate any high-level waste, although the state's first and only nuclear plant, the Wolf Creek reactor near Burlington, is scheduled to begin power production sometime in 1985.

Nevertheless, nuclear waste is a recurring issue in Lyons— a subject that periodically mobilizes the town, then goes away, only to return to galvanize the citizenry anew. This is because Lyons has an abandoned salt mine that exercises a powerful pull on those in search of places to bury radioactive garbage.

In the 1960s, it was the federal government. For eight years, from 1963 to 1971, the government pinned its hopes of establishing an underground repository for high-level waste on the Lyons mine. It dispatched teams to study the salt formation, to place used fuel rods in the mine floor to gauge the effectiveness of the storage site, and to analyze the reams of data that resulted.

On the basis of those tests, the AEC announced in 1970 that the mine had been tentatively selected to become the nation's first repository. A year later, the project was scrapped when Kansas officials detected a serious geological flaw that the AEC had overlooked.

Now the Lyons mine is again being talked of as a waste center, only this time for low-level waste. It is a prospect that has many residents apprehensive, given their initial encounter with nuclear planning in the 1960s. A Kansas company called the Rickano Corporation has an application pending with the state Department of Health and Environment to store low-level nuclear trash in the mine, which could give Lyons and Kansas the distinction of becoming the home for the first such facility to open in the 1980s. The DOE believes that only large companies with substantial resources will be capable of constructing low-level-waste facilities in the future. "I know Westinghouse is very interested," a department official said. "I can only guess that there are probably a lot of big architectural and engineering firms that will be making proposals." Rickano is definitely at odds with the department's vision. The company began business in a rented office on the Lyons square, with a stockholders equity of $131,985. That's less money than is ordinarily invested to open a single McDonald's fast-food outlet. Records filed with the Kansas secretary of state's office listed ten stockholders, seven of whom were identified only by their initials and addresses. They included the following:

M. F. Farrens, 707 Sanford, Richland, Washington. M. F. Farrens is Mary Farrens, who is identified in local city directories as a retired nurse. Along with her husband, also retired, she lives in a one-story frame house in the south-central Washington city of Richland. Mrs. Farrens, who is listed as the owner of 89,000 shares of Rickano stock, described herself and her husband as "poor people."

J. L. Rattray, Rt. 3, Box 3421, Kennewick, Washington. J. L. Rattray is Janice L. Rattray, a housewife and mother of three small children who, with her husband, lives in a ranch house on the outskirts of Kennewick. She owns 80,030 shares of Rickano stock.

M. L. Graff, P.O. Box 186, Prosser, Washington. Although it is possible that there are other M. L. Graffs in Prosser, the only one in the area who could be located is Mary Lou Graff, a housewife who lives outside the town, and who says that she does not own any Rickano stock. M. L. Graff is listed as the owner of 90,023 shares.

M. Murray, P.O. Box 279, Grandview, Washington. Postal officials in Grandview (pop. 3,500) said that no one by the name of Murray has rented Post Office Box 279 in recent years and that no one by that name received mail at that box. M. Murray is listed as the owner of 90,030 shares of Rickano stock.

Far from being the Fortune 500 enterprise envisioned by federal officials, Rickano is the latest attempt of Fredrick P. Beierle, the nation's nuclear-waste supersalesman, to establish another low-level-waste facility. Much of the stock is owned by Beierle and his family, a not uncommon business practice. Mrs. Farrens is his mother-in-law. Mrs. Rattray and another shareholder, Jennifer Burrell, are his daughters. Mrs. Graff, although she says she has never owned any Rickano stock, is a cousin of Beierle.

The Lyons mine, the object of Beierle's latest marketing effort, was worked by the Carey Salt Company from 1891 to 1948, when some twenty miles of tunnels were carved out. The caverns, which take up only a fraction of the salt formation beneath Lyons, are large enough to hold the cumulative low-level waste that has been buried at all commercial sites over the last two decades. The mine is part of the Permian salt basin, a kidney-shaped deposit stretching in a great arc from central Kansas through parts of Oklahoma to the Texas Panhandle. The formation, which runs from one thousand feet to a mile below the surface, is considered one of the country's richest veins of bedded salt.

Beierle, who for years persuaded public officials and small

towns that dumping low-level waste in the ground was an appropriate method for dealing with it, now claims that this technique is not the "best." A news release distributed in Lyons after the Rickano application was filed in 1978 stated, "Rickano Corporation realizes that shallow land burial, although adequate, is not the best method for long term disposal of low level radioactive waste materials, especially in high rainfall areas. Rickano has been researching alternate methods and this research has led to the conclusion that salt formations appear to be the most attractive disposal medium."

At Sheffield, Illinois, where Beierle established a low-level burial ground in 1967, he contended that the area's impermeable clay would act as a strong bond to contain radioactivity. As his company said in its license application; "No increase in the natural radioactivity will be measured outside the Sheffield Nuclear Center due to the burial of radioactive wastes." Illinois health inspectors found traces of radioactive tritium in wells outside the trenches in 1976. By early 1982, the tritium had seeped off the property and contaminated nearby land. Beierle now says that underground mines like that at Lyons represent a "significant environmental improvement over the current land fill process."

Although Lyons's business community initially welcomed Beierle, his proposal soon provoked widespread opposition in central Kansas. The plan was attacked at public meetings. A grass-roots group called Rice County Concerned Citizens circulated a petition that 3,000 people signed—more than half of the county's registered voters—opposing the application.

Dr. Jack C. Dysart, a practicing physician in Rice County who helped lead the opposition, summed up the general concern in testimony before a state legislative committee in 1980: "The Carey mine is located under a busy town . . . surrounded by a thriving agriculture and cattle area. It is near a major aquifer, within 500 yards of a working salt mine, and the geological area is fractured. . . . Granting such a license opens a Pandora's box of . . . problems."

SALT VAULT BLUNDER

Lyons did not always feel this way about radioactive waste.
That it now does is a reflection of how past mistakes by nuclear-
waste professionals have made average citizens increasingly
wary of their claims. The movement from trust to distrust is
very evident in Lyons.

When the AEC began studying the Carey mine in the 1960s,
the town encouraged and supported the program. The townspeople believed a high-level-waste repository would create jobs
and stimulate the economy. More important, they had faith
that the federal government knew what it was doing. "I trust
my government," a Lyons banker told a correspondent of the
New York Times in 1971. Another businessman said the government scientists were not only "trustworthy" but "good guys,
good neighbors."

The AEC study was part of a program called Project Salt
Vault. Government plans then called for used fuel rods from
commercial reactors to be reprocessed and the leftover liquid
waste solidified and stored underground. For several reasons,
scientists considered bedded salt the geological formation best
suited for the permanent burial. The deposits had been in place
for 200 million years; they were dry and, it was believed, resist-
ant both to earthquakes and to water infiltrating from the outside. Because of its plasticity, salt was capable of sealing frac-
tures and changing shapes. Since all formations were found
deep in the earth, salt also afforded a secure way to isolate the
waste from man, animal, and nature.

In 1965, a small number of metal canisters containing used
fuel from an AEC test reactor in Idaho and other electrically
heated canisters were placed in twelve-foot-deep holes drilled
into the floor of the Carey mine. The AEC's 1965 annual report
described the purpose thus: "This two-year experimental project is designed to demonstrate the suitability of rock salt deposits for the long-term storage of solidified high-level radioactive
wastes such as those from power reactor fuel reprocessing.
. . . At the end of the two-year program, sufficient data should

be available on which to base a detemination of the feasibility of using underground salt mines for the full-scale disposal of high-level radioactive waste."

The used fuel assemblies were lowered 1,000 feet by elevator to the mine floor, where they were transported by a specially built tractor and trailer. The two vehicles had been taken apart, lowered piece by piece into the mine, and reassembled. The tractor and trailer carried the assemblies to the test area, where they were monitered by instruments. The assemblies were replaced every six months with freshly used fuel to "insure a high radiation dose to the salt for determining the long-term effects of radiation on salt formations."

Although limited in scope, the Lyons experiment remains a benchmark in nuclear-waste planning. To this day, it is the only study in which fuel rods were actually placed in a salt bed. Moreover, the government has no intention to conduct another such field test—even though it is now committed to constructing a repository. In reality, it is unlikely that a repository will be built, at least in this century, because of loopholes in the Nuclear Waste Policy Act of 1982 that give states various ways to block such a project.

Still, the act requires the president to recommend a site to Congress by March 31, 1987. Even then the DOE does not intend to test used fuel rods or other radioactive waste at a potential repository location. Critz H. George, a DOE official active in the research for suitable geological formations, explained why. "It is quite troublesome to deal with these [radioactive] materials," he said. "Whenever you can get away without doing it, you don't do it, and we wouldn't need to do it in these cases. We have already done enough tests."

During the Lyons experiment, the AEC monitored the fuel packages implanted in the mine for about eighteen months before removing them and going over the data. There were extensive cracks and substantial corrosion in the steel walls of the canisters, but not to a degree that shook the AEC's confidence in salt as the medium best suited for interring high-level waste. The commission pronounced Project Salt Vault a success

The Carey salt mine, Lyons, Kansas, during Project Salt Vault. *U.S. Department of Energy*

Used-fuel-assembly test in the Carey mine, Lyons, Kansas, 1965. *U.S. Department of Energy*

in 1967, saying, "It appears that this type of storage may provide safe and efficient ultimate storage for high-level radioactive wastes."

This optimistic appraisal notwithstanding, the agency for two years made no move to actually go forward with the repository. When it did, the impetus came not from any long-range timetable but from a nuclear mistake. A major fire in 1969 at the AEC's Rocky Flats plutonium-processing plant near Denver, Colorado, forced the agency to dismantle contaminated buildings and ship the waste to agency facilities at Idaho Falls. The sudden influx of the long-lived atomic waste ignited a controversy in the state. As a result, Frank F. Church, Idaho's Democratic senator, extracted a promise from Glenn T. Seaborg, the AEC chairman, to remove the plutonium-contaminated waste from Idaho by 1980. The pledge forced the commission to begin energetically planning for underground storage of the Rocky Flats material, as well as of the burgeoning volume of high-level waste.

Less than a year later, in June 1970, the AEC designated the Carey mine as the tentative site for America's first high-level repository. Later that year, after reviewing Project Salt Vault data, the Committee on Radioactive Waste Management of the National Academy of Sciences, endorsed Lyons. The committee's report said that "the use of bedded salt for the disposal of radioactive waste is satisfactory" and that "the site near Lyons, Kansas, selected by the AEC, is satisfactory, subject to the development of certain additional confirmatory data and evaluation."

Congress gave $3.5 million to the AEC in 1971 to buy the mine, to acquire an additional 800 acres around it, and to prepare a conceptual design of the repository, which Commissioner James T. Ramey confidently predicted would "last for centuries." The project had broad support in Congress. "There is a strong feeling in the Atomic Energy Commission," said John O. Pastore, a Republican senator from Rhode Island, "that this is the proper place for storage because of the very nature and character of these salt formations which I understand are rather impervious."

The AEC dangled the prospect of a bounty of economic benefits before Lyons if the facility was built. "The projected full scale operation of the repository will require perhaps 200 employees," the commission said in its environmental statement. "It is possible that the presence of the repository may attract other commercial or nuclear related activities to this area."

If it had been left to the AEC, there might be a repository in Lyons today. As it was, the project collapsed in 1971 because of other scientific findings. The Kansas Geological Survey, which had been hired to make a final assessment of the property, came up with a disquieting discovery that had somehow eluded federal officials in eight years of study.

The land above the mine had been heavily drilled for oil and gas, and some of the boreholes had not been properly plugged. Dr. William Hambleton of the Kansas Geological Survey described the earth as "a bit like a piece of swiss cheese." If water were to penetrate one of the boreholes and seep down into the salt mine containing the nation's high-level waste, radioactive brine could flow out of the repository and into nearby groundwater supplies.

It was also determined that salt was not as impermeable as had been thought. Less than half a mile to the south, at an active salt mine, the owner reported that 175,000 gallons of water that had been injected into the mine to dissolve salt for a new cavern had never flowed back to the earth's surface, as had been expected. The water had vanished, and no one knew where it had gone. Obviously, underground salt beds still contained mysteries for geologists.

Of even greater concern to Kansas geologists was the scientific approach employed by federal officials and private contractors to evaluate the mine's suitability. The state agency was especially critical of Oak Ridge National Laboratory, in Tennessee, which was overseeing the project for the AEC. Kansas officials complained that Oak Ridge scientists had not sufficiently researched the question of how heat from high-level waste would affect the surrounding salt and rock.

"The State Geological Survey regards solution of this problem as crucial to the safety of the repository site," the survey's director reported to Gov. Robert B. Docking of Kansas in December 1970. "It has seemed to us at times that the AEC has been more interested in convincing the public of the safety of the Lyons site rather than using these funds needed to carry studies to a conclusion."

The AEC also came in for stiff criticism from an unexpected quarter—the Department of the Interior. Commenting on the commission's environmental statement, Hollis M. Dole, an assistant secretary of the interior, wrote on February 3, 1971, "Such a permanent commitment of the wastes requires a very strong and scientifically convincing demonstration that the wastes will remain in a geologically relatively undisturbed and hydrologically isolated position for the several thousand years required for the decay of high level [waste]. . . . Such a scientific and engineering demonstration does not appear to be impossible at all, but it will require a more thorough and better documented approach than is presented in the draft environmental statement. . . . We believe that additional significant studies and confirmatory data concerning the geology and hydrology of the salt deposits and overlying rocks, at and near Lyons, Kansas, and the effects of construction of the waste disposal facility will be necessary to demonstrate conclusively, beyond a reasonable doubt, that these deposits are indeed suitable for the final repository."

The storm these disclosures provoked in Kansas forced the AEC to back away from Lyons in late 1971 and to start looking elsewhere for an underground formation. Fourteen years and millions of dollars later, the government is still looking. Meanwhile, the plutonium-contaminated waste that the AEC promised would be removed from Idaho no later than 1980 is still sitting in barrels in Idaho Falls.

SECOND TIME AROUND

If Lyons found the experience with federal high-level-waste planners disillusioning, the town has been nearly as bewildered by Beierle's proposal. Beierle arrived in the spring of 1978, when the government and nuclear industry were troubled by a looming shortage in low-level-waste-burial capacity.

Three of the six commercial dumps had closed in a three-year period leading up to 1978. Simultaneously, the volume of low-level waste was soaring. In 1975, when all six graveyards were open, 1.7 million cubic feet of low-level waste was buried annually. By 1978, the volume had risen to 2.8 million cubic feet a year, a 65 percent increase. Furthermore, the Department of Energy estimated that production would rise to 5.9 million cubic feet by 1990, an amount "significantly exceeding the capacity of the three currently operating commercial sites."

Lyons had a special attraction to Beierle, in addition to being rural and eager for any new industry an outsider might bring. The town was about a hundred miles south of the geographical center of the continental United States. A low-level-waste facility there would occupy an enviable central location in an industry where transportation costs are a major expense.

On his arrival in Lyons, Beierle applied his special brand of salesmanship and promotion. On August 31, 1978, he and his wife, Vesta, bought a one-story brick house. They registered to vote. Beierle hired the director of the local economic development board as an assistant. He told townspeople that his low-level waste venture would generate jobs. He promised to locate other "business operations" in the county if the state approved his application. And he offered to buy a parcel of land from the chamber of commerce, not because he needed it, but, as a local attorney representing Beierle said in a letter to the group, "primarily to assist the Chamber financially."

The original application, filed on May 22, 1978, was made in the name of the SouthWest Nuclear Company, a Texas corporation based in Pleasanton, California. Beierle had helped found SouthWest Nuclear in 1975, and it is headed by one of his longtime associates, James L. Harvey. Over the years, Beierle has served variously as its president, chairman, and chief executive officer.

After the rise of initial opposition, Beierle incorporated Rickano, with himself and Harvey as officers, and resubmitted the application under the Rickano name on November 8, 1978. Rickano—a contraction for the county, Rice, and the state, Kansas, where the mine is located—first listed its address as 205 West Commercial Street, Lyons. Later papers filed with the Kansas secretary of state's office gave the address as 7066-A Commerce Circle, Pleasanton, California. That is also the address of the offices of SouthWest Nuclear.

From the start, there was confusion about the type of low-level waste Rickano intended to put in the mine. The original application appeared to be quite specific on that point, stating, "Radioactive waste materials will primarily come from hospitals, research institutions, nuclear power plants, naval shipyards, and others who offer services to the nuclear industry." When Kansans expressed some unease about waste from nuclear plants, Rickano changed its position. In a November 16, 1979, letter to Kansas authorities, Harvey, Rickano's vicepresident, wrote, "We do want to make it clear that we intend for the Lyons Low-Level Retrievable Storage Facility to be an exclusive repository for institutional type radioactive wastes. Consequently, comparison to the types of waste that are received at shallow land burial facilities is not an accurate comparison, and this facility should be analyzed strictly on the basis of the type of waste materials that are generated at institutional facilities." "Institutional" waste, the industry's term for the low-level material produced by hospitals and research laboratories, is generally less hazardous than low-level waste from power plants.

At a 1979 public meeting in Lyons, Rickano officials distributed a fact sheet saying that the company's customers would be primarily "hospitals, universities, and research labs." It added, "Items to be stored include old lab coats, medicine bottles, hypodermic syringes, etc." Rickano has since reversed itself again. Harvey, in an interview with the *Philadelphia Inquirer* late in 1982, said that Rickano would bury all forms of low-level waste, including that from atomic power plants.

At this point, it appears difficult to say just what type of waste might ultimately go into the Lyons mine, but then

Volume of Low-Level Waste Produced by Power Plants
(In Cubic Feet)

1	Illinois	142,887	14 California	43,340
2	North Carolina	138,762	15 Minnesota	30,673
3	Pennsylvania	137,198	16 Nebraska	27,808
4	New York	134,861	17 Arkansas	25,069
5	Massachusetts	114,347	18 Iowa	21,311
6	Alabama	106,135	19 Oregon	14,972
7	South Carolina	105,316	20 Vermont	13,991
8	Virginia	98,558	21 Wisconsin	13,651
9	New Jersey	92,180	22 Maine	12,080
10	Connecticut	90,260	23 Maryland	11,936
11	Michigan	70,341	24 Ohio	8,693
12	Florida	65,923	25 Tennessee	787
13	Georgia	51,657	Average	62,910

Source: Compiled from U.S. Department of Energy records.

These tables show the volume and radioactivity of low-level waste produced each year by power plants in the twenty-five states with nuclear generating stations. The figures are annual averages for the years 1979–1982.

Radioactivity in Low-Level Waste Produced by Power Plants
(Figures in curies)

1	Illinois	56,881	14 New Jersey	2,448
2	New York	12,499	15 Maine	1,935
3	Pennsylvania	6,731	16 Arkansas	1,619
4	Alabama	6,560	17 Wisconsin	1,512
5	Massachusetts	6,512	18 California	1,199
6	Florida	5,924	19 Maryland	1,031
7	North Carolina	5,793	20 Iowa	956
8	Michigan	5,149	21 Vermont	809
9	Minnesota	4,469	22 Nebraska	546
10	South Carolina	4,118	23 Oregon	361
11	Virginia	3,544	24 Ohio	23
12	Connectiuct	2,737	25 Tennessee	4
13	Georgia	2,545	Average	5,436

Source: Compiled from U.S. Department of Energy records.

that is in keeping with experiences at other low-level burial plots.

The confusion over the type of waste destined for the Carey mine has engendered yet another anxiety in central Kansas. Some residents fear that the mine will, after all, wind up as a repository for used fuel rods from reactors—even though the federal government ostensibly ruled that out in 1971. The fear may sound farfetched, but there are some facts that feed it. Consider the following:

- After years of research and the expenditure of millions of dollars on exploratory studies, the federal government still has not been able to select another potential repository site in bedded salt.
- Federal waste planners and private contractors have continued to produce conceptual studies of a salt-based repository using data from the Carey mine.
- The government's accumulated data on storing intensely radioactive waste in salt come almost exclusively from Project Salt Vault.
- Although the Department of Energy insists that Lyons is not being considered as the site of the nation's first repository, the department wants to build additional repositories, and Lyons could be nominated to serve as one of them.

Despite the poor prospects for the construction of even one high-level waste vault, some Kansans remain convinced that Beierle's plan to bury low-level garbage is merely a foot in the door for the federal government. Most suspicious of all is Max McDowell, a former press secretary of Governor Docking, who was in office when the Carey mine was first selected for high-level storage. McDowell lives in the town of Elmdale, eighty miles east of Lyons. Shortly after Beierle settled on Lyons for "low level radioactive waste retrievable storage," McDowell began to delve into the mine's history.

He believes that the federal government never gave up on the Carey mine as a high-level repository and that Beierle is merely a vehicle that would allow federal scientists and contractors entrée once again. "The federal government needs access to the Carey mine," McDowell said, "to validate their computer models on a salt repository. This is the only place in the world they have implanted spent fuel in salt. They have twenty years of research based on that mine, and they don't have time to start over somewhere else."

Beierle has maintained that he has no such intentions. A fact sheet distributed at a public meeting in Lyons in 1979 said, "Absolutely no nuclear fuel will be received at this facility. High-level nuclear waste storage is, strictly, a federal government responsibility. No licensing procedure exists that allows a firm such as ours to store high-level nuclear waste. You can be sure Rickano would be the most vocal opponent of such a move."

Even if Beierle's proposal aims exactly at what he said—the storage of low-level radioactive waste—its history illustrates the labyrinthian regulatory structure that governs the licensing of such facilities. To secure a permit to put nuclear waste in the mine, Beierle applied to the Kansas Department of Health and Environment. The application was made to the state rather than to the federal Nuclear Regulatory Commission because Kansas is an "agreement state"—that is, one of the twenty-six states that have voluntarily taken on some regulatory functions over low-level waste, including the licensing of burial and storage facilities. In "nonagreement states," the federal government does the regulating. This division grew out of a 1959 amendment to the Atomic Energy Act that a handful of states, notably New York, sought in order to gain a foothold in what was then expected to be a booming new atomic industry.

Although, as an agreement state, it is responsible for ruling on Beierle's application, Kansas did not have the staff or the budget to evaluate the proposal. There are only four full-time professional workers in the state's radiation-control division. So it asked the NRC for help. NRC staff members traveled to Kansas to inspect the property and to interview Beierle and his associates. As is typical of the regulatory entanglements of nuclear-waste management, the NRC's questions about the mine's suitability and the company's qualifications were directed to the state of Kansas rather than to Beierle or Rickano.

That's because regulatory protocol makes the state the lead party in ruling on the application, even though the NRC did most of the initial work. Kansas has the option of following up on questions raised by the NRC or of ignoring them. The double layer of regulatory review has complicated the process of assessing the application.

NRC documents show that Lyons residents were not the only people baffled by Beierle's proposition. Federal officials were equally puzzled about some aspects, including why Rickano would even consider the mine for only hospital and institutional waste—a plan the company now says has changed. "The waste that Rickano has asked permission to store represents a very small percentage of low level waste generated in the United States [our estimate is about 3 percent of the total] and contains mostly short lived isotopes," wrote R. Dale Smith, chief of the commission's low-level licensing branch. "If there is a mismatch, it is because the isolation characteristics of the site are much more than are needed for the type of waste."

Beierle's start-up costs, the NRC said, would be "significantly higher" than those for shallow land burial. The mine shaft would have to be refurbished, a new shaft would have to be drilled, and ventilation equipment would have to be installed. "If the volume is small, and the expense of rehabilitating the mine is high, why is Rickano interested in developing the facility?" Smith asked.

After a preliminary review, the NRC informed Kansas authorities on July 10, 1979, "We believe the concept of a mined cavity waste facility has merit. . . . However, the applicant has made only superficial efforts to describe the planned design and operation of the facility."

Of concern to the NRC was Rickano's failure to take note of special requirements for storing waste in a mine. "Flammable materials may well have to be excluded due to the warehouse-like operation of the mine," and NRC official wrote. "Flammable materials and containers may have to be [incinerated] on the surface or excluded from the mine if adequate fire protection is not designed into the facility. Some of these wastes can undergo spontaneous combustion and no amount of engineering will make them acceptable. Biological wastes, scintillation vials, and other nonsolidified wastes . . . can give off toxic or hazardous fumes. Strict measures for ventilation, filtration, and personnel control must be added if these wastes are not to be excluded." On the basis of the application, the NRC concluded, "it appears that many major waste types may be unsuitable for storage or disposal."

While his application was pending, Beierle went about business as usual. In November 1980, Rickano bought the Carey mine for $350,000. Then, in February 1981, Beierle announced in the local press that Rickano would spend up to $1 million to repair the main shaft, which was blocked at the 700-foot level. A month later, workmen showed up from a company identified as the American Mining and Drilling Company of Tuscon, Arizona. According to published reports, American Mining described itself as the United States subsidiary of a Scottish company that repaired mine shafts around the globe. Crews spent several months working on the shaft.

If Beierle's proposal is approved, the Carey mine will become the first low-level dump to open since 1971, when Barnwell—also a Beierle venture—went into operation. As matters now stand, though, it is not clear which states might have access to it. This is due to the uncertainty among the states about how to comply with the Low-Level Radioactive Waste Policy Act of 1980. The act made states responsible for the waste they generate and urged them to set up regional burial grounds.

Kansas and eight other states in the central part of the country are eligible for the Central Interstate Low-Level Radioactive Waste Compact. By the summer of 1984, Kansas, Louisiana, Arkansas, Nebraska, and Oklahoma had enacted legislation to join it. Iowa and Minnesota were also eligible but had voted to align with the Midwest compact. Two other states, North Dakota and Missouri, had not taken action on either.

Once established, the Central Interstate compact could designate the Carey mine as the region's low-level burial center and, if it chose, refuse to accept waste from nonmember states. The 1980 law gives compacts that authority. But it is unlikely that the mine would be economically viable under those conditions. The five states that have ratified the agreement generate a small volume of waste. From 1979 to 1982, they averaged 58,677 cubic feet a year. Even if North Dakota and Missouri were added, the volume would rise only to 67,894 cubic feet— 2 percent of the national total.

The lack of sufficient waste to make a commercial burial business profitable would be overcome if the Central states agreed to take in waste from other states. Two possibilities are the Midwest compact or Illinois, a state that by itself produces 8 percent of the country's radioactive refuse.

Kansas officials said that no action would be taken on Beierle's application until Congress approved the Central Interstate compact. In the meantime, Beierle transferred ownership of his Lyons house to Rickano and returned to his home base in Prosser, Washington. A son, William Beierle, moved to Lyons and worked briefly for Rickano before his death in April 1981. (Lyons police say that young Beierle, twenty, bled to death from a cut received when he broke into a house after a day-long binge on alcohol and drugs, including LSD and methamphetamines.)

Beierle declined to discuss his business affairs with the authors, reporters for the *Philadelphia Inquirer.* During one attempt to reach Beierle by telephone at his Prosser office, a woman identifying herself as Mrs. Beierle said her husband would not be interviewed.

"He will not speak with you," she said. "Newspaper people per se, as well as TV people, they always like to edit something so that it's very negative. We're not negative about the nuclear business. We think it is a good business, and our children are working in it. If we thought it was poor, we certainly wouldn't have our children working in it, would we?"

Mrs. Beierle confirmed that the Kansas application was still pending. "Of course it's still pending," she said. "As far as I know it is the only application pending in the United States. Yet Kansas refuses to act on it. I don't know what the industry is going to do if something doesn't happen. I don't know what is going to happen to nuclear medicine. I don't know what is going to happen to power plants."

James L. Harvey, Beierle's associate in Rickano, did say that the company is waiting for more states to ratify the Central compact before doing any more work on the mine. "Sometimes it comes back to haunt me, but I want to be completely candid with you," Harvey said in a telephone interview in November 1982. "This was an election year so we didn't do too much at the mine, because the first thing you know is that some politician who is running behind would grab that and make an issue out of it. So this year we have been very quiet. And besides we don't have much money right now."

Asked whether he was optimistic that Rickano's application would be approved, Harvey answered, "I am optimistic, or we would not have spent the money or the time. There have got to be more disposal sites." He estimated that after a permit was granted, Rickano could begin storing waste in six months to a year. "There is 50 million cubic feet of storage space in the mine," he said. "There are actual rooms down there. You could store it by customer or by type of material or any way you wanted to. It would just be a beautiful operation. If a customer wanted to come back in ten years and play with his waste, we could tell him exactly where it was and let him have at it."

Harvey said he and Beierle were also considering more sites in other states. "We have a couple of plans," he said, "but nothing we want to divulge, because of the competitiveness of the situation."

12
Radiation, Waste, and the National Health

THE GREAT UNKNOWN: LOW-LEVEL RADIATION'S EFFECTS

Experts in government, industry, and science claim to know more about radiation than about any other potential health hazard. James L. Liverman, acting assistant secretary for environment in the DOE, told a House Science and Technology subcommittee in June 1978 that "it is generally agreed that radiation is the most exhaustively studied single environmental insult worldwide." Cyril L. Comar, director of the environmental-assessment department in the Electric Power Research Institute, told two House Science and Technology subcommittees in June 1979 that "we know more about the effects of ionizing radiation than about the effects of practically any other toxic agent or carcinogen that man exposes himself to." A pamphlet distributed by the American Nuclear Society in February 1981 stated that "the effects of radiation are better known than those of practically all other harmful agents and the regulations and monitoring measures to protect us against these effects are more complete and more advanced."

If all this sounds familiar, it should. The experts, after all, made the same sweeping claims about their knowledge in all other phases of the nuclear-waste business, from reprocessing and solidification to shallow land burial. Those faulty judgments have cost Americans billions of dollars, and will cost them billions more. Should the assurances on radiation prove no more accurate, the cost will be measured in human lives and will be paid by the children of generations to come.

Radiation is the most widely studied of all cancer-causing agents. Scientists and researchers have cataloged scores of radioactive materials, itemized their chemical and physical characteristics, and determined the length of the hazard. They know that technetium 99m will lose half its radioactivity every six hours, so that 10,000 curies will decay to an insignificant fraction of one curie in five days. They know that neptunium 237 will lose half its radioactivity every 2,140,000 years, so that 10,000 curies will decay to the same insignificant level only in 42,800,000 years.

They know that radiation causes leukemia and almost every type of cancer and that it will shorten a person's life span by months, years, or decades. They know that it will cause cataracts and weaken bodily defenses. They know that, if ingested or inhaled, some radioactive substances will be more harmful to certain body organs than to others. Strontium behaves like calcium and is absorbed in the bones. Radioactive iodine concentrates in the thyroid gland. Radon gas clings to particles that lodge in the lungs, as does plutonium. Radioactive sodium spreads through the body. The tiniest amount of radiation to the reproductive cells will cause mutations. And as the National Academy of Sciences once put it, "the more radiation, the more mutations. The harm is cumulative."

Scientists know all this and much more. Yet their ignorance dwarfs their knowledge. No one understands why radiation is more harmful to the young than to the old, or why some people develop cancer from small doses of radiation and others do not. No one can identify those who are most susceptible to radiation-induced cancer. On the most elementary level, it is impossible to say why radiation will cause a single cell to become cancerous and over time reproduce billions of other cancerous cells. The one cancerous cell cannot be pinpointed, nor can the first hundred or the first thousand.

Decades often elapse between the time when cancer is induced by radiation and when it is finally detected—often too late. Scientists do not know why some cancer cells proliferate more rapidly than others. They do not know why some cells are more sensitive to radiation than others. Most important of all, they do not know how small a dose of radiation is required to turn a healthy cell into a cancerous cell. It may be ten rems or one rem.

This last unknown has sparked great controversy in scientific circles. There is no irrefutable physical evidence to demonstrate the effects of low-dose radiation. Medicine and science must rely on epidemiological surveys, on the pattern of disease across large groups of people, to draw their conclusions. There are so many variables in such studies that the results are often used to support a variety of positions. Thus, some government and health authorities maintain that the permissible exposure limit for workers in the nuclear industry, set at five rems a year, is harmless, while other government and health authorities maintain that that amount of radiation, and less, is killing people and that there is no safe dose.

Although there are exceptions, the experts in this debate are divided essentially along the following lines. Scientists and researchers who work for industry and some government agencies, either directly or under contract, and medical specialists such as radiologists, whose fields are based on radiation science, generally hold that existing standards not only are safe but could be relaxed. Scientists and researchers who work for private organizations or are engaged in the public-health field, including many formerly employed by the federal government, believe that existing standards are leading to cancer, birth defects, and other ills and need to be tightened.

In the past, the debate affected mainly nuclear workers, people who had decided a job was worth the risk of contracting cancer or a shortened life span, much as coal miners accept the possibility of getting black lung disease. Now the entire population will risk increased exposure to radiation without any individual benefit and, in many cases, without ever knowing it, because of the growing use of nuclear materials and mounting stockpiles of commercial radioactive waste.

The radiation controversy has embarrassed the National Academy of Sciences. During the 1970s, the academy issued three reports on the health effects of radiation, the first in 1970, the second in 1972, and the third in 1979. All three adhered to roughly the same formula in the calculating of health risks. But the 1979 report was recalled shortly after its release as a result of a heated dispute between those academy members who believed the document overstated the cancer risk from low-level radiation and those who believed that it understated it.

Dr. Philip Handler, the academy's president, was quoted at the time as saying, "I was quite surprised when I learned that there were two groups so bitterly opposed to one another on the committee [that prepared the report]. I kept asking how many people were involved and the numbers kept changing. We encourage individual dissent on reports like these, but when the voting comes out so close, it tells me that the evidence being considered doesn't compel any conclusion." It may have only been coincidental, but the academy's 1979 report was recalled after the Three Mile Island accident, when residents in the area were exposed to radioactive gases released by the plant. An amended report that slightly downplayed the health risks of low-level radiation was published the following year. It satisfied neither faction.

WHO SPEAKS FOR THE UNBORN?

Since the health effects of low-level radiation cannot be conclusively proven, some in science and government believe that it is fair to assume there are none and that people could be safely exposed to larger radiation doses. Joe Skeen, a Republican representative from New Mexico, spoke for many of those people when he complained about unnecessarily restrictive regulations to his House colleagues in December 1982. "There is no evidence that demonstrates that exposures to radiation at these levels is hazardous at all," Skeen said. "The hazard is purely hypothetical."

That view has a long history in the medical literature on the health effects of radiation and of a variety of other substances. Medical researchers used nearly identical language in the 1950s and 1960s to discount a link between cigarette smoking and cancer. A 1953 study published by one medical journal asserted, "It may be said that in our opinion the data available today do not justify the conclusion that the increase in the frequency of cancer of the lungs is the result of cigarette smoking."

More than a quarter of a century ago, the National Academy of Sciences warned of the folly of ignoring radiation's unseen effects. "We should not disregard a danger simply because we cannot measure it accurately," the academy said, "nor underestimatate it simply because it has aspects which appeal in differing degrees to different persons."

Those who believe that present radiation-protection standards are adequate also point to the risk factor to buttress their case. The automobile, because it is involved in many thousands of deaths each year, is far more lethal than radiation or nuclear waste, they say. Since the chance of dying in an automobile accident is much greater, they argue, the concern about radiation is misplaced. Furthermore, they reason, the benefits of nuclear materials to society far outweigh the risks of radiation exposure. Left unmentioned in this argument are several critical differences. First, in the case of the automobile the driver or passenger consciously assumes the risk, whereas in the case of radiation the government accepts it on behalf of everyone. There is no individual choice.

At House Science and Technology subcommittee hearings in June 1979, Jerome A. Ambro, Democratic representative from New York, spoke of the dilemma confronting Congress in its attempt to determine how much radiation the public should be permitted to receive. "When you use a phrase such as the risk that you will allow," Ambro said, "that becomes difficult to deal with politically. How do you do it? Do you go to five miles out from Three Mile Island and say to the people who live in that area . . . that over the next ten years seven of them will die of cancer. Now, let's have a referendum to determine whether or not you are going to continue to permit this kind of dose. Then do we go to the community between ten miles and forty miles out, and say three of you will die, let's have a referendum and see if you will accept that. . . . Or do you say, well, I have been elected by you and I will make that judgment, and then have them say the hell with you, you won't make that judgment."

What is the risk, as best as it can be determined from all the conflicting studies, that Congress and federal agencies have accepted for the public? If 234 million Americans each received the 170 millirems of radiation from nuclear power, nuclear waste, and other man-made sources allowed by law, approximately 8,000 men, women, and children would die of cancer.* That figure is a middle-of-the-road estimate based on one medical-risk assessment. Some physicians and scientists, applying a different formula, would put the number of deaths at 4,000 or fewer. Other physicians and scientists, using yet another formula, would put the number of deaths higher, at 24,000 or more. Whatever the figure, it represents only fatal cancers. It does not include occurrences of those like thyroid cancer that are considered curable.

More important, the cancer estimates deal with only one part of the problem. The other involves a greater unknown— the genetic damage to future generations. It is this hazard that undermines the analogy with the automobile driver. The person exposed to radiation assumes both a personal risk and one for future generations, which may be afflicted with physical and mental handicaps or other genetic abnormalities. Even the EPA, which has largely ignored genetics, grudgingly acknowledged this moral dilemma in proposed regulations for a high-level waste repository. "Most of the benefits derived in the

---

*There are 1,000 millirems in 1 rem.

process of waste production fall upon the current generation," the EPA said, "while most of the risks fall upon future generations. Thus, a potential problem of inter-generational equity with respect to the distribution of risks and benefits becomes apparent."

That equity issue looms large. "The spectrum of radiation-caused genetic disease is almost as wide as the spectrum from all other causes," says the National Academy of Sciences. Some genetic defects would appear in the children of the exposed person, but others would be postponed to later generations. The effects would include extra fingers and toes, dwarfism, progressive involuntary movements, mental deterioration, muscular dystrophy, anemia, eye cancer, embryonic death, mental retardation, and an inherited predisposition for a catalog of diseases, including diabetes, schizophrenia, cancer, impaired mental or physical vigor, and malformation of some organs.

Just as there are those who shrug off radiation's cancer-causing effects as unimportant, there are those who dismiss the genetic consequences. Some have suggested that massive irradiation, such as in a nuclear war, might be a good thing, a sort of survival-of-the-fittest experiment. One scientist explained to the Joint Committee on Atomic Energy in 1959, "Fortunately, the human race has the power to go on leaving the fallen behind, cleansing itself gradually of genetic injury inflicted, and we can even draw an ideal picture of the survivors of worldwide irradiation emerging as a bigger, stronger, wiser, gentler, healthier race than would otherwise have developed." Conceding that many people would die, he added that "the biological law has sometimes been stated, evolution goes rapidly only in times of stress, and we go on from the Biblical, the wages of sin is death, to the profane scientific, the price of selection is deletion."

Presumably, few in the medical and scientific communities would subscribe to that judgment today. The more widely held view is that any mutant gene is bad. "Virtually every mutant that has been studied has some harmful effect if it has any overt effect at all," according to Dr. James F. Crow of the Department of Genetics at the University of Wisconsin. "There are very likely some new mutant genes that are beneficial in special combinations. But it is abundantly clear, despite the fact that knowlege of this much-studied and much-discussed subject is far from complete, that the net effect of mutation is harmful."

In part because of the genetic threat, Dr. Edward P. Radford, an epidemiologist who was then with the Graduate School of Public Health at the University of Pittsburgh, wrote a strongly worded dissent to the 1980 National Academy of Sciences report that found no reason to change the permissible radiation dose of five rems. Radford believes that it should be reduced, and reduced sharply for younger workers in their reproductive years. "We have to lean over backward to be protective," he says, "because the genetic effects are still sitting there, and they are part of the total cost to the people, whether they are willing to consider it or not."

But there is little political support for standards to protect unborn voters. That's understandable, especially, as Radford observes, "when you consider the extent to which people can psychologically fluff off the evidence on cigarette smoking, where you're talking about something that could affect them, but twenty years hence, and they still will smoke. So now you start talking about things that are going to happen in two or three generations; it's something that the average person—I suppose you and I too,—are inclined to tend to discount."

To further obscure the hazards, genetic defects caused by radiation, like cancer caused by radiation, are indistinguishable from those caused by other factors. As a result, the National Academy of Sciences once noted, thousands of handicapped and deformed children "would be lost in the crowd" because "no one could trace the direct connection between their special handicaps and the raddiation dose." The academy said in yet another report that "only if all the affected persons in future generations could somehow be identified and brought together at one time and place could the total impact of the mutations be apparent."

Like others in the public-health field, Radford believes that the permissible radiation dose should be graduated according to age, rather than fixed at a flat five rems a year for all workers. He recommended in congressional testimony that people under age thirty-five receive no more than 500 millirems a year, one-tenth the present allowable level. He suggested that the permissible dose be one rem for workers between thirty-five and fifty, and two rems for those over fifty. This is just the opposite of what has been happening in industry; traditionally, younger workers have received the largest radiation doses.

DISREGARDING DANGER

No one knows, or will know with any certainty for many years to come, whether Radford and his supporters or whether their opponents, who argue for more-relaxed standards, are correct. But if history is any guide, the odds are with those who maintain that the present standards are unsafe. Ever since radioactive materials were first used, government, science, and industry have tended to downplay or disregard potential health hazards, only to discover later that they had vastly underestimated the danger, often with tragic results. To appreciate this recurring failure, it is worth going back to the early part of this century, when a line of new health supplements captured the fancy of American consumers.

Starting around 1915 and continuing through the 1920s, ambitious salesmen hawked patent medicines and bottled water spiked with a marvelous new medicine—radium. These products, they boasted, would cure almost any ailment, including rheumatism, bowel trouble, indigestion, tuberculosis, high blood pressure, diabetes, piles, nervousness, and lagging sexual powers.

Associated Radium Chemists Inc. of New York, a typical company, marketed a variety of tablets and ointments that contained "genuine radium certified by the United States government." There was Arium, a sort of all-purpose tablet; Dentarium, "radium for the teeth and gums"; Ointarium, "radium for skin eruptions"; Linarium, "radium for palms and soreness"; and Kaparium, "radium for the hair and scalp." An advertising circular touted the curative powers as follows: "Radium is the greatest example in the world of concentrated energy, and it must be remembered that this enormous energy is obtained from millions of tiny rays that are constantly being thrown out by radium, traveling sometimes at the rate of 100,-000 miles a second, and that even the amount of radium in each Arium tablet will throw out millions of these rays of energy for thousands of years."

Physicians endorsed radium restoratives. "I believe that radium water has a definite place in the treatment of certain diseases, and I prescribe it when I deem it necessary," said a Pittsburgh doctor. Skeptical citizens asked the federal government for guidance. Many accepted the medical testimonials for radium and wanted to know only whether the advertised products actually contained the wonder element. A Dixon, Iowa, drugstore proprietor wrote to the U.S. Bureau of Standards in March 1926, "I wish to inquire as to whether your office certified all the radium used in Arium as to its radioactivity. . . ." The director of the bureau replied, "[A]n alpha-ray test was made on a number of Arium tablets submitted by the Associated Radium Chemists in September 1922. The material was found to be radioactive. We have had no further dealings with the company."

Some citizens worried about the safety of such products. To a Chicago man who wondered whether radioactive water "is injurious to the body years or any length of time after drinking [it]," the Bureau of Standards wrote in April 1926, "This bureau has never heard of any cases of harmful effects due to drinking water which has been made radioactive." Although the bureau never said that radioactive medicinals were beneficial, it implied as much. After it confirmed that a product advertised as radioactive in fact was not, the bureau referred the case to another federal agency for legal action.

The federal government allowed sales of the radioactive cure-alls to flourish until about 1932, when Eben M. Byers, a Pittsburgh steel manufacturer and onetime national amateur golf champion, died in a New York hospital at age fifty-one. The cause of death was radium poisoning. Two years earlier, Byers had started drinking Radithor, a radioactive elixir consisting of distilled water spiked with radium and mesothorium, another radioactive compound. Within a year, Byers started to lose weight. He complained of severe headaches and pain in his jaw. Several of his teeth dropped out. The radium and mesothorium in the tonic—promoted as a cure for more than a hundred ailments—built up in Byers's bones and slowly ate away his body.

Because of Byers's prominence, his death touched off federal investigations into radioactive cure-alls. The medical and scientific establishments, which had for the most part kept silent throughout the 1920s, immediately denounced the products. No one will ever know how many people died from radioactive nostrums during those years. By the late 1920s, radium was included not only in patent medicines but also in chocolate candy. The long delay in response from the government and the medical and scientific communities was all the more remarkable considering what was happening in another industry.

Hazel Kuser was sixteen years old in 1916, the year she went to work at the U.S. Radium Corporation in Orange, New Jersey, painting luminous faces on watches. It had been just three years since the formula for the radium paint that glowed in the dark had been developed by Dr. Sabin A. von Sochocky. Demand for luminous products boomed, partly in response to the need for instrument dials during World War I and partly because the public had become enchanted by anything that glowed, from watch dials to house numbers. About 8,500 luminous dials were turned out in 1913. By 1919 production had soared to 2.2 million. For the dial painters, mostly young women like Hazel Kuser, the job was simple. They applied the luminous paint over printed numerals with fine-tipped brushes, which they repeatedly pointed by moistening them between their lips. Many of the women became quite adept at this piecework, painting from 250 to 300 dials a day.

In 1920, because of an inexplicable deteriorating physical condition, Mrs. Kuser left U.S. Radium at the age of twenty. Three years later, while extracting several teeth, her dentist noticed that her jawbone was rapidly decaying. He labeled the disease "radium jaw" and linked it to her work. On December 9, 1924, Mrs. Kuser died, at age twenty-five. By then, much of the rest of her body had been eaten away by cancer. U.S. Radium officials denied any connection between her death and their luminous paint. As other dial painters developed cancer and died, the company kept issuing denials. The New Jersey Department of Labor investigated the plant and reported that it found no health hazards. The U.S. Public Health Service, asked to make a similar inquiry, did not consider the situation serious enough to examine.

Industry rushed to support U.S. Radium. William J. A. Bailey, director of the Bailey Radium Laboratories in East Orange, New Jersey, said that "no one has worked longer or with greater amounts of radium than has Mme. Curie. For over twenty-five years she has toiled unceasingly in her laboratory and today she is not only much alive but reported recently to be in excellent health." (Nine years later, Marie Curie, the codiscoverer of radium, died of leukemia caused by radiation; a daughter, Irene, who also worked with radioactive materials, died of leukemia in 1956.) Dr. von Sochocky himself, cited as a world-renowned authority on radium, said there was no possible association between his paint and the deaths of those working at the radium-dial plants. Time would prove all the experts wrong. By then, it was too late. Scores of people were dead or dying. Hundreds of others had either developed, or would develop, cancer as a result of their employment at U.S. Radium and similar plants in other states.

During those early years, many such deaths were attributed to other causes, because physicians failed to recognize a connection between radiation and the diseases they were treating. The primary cause of one woman's death was labeled ulcerative stomatitis, with syphilis as a contributing factor. Years later, when her body was exhumed and an autopsy performed, pathologists found radium deposits throughout her body and no evidence of syphilis. Even Dr. von Sochocky, who rejected the idea of any link between the deaths and radium, died of cancer at the age of forty-six. The level of radium in his body exceeded that found in the bodies of many dial painters.

The failure to recognize that radiation exposure caused the deaths was related to prevailing medical practices. At the time, physicians themselves were entranced by the potential curative values of radiation, in the form of radium and X-rays. They recommended both for treating an assortment of non-life-threatening ailments. As one doctor explained in a medical-journal article, "There seems no question but that certain forms of gout, rheumatism, chronic arthritis and neuralgia can be greatly helped by its [radium's] use." Physicians applied radium-filled tubes to the jaws of adults for up to twelve hours to reduce enlarged tonsils; children under twelve received about half the dose. If that did not work, they inserted radium-tipped needles directly into the tonsils for up to ninety minutes. And if that failed, they implanted the radium directly into the tonsils, although it was noted that this method "will result in a rather severe reaction." They used radium to treat women, even teenage girls, with prolonged menstrual cycles, while they dismissed fears of possible sterility as "unfounded." One medical team injected radium salts into patients in a mental institution to establish that radium would lower high blood pressure. Much of the debate among doctors was not over any possible harmful effects but over which source of radiation gave the best results—radium or X-rays.

That Americans who were treated with radium or X-rays, who drank elixirs, or who worked in dial-painting factories, were allowed to suffer their fate can be explained in a word—ignorance. So little was known about radiation at the time that few had any concept of the danger. Even as knowledge about radiation grew, government and health authorities continued to downplay the hazard and suppress evidence pointing to it. This happened in the 1950s and 1960s, when the victims were both humans and sheep. First the sheep.

Utah ranchers charged in 1953 that fallout from atomic bomb tests in Nevada had killed more than 4,000 sheep grazing 40 to 160 miles from the above-ground explosions. The AEC, which oversaw the tests, denied any responsibility. After investigating the allegations, the commission reported that "on the basis of information now available, it is evident that radioactivity from atomic tests was not responsible for deaths and illness among sheep in areas adjacent to the Nevada Proving Grounds. . . ." The U.S. Public Health Service agreed.

Government officials, in fact, had no qualms about the public's exposure to radioactive fallout. In an AEC memorandum of July 11, 1951, originally classified secret, a commission official who set protection standards for weapons tests spelled out his views on radiation dosage. "It would cause me personally very little concern if some of these people[the general population beyond the forty-mile test site]," he said, "should by chance receive as much as five or ten rem total dose." (The ten-rem figure is nearly sixty times greater than the dose recommended today for the population at large.)

Willard F. Libby, an AEC member, agreed. He observed during a commission meeting in February 1955 that "people have got to learn to live with the facts of life, and part of the facts of life are fallout." Eight years later, in January 1963, the AEC argued against reducing the permissible exposure level for people in the vicinity of atomic bomb tests. In a document classified at the time, the agency stated, "We do not recommend any new radiation protection guides for nuclear weapons testing at this time. . . . To change the guides would require a re-education program that could raise questions in the public mind as to the validity of past guides."

The AEC was saying that the approved dose should not be lowered, because people would think the old limit had not been safe. It was not. Looking back on those years, F. Peter Libassi, general counsel for the former Department of Health, Education, and Welfare, told a joint congressional subcommittee in April 1979, "The American people were not informed of the evidence that was gathering during the 1950s and 1960s of the uncertainty as to the health effects of radiation from these atmospheric nuclear tests. . . . I would say there was a general atmosphere and attitude that the American people could not be trusted to deal with the uncertainties and therefore the information was withheld from them. I think there was concern that the American people, given the facts, would not make the right risk-benefit judgment."

It was against this background that the AEC rejected the Utah ranchers' claims that fallout had killed their sheep. In 1955, the ranchers thus sued the government in the U.S. District Court in Salt Lake City. The judge, A. Sherman Christensen, later recalled how a parade of government experts came before him to express "convincing judgment that radiation damage could not possibly have been a cause" of the sheep deaths. Other government witnesses testified that scientific experiments on the effects of fallout on sheep had been carried out at the federal Hanford Reservation. These experiments, they said, showed that the Utah sheep had not died of radiation.

The ranchers' attorney, Dan S. Bushnell, suggested that the government had covered up information and that the experts "got their conclusions and proceeded to substantiate it." Judge Christensen then asked, "Now, Mr. Bushnell, if the government witnesses . . . either knew or suspected the possibility of that extent of fallout, and those consequences to animals . . . and realizing also that not only the welfare of the people in that area but the welfare of future generations . . . would be jeopardized by a false appraisal of the situation, in that respect, do you want me to believe that they aren't giving their . . . objective opinion with reference to the effects, if any, of radiation?"

"I do," replied Bushnell.

Largely on the basis of the testimony of the government's experts—who said the sheep had died of malnutrition, disease, and drought—Judge Christensen rejected the ranchers' claims. That was the end of the matter for more than twenty years, until two parallel investigations in 1979 turned up new evidence. The probes were conducted by a congressional subcommittee and the Department of Health, Education, and Welfare;

both wished to examine the health effects of low-level radiation, particularly from fallout.

The subcommittee, a part of the House Interstate and Foreign Commerce Committee, held a series of hearings and assembled previously undisclosed documents from AEC files. A report by an AEC consultant, a veterinarian, said it was certain the sheep injuries had been caused by "another 'accidental fallout' of radioactive material." He added, "The conclusion that I have drawn from this inspection [of the sheep] are [*sic*] that these ranchers have a very legitimate claim."

When one of the ranchers asked for a copy of the report and indicated he intended to sue the government, there followed, within the AEC and between the AEC and the Department of Justice, a flurry of letters and memoranda explaining why the document should be kept secret. One such memorandum, dated January 16, 1953, stated in part, "Since this report, which was made to the commission by one of its consultants, contains some conclusions concerning the merits [of the claim] . . . we do not believe that any portion of this report should be made available to the [rancher]."

Following its investigation, the House subcommittee concluded that "the government knowingly disregarded and suppressed evidence correlating the deaths of the sheep to radioactive fallout." HEW reached a similar conclusion, declaring that the AEC's original inquiry "was not designed to investigate the possible role of radiation in sheep deaths." Dr. Donald S. Fredrickson, director of the National Institutes of Health, after reviewing the AEC's previously secret reports, testified during a congressional hearing that "it would have been extremely difficult, probably impossible, to conclude that radiation did not at least contribute to the cause of death of the sheep."

Armed with this fresh evidence, the ranchers, again represented by Bushnell, returned to federal court in Salt Lake City and sought to have the earlier judgment set aside. Bushnell charged that the AEC had committed a "fraud upon the court" in the original trial. He said the commission had engaged in a conspiracy that included "classifying and suppressing evidence that radiation was causally involved [in the sheep deaths]; tampering with potential witnesses to change their opinions, and issuing false and misleading public statements that radiation could not have been involved. . . ." He also charged that "government attorneys knew of and participated in this fraud by influencing the testimony of potential witnesses and issuring knowingly false answers to [questions]."

Among the documents produced were internal memoranda of the AEC and the Department of Justice that described the government's efforts to persuade some witnesses who had said they thought radiation contributed to the sheep deaths to change that opinion, or at least to say that they were not qualified to make such a judgment. A six-page letter from the Department of Justice to the AEC, dated June 20, 1955, summarized meetings between government lawyers and potential witnesses. The letter pointed out that one veterinarian who had at first expressed the belief that radiation contributed to the sheep deaths "had amended his findings." Although another veterinarian continued to maintain that radiation was a factor, he agreed to "be disqualified" as an expert and to testify that he did not have enough data "to be qualified to give an opinion." The letter was signed by the assistant attorney general in charge of the Department of Justice's civil division, Warren E. Burger, now chief justice of the United States, and by Bonnell Phillips, chief of the torts section.

When the ranchers went back to court, the case came before Sherman Christensen, who had presided over the original trial and who was still a federal judge. Christensen ordered a new trial, declaring that the government had "perpetrated a fraud upon the court" in the original proceedings. In a sixty-page opinion in August 1982, he wrote, "It appears by clear and convincing evidence, much of it documented, that representations made as the result of the conduct of government agents acting in the course of their employment were intentionally false or deceptive, that improper but successful attempts to pressure witnesses not to testify as to their real opinions, or to unduly discount their qualifications and opinions were applied

. . . that there was deliberate concealment of significant facts with reference to the possible effects of radiation upon the plaintiffs' sheep. . . ."*

HANFORD'S DEAD WORKERS

On the surface, the sheep who died of exposure to radioactive fallout in the 1950s—like the men, women, and children in Utah, Nevada, and Arizona who subsequently became ill with cancer or died—would seem to be little more than an interesting historical footnote. But it is part of a pattern.

This was reaffirmed in 1974 after a Washington State epidemiologist discovered that workers at the Hanford Reservation, where the government produced plutonium for nuclear weapons, were dying of cancer at a higher rate than the general population, even though their exposure to radiation was well below permissible limits. The researcher submitted a draft report on his findings to the AEC, which reacted much as it had two decades earlier in the Utah sheep case. At first, the commission urged the researcher to keep his report confidential, saying that it was conducting its own study at Hanford and that the findings were expected shortly. That was true, at least in part. Dr. Thomas F. Mancuso, a University of Pittsburgh epidemiologist, had been compiling health and radiation-exposure data on Hanford workers since 1964 under a long-term AEC contract.

Although Mancuso's work was not finished, the commission asked him to issue a preliminary report saying that the rate of cancer deaths among Hanford workers was not above normal. That, at least, was what the AEC expected him to conclude. Earlier, Mancuso's contract officer at the commission

---

*The U.S. Department of Justice appealed Christensen's decision. In November 1983, the U.S. Court of Appeals for the Tenth Circuit sided with the government and reversed the order for a new trial, declaring "that nothing was demonstrated which would constitute fraud on the court." At the request of the ranchers, the appellate court granted a rehearing in March 1984. The case was still pending in November 1984.

had written in an internal memorandum that "[Mancuso's project] should permit a statement to the effect that a careful study of workers in the industry has disclosed no harmful effects of radiation, if the results are negative, as they are likely to be."

After Mancuso refused to rush out the report, his contract officer, who was now with the Energy Research and Development Administration, which along with the Nuclear Regulatory Commission had assumed responsibility for nuclear matters handled by the abolished AEC, informed him that his contract would be terminated in 1977. With time running out, Mancuso brought in two other researchers to assist him, Dr. Alice M. Stewart and Dr. George W. Kneale of the cancer epidemiology research unit at the University of Birmingham in England. Dr. Stewart, an internationally recognized British epidemiologist, had in the 1950s reported a correlation between X-rays of pregnant women and cancer in their children—a finding at first dismissed by the medical and scientific communities, and years later accepted as valid.

Mancuso, Stewart, and Kneale released the results of their study in 1977: Hanford workers exposed to radiation doses within government safety standards were dying of a variety of radiation-induced cancers. Federal energy officials promptly canceled Mancuso's contract and transferred responsibility for the Hanford study to the Battelle Memorial Institute's Pacific Northwest Laboratory. While Battelle had never before conducted large-scale epidemiological research, the institute was the beneficiary of hundreds of millions of dollars worth of other government contracts; still later, it received a half-billion-dollar contract to oversee the search for a high-level-waste repository. The Battelle official placed in charge of the radiation research was Mancuso's former government contract officer. Since that time, Hanford researchers working under Battelle's direction have judged the Mancuso study faulty.

The Battelle researchers found no connection between radiation and the deaths of Hanford workers from lung cancer and myeloid leukemia, which have been associated with radiation exposure, or eleven other forms of the disease. The study did confirm the "correlation of radiation exposure with multiple myeloma and cancer of the pancreas," but it claimed that the results were not conclusive.*

These two stories—about the dead sheep in Utah and the dead workers at Hanford—share a principal character. It is Dr. Sidney Marks. He was one of the authors of the 1953 Hanford study cited by the AEC as evidence that the Utah sheep did not die from radiation exposure. He was the AEC contract officer who wrote the memorandum expressing confidence that Mancuso's research would show no connection between radiation exposure and cancer among Hanford workers. He was the ERDA official who informed Mancuso that his contract would be terminated. He was the Battelle official placed in charge of continuing the study of Hanford workers, a study that found no connection between radiation exposure and most cancers.

Marks stands by his work, and Mancuso stands by his. Marks declined to be interviewed about either the sheep research in the 1950s or the continuing cancer study at Hanford. After consulting with the public relations staff at Pacific Northwest Laboratory, Marks told the authors, "I've been advised on the sheep situation that I'm a former GE employee [General Electric managed Hanford at the time]. GE is a defendant in a lawsuit that deals with the issue, and therefore it would be inappropriate for me to say anything about it." Regarding the Hanford cancer study, he said, "I'm in an administrative capacity here mostly, and I've been working on other projects, so that I don't stay close to it. . . ."

Marks did acknowledge that there were significant differences between the Battelle and Mancuso findings, two studies based on the same records. Asked how the average person could decide what to think when one team of medical researchers says that low radiation doses cause certain cancers and another says they do not, Marks replied, "I don't know how the layman can assess that. It's almost a hopeless thing. The tendency seems to be to accept the things that are of a more damaging nature.

---

*See page 338 for detailed note.

That's a trend, I think, everywhere. It seems to be furthered by the media, naturally."

THE GOVERNMENT'S "SAFE" DOSE

The United States government first set guidelines on radiation exposure in 1934. As the death toll mounted from radium-based paints and patent medicines, the government gradually recognized the need for standards, at least for those exposed to radiation in their work. Using a new unit of measure, the rem, the Bureau of Standards fixed the allowable dose at one-fifth of a rem daily, or fifty rems a year.

Medical and scientific authorities at the time widely assumed that this was the safe dose of radiation, that any person exposed to fifty rems yearly would suffer no ill effects. Two years later, in 1936, the federal government cut the "safe" dose in half, to one-tenth of a rem daily, or twenty-five rems a year. Although there now was uncertainty over the safety of fifty rems, the Bureau of Standards suggested that twenty-five rems was innocuous. "Continued exposure of technicians for a number of years [at one-tenth rem per day]," the bureau said, "has been found to be safe at Memorial Hospital, New York, New York."

The twenty-five-rem limit remained in effect through the 1940s. The AEC, in one of its periodic reaffirmations of the safety of that exposure, reported in 1949 that "many years ago medical scientists agreed that a normal human being could sustain a continuous day-in-and-day-out whole-body external exposure of one-tenth roentgen per day [twenty-five rems a year] without any detectable effects."

One year later, the government decided that dose was not so safe after all. Now there was a fresh concern—radiation's genetic impact on future generations. In 1950, the government therefore again reduced its protection standard, from one-tenth of a rem daily to three-tenths per week, or fifteen rems a year. The AEC continued to refer to this as a "harmless" dose. "Through long study of the effects of such exposures," the commission said, "it has been determined that a dose of 0.3 roentgen per week [fifteen rems a year] may be delivered to the whole body for an indefinite period without hazard. The maximum permissible weekly rate of exposure is designed to assure safety for persons regularly exposed to penetrating radiation over periods of many years."

Government research laboratories endorsed this position. Studies of "the harmful effects of radiation to the human body have led to the establishment of safe levels of exposure in radiation work," the Livermore Research Laboratory declared in June 1954. The laboratory said the fifteen-rem limit, was "considered safe for repetitive daily exposure without measurable harmful effects."

Two years later, in 1956, the government concluded that fifteen rems was not a safe dose either. This time, it cut the allowable dose from three-tenths of a rem per week to one-tenth, or five rems a year, where it remains today. Over a little more than two decades, the record looked like this: in 1934, the Bureau of Standards said fifty rems a year was safe; in 1936, twenty-five rems a year was safe; in 1950, fifteen rems a year was safe; in 1956, five rems a year was maybe not safe, but "permissible." Why did it reduce the permissible dose to five rems? "To lessen the possible incidence of certain types of [physical] damage," the bureau said, "for example, radiation-induced leukemia and shortening of life span."

The permissible dose for workers in the nuclear industry remains where it was set in 1956, at five rems a year. That the "safe" standard has remained constant the last twenty-nine years after having been reduced three times in the preceding twenty-two years, might suggest that no further reduction is needed. In fact, that is what industry and its supporters maintain.

Dr. G. Hoyt Whipple, a member of the staff of the School of Public Health at the University of Michigan and a consultant to the Atomic Industrial Forum, the nuclear-industry trade association, told House Science and Technology subcommittees in June 1979, "There is no evidence that people working under the present radiation protection standards have experienced any ill effects from such work."

Dr. James L. Liverman, of the DOE, told a House Government Operations subcommittee in July 1978, "No radiation injuries have been established in man under exposure conditions compatible with current radiation protection guidelines."

In their words, there is an eerie refrain. Dr. Frederick B. Flinn, a prominent New York physicist, reporting on a study of conditions at the U.S. Radium Corporation plant, wrote in the *Journal of the American Medical Association,* the bible of the medical profession, in December 1926, "From the facts here presented, I believe we are justified in arriving at the conclusion that an industrial hazard does not exist in the painting of luminous dials."

But there also may be another explanation for the maintaining of the five-rem limit. When that figure was agreed upon in 1956, most people who handled radioactive materials worked for the federal government. The private work force, outside of medical and educational institutions, numbered in the hundreds. Now all that has changed. Since the advent of the commercial nuclear-power industry in the late 1950s, the private work force has grown to include tens of thousands of workers. A further lowering of the five-rem limit would have a major economic impact on the nuclear industry.

For workers and their offspring, the five-rem dose will become increasingly important. Just as radioactive waste is growing, so is the number of workers exposed to radiation. The federal Bureau of Radiological Health in 1977 described the results of this trend as follows: "The greater the number of people exposed to low-level radiation, whether from industrial applications, consumer products or medical sources, the greater the number who will suffer the long-term consequences."

The statistics for the atomic-power industry offer some insight into the changing nuclear workplace. As recently as 1970, only 2,661 workers at nuclear power plants were reported to have been exposed to measurable radiation, according to NRC records. By 1981, that figure had soared to 82,183 workers, an increase of nearly 3,000 percent. During those years, the number of reactors put into service also rose sharply, from ten in 1970 to seventy-seven in 1981. Still, only half the increase in the work force was attributable to the building of new plants. The other half resulted from the growing "dirtiness"—industry jargon for radioactivity—of power-plant jobs.

NRC records show that 2,514 workers received a radiation dose of two rems or more in 1973. That figure shot up 179 percent, to 7,014 workers, in 1981. More important, a total of 14,780 power-plant workers were exposed to measurable radiation in 1973. Their collective doses amounted to 13,963 rems. That worked out to an average of 945 millirems for each worker, the highest level since the federal government began compiling statistics on individual exposures.

By 1981, the 82,183 power-plant workers had received collective doses totaling 54,142 rems, up 288 percent from 1973. That averaged out to 659 millirems per worker, a seemingly significant improvement over the 1973 average of 945 millirems. But the figure is misleading. To bring the average dose down, electric utilities recruited more workers to perform radiation-related tasks. In other words, they spread the radioactivity around to a greater number of people. If the utilities had limited the number of employees per reactor to the 1973 level, the average exposure in 1981 would have been 1,300 millirems, or 1.3 rems—the highest in history. The power companies may be compelled to further increase employment at reactors because as the plants age, they require more maintenance. If that happens, the number of workers exposed to measurable radiation could by the year 2000 top the quarter-million mark.

More Faulty Statistics

Although there is no question that the total radiation exposure is growing, the absolute amount is debatable. That's because the techniques for measuring exposure are about as primitive as most nuclear-waste-management practices. The doses are calculated from readings taken from monitoring devices that are worn by workers and visitors at nuclear facilities. The badges are processed much like film, or scanned by machines, to calculate individual doses.

Surveys have shown that laboratories that process the badges misread 50 percent or more of them. Even if the processing were expert, many radiation readings would still be inaccurate because dosimeters vary in effectiveness with the type of radiation. That was established during the Three Mile Island accident, when the accuracy rate of dosimeters dropped below 20 percent. Furthermore, the badges cannot measure low radiation doses. An employee could receive as much as one-half the dose permitted in a year, while his dosimeter would register no radiation exposure at all. Even the NRC has acknowledged that current practices leave much to be desired. In regulations for dosimetry standards proposed in January 1984, the agency said that "tests have indicated that a significant percentage of personnel dosimetry processors may not be performing with a reasonable degree of accuracy."

Despite the faulty numbers, the federal government relies on them to show that nuclear workers are not exposed to more radiation than legally allowed. The Department of Energy declared that 45,054 employees at federal nuclear installations received a measurable dose of radiation in 1980. Of that number, 29,384 reportedly received less than one-tenth of a rem, while 16 received between 3 and 4 rems—the highest exposure. The NRC compiles similar information on workers at nuclear power plants.

Some of the most damaging evidence of the crude state of radiation measuring came in a 1982 trial in Salt Lake City. The litigation was initiated by families who lived in Utah, Nevada, and Arizona during above-ground atomic bomb tests. They claimed they were exposed to harmful levels of radioactive fallout. U.S. District Court Judge Bruce S. Jenkins handed down a historic decision in the case in May 1984, becoming the first judge to hold that government-approved levels of radiation exposure caused the deaths of unsuspecting citizens. Jenkins found that fallout had induced the cancer that led to the deaths in ten of the twenty-four cases consolidated for the trial but that it was not a factor in the other fourteen cases. He awarded $2.66 million in damages to the families of nine victims; the amount for the tenth, who died after the trial, was to be fixed at a later date. The case was the first in what is expected to be a series of trials growing out of nearly four hundred lawsuits filed by cancer victims or their families.

After hearing thirteen weeks of testimony, Judge Jenkins took seventeen months to write a formidable 419-page opinion. One of his critical findings centered on the veracity of the government statistics that purportedly showed how much radiation each victim had received—even though it had not monitored them or anyone else in the general population at the time of the tests. He wrote, "The negligence reflected in the monitoring program is highlighted by the fact that even now we have more direct data concerning the amount of strontium 90 deposited in the bones of the people of Nepal, Norway or Australia than we have concerning residents of St. George, Cedar City or Fredonia." Regarding the AEC's decision to give dosimeters to government employees involved in the tests but not to people living in the vicinity, the judge said, "[T]he scientific justification for monitoring workers directly, but not the people around them, especially children, defies the imagination."

Although the government took no readings of people at the time, it still introduced precise figures for the amount of radiation that the victims had received more than twenty years earlier to support its contention that fallout could not have caused the cancers. With the aid of computer models, it also calculated the radiation exposure to specific organs in the victims' bodies. Judge Jenkins singled out the data on one person, Glen S. Hunt, to show the absurdity of the calculations. Born in 1920, Hunt lived in Utah from 1951 to 1959, when the tests were carried out. He was diagnosed as having cancer of the pancreas in 1978 and died in 1980. An elaborate government chart entered into the record listed the exact amount of radiation that Hunt's organs received from twenty radioactive substances. For example, the government chart showed that

Hunt's pancreas received 0.00126 rems of radiation from cesium 137.

"There are at least two aspects of this evidence which can be misleading," Judge Jenkins wrote. "The use of 'significant' figures, a strontium 90 dose to the pancreas of 0.0000220 rads, not 0.0000222 or 0.000018, or some different amount, [and] the precision of the stated figure is betrayed by its potential for inaccuracy. The potential error in the stated figure compared to whatever actual dose was received is far greater than the figure itself. The real amount may vary by a factor of 2, 5, 10, 100 or more, depending on real, unreconstructable events."

But there were more telling entries in the chart than the computerized guesswork. Government experts had calculated that Glen Hunt's ovaries had received a radiation dose of 0.-0000574 rads from cesium 137, and that his uterus had received a dose of 0.0000715 rads. Judge Jenkins, who had a clearer grasp of anatomy than did government scientists, observed, "Glen Hunt, like almost all men, had neither ovaries nor a uterus."

THE UNSEEN THREAT

More than a quarter of a century ago, the National Academy of Sciences looked into the future and described the challenge of managing nuclear waste and controlling radiation. The academy declared, "Radiation in the general environment has not yet become a serious problem. In a few decades, however, radioactive waste products from atomic power plants will represent an enormous potential source of contamination. How much of that radioactivity will actually reach the population depends on how successfully it can be kept out of the great network—ocean and air currents, food and water supplies—which connects man to his surroundings."

Today, the Environmental Protection Agency, which is responsible for setting radiation standards, confidently predicts that when all the nation's high-level radioactive waste is finally buried in an underground repository, it will be isolated from man and the environment for longer than civilized society has existed. To guarantee the public's protection, the EPA has issued proposed regulations specifying that any repository must contain the waste for 10,000 years. "We believe that a disposal system capable of meeting those requirements for 10,000 years," the EPA said, "will continue to protect people and the environment beyond 10,000 years." Authorities in and out of government have prepared computer studies to demonstrate on paper a repository's safety. One researcher estimated the possibility of an atom's escaping from an underground burial vault at "one chance in five trillion per year."

Perhaps. But the government's past forecasts inspire little confidence. Indeed, the government's record for keeping even small quantities of waste out of the environment has not been good. The scientific community has fared no better in predicting the behavior of radioactive waste once it is buried. This is of special concern because of the possibility that waste will slowly work its way into food and water supplies. If that happens, the consequences may not be known for a very long time.

The likelihood that radiation will go undetected is one of its greatest threats. Other toxic agents are often identified quickly because their effects can be seen, smelled, or tasted. Not so with radiation. The AEC, which seldom expressed concern, had a few words of caution on this point in 1960. "Key factors in the hazards of atomic wastes," the commission said, "are that radiation is not detectable by the unaided human senses, except at extremely high levels; that only time can destroy radioactivity; that toxic effects often are cumulative, and that injuries resulting from radiation may not become evident for some time."

Because radiation is so elusive, contaminated products often find their way into the marketplace. Radioactive jewelry turns up periodically, most recently in Virginia stores in 1983, where necklaces, belt buckles, and other items were decorated with radium-based paint. Health officials warned that the repeated wearing of the jewelry could cause skin cancer. That happened to a fifty-four-year-old Bradford, Pennsylvania, man who learned in 1977 that the ring he had worn for years was made from radioactive gold. Although his arm was amputated, the cancer continued to spread and he died five years later.

Just how difficult it is to track radiation was borne out in December 1983 and January 1984 when truckloads of contaminated products were brought into the United States from Mexico. A foundry in Chihuahua manufactured thousands of tons of steel reinforcing rods from scrap metal contaminated with radioactive cobalt. It shipped the radioactive bars to Arizona, California, Colorado, New Mexico, Texas, Utah, and other western states for use in construction projects, including homes and office buildings. At the same time, another Mexican foundry in Juárez produced table legs from similarly contaminated metal. It shipped thousands of radioactive pedestals to restaurants, hotels, nursing homes, department stores, and other establishments in more than two dozen states, from Virginia to California, from Michigan to Florida.

Thousands of people would today be eating their meals at radioactive dining tables, working in radioactive office buildings, and living in radioactive homes had it not been for a driving error. When a truck loaded with steel rods took a wrong turn at the Los Alamos National Laboratory in New Mexico in January 1984, it tripped a radiation-detection device. That sent federal officials scurrying to find the source of the radioactive steel, a trail that eventually led back to a Juárez junkyard, which had purchased a cylinder from a radiation-therapy machine that contained about 1,000 curies of cobalt 60. The cobalt consisted of some 6,000 pellets smaller than a pencil eraser, most of which were compacted with other metal and sent to the two foundries.

Following a quiet search for the contaminated products, the NRC erroneously assumed that all the table legs were still in warehouses in the United States and had not yet been shipped to commercial and retail outlets. Then a second fortuitous incident occurred. A radiation-detection device in the car of an Illinois state policeman, parked on I-294 near Chicago, went off when a truck passed by. The truck was carrying radioactive table legs bound for a suburban Chicago restaurant. "I could've been in a thousand places other than where I was at that particular time," the trooper said to reporters. "I just happened to be in the right place at the right time."

After Illinois officials disclosed the incident, radioactive table legs were found in scores of public places. As the NRC intensified its efforts to track down the table legs and steel, a recurring phrase ran through news accounts. When the contaminated steel was found in Tucson, the *Arizona Daily Star* reported that officials said "the steel does not present an immediate health problem." When the table legs turned up in Michigan, WJRL-TV in Flint reported that "the state health department says the contaminated parts contain relatively low radiation and have caused no visible injury." *USA Today* quoted an NRC representative as saying the table legs "aren't extremely hazardous. It's just that it's unnecessary exposure that offers no benefit."

When government and industry discuss mistakes in handling radioactive materials or waste, the phrase "no immediate" health threat is used over and over again. When mill tailings were discharged into the Animas River in Colorado in the 1950s, the AEC announced that "no immediate health hazard exist[ed]." In 1978, the DOE said radiation from mill tailing piles did "not pose any immediate health hazard." When radioactive waste was discovered along a stream in Wayne, New Jersey, in 1983, the *New York Times* quoted officials as saying there was "no immediate hazard."

Another favorite practice of government and industry is to compare radiation exposure from an accident or a mistake to that from a medical X-ray. Thus, when the radioactive table legs were found in one state after another in 1984, the *Wall Street Journal* quoted an NRC spokesman as saying the highest level of radiation measured was "about 2.5 times that of a typical chest X-ray."

All these statements were true. There was no "immediate hazard," no "visible injury," due to exposure to the contaminated products or the waste. But, in time, some exposed persons could develop cancer, give birth to children with physical deformities or other genetic defects, or suffer from some other disease and never know the reason.

The story of the contaminated steel and table legs is a microcosm of what is wrong with the nation's nuclear-waste and radiation-protection programs, as well as a window onto the future, when such accidents may well become commonplace and go undetected.* The United States government had no idea that the radioactivity was present. Its initial response was to blame Mexico for permitting nuclear materials to go astray. But it was a Fort Worth company that had sold the therapy machine to a medical clinic in Juárez. The machine was never used, and the cylinder containing the cobalt was sold for scrap. The government discovered the contamination by accident, since there is no systematic radiation-screening program.

After the contaminated steel and pedestals had become public, the NRC and some state health authorities downplayed the potential hazard. To do this, they selectively described what would happen to a person exposed to the radiation only once. They neglected to mention that some people would be exposed to it continually, either in living or working conditions, and they misrepresented the government's standards.

Consider the table legs that were intercepted en route to a suburban Chicago restaurant. Anyone who ate at the restaurant once would have received a radiation dose equal to about 3 X-rays, just as the NRC said. Anyone who ate there twice would have received the maximum radiation dose government regulations allow for the public at large—a comparison the NRC avoided. A person who ate there daily would have been exposed to the equivalent of 15 X-rays in one week. Over a year's time, an unsuspecting diner would have received the equivalent of 750 X-rays, five times the radiation dose allowed for workers in the nuclear industry. Waitresses and other employees in the restaurant would have received even larger radiation doses. Pregnant women and children, more vulnerable to radiation, would have been at greater risk.

---

*See page 340 for detailed note.

Because the contaminated products were detected in time, only a few hundred persons were exposed. The most serious cases were in Mexico. According to NRC records, "five persons, including three or more employed at the junk yard, received estimated whole body doses in the range of 100 to 450 rem. One individual involved with the disassembly of the teletherapy unit has severe radiation burns on one hand." Some of the cobalt pellets were left in the back of a truck parked in a residential neighborhood. Radiation levels three feet from the truck measured fifty rems an hour. Adults who worked or children who played near it could have received a lethal dose in several days. In addition, sixty-two of the cobalt pellets were found in Juárez streets. Nearly a dozen people tested have showed chromosomal damage. The test itself is a measure of what medicine and science do not know. It shows only whether a person has been exposed to radioactivity. It cannot tell the consequences of an exposure.

Epilogue

WHAT THE FUTURE HOLDS

For the first forty years of the atomic era in the United States, radioactive waste touched few lives directly. Growing stockpiles of used fuel assemblies at nuclear power plants went largely unnoticed. The few sites where other radioactive waste was stored or buried were either far from major population centers or near isolated pockets of strongly pronuclear citizens. No one cared much about nuclear waste.

Those days are gone. Over the next decade, the radioactive-waste issue will disrupt the lives of a majority of Americans. The Department of Energy plans to build at least two massive underground repositories to hold the swelling backlog of radioactive fuel rods. One of those installations is planned for somewhere in the East, near millions of people. Trucks hauling the high-level waste to both repositories would become as familiar on the nation's highways as ordinary tractor-trailers are today. In addition, all fifty states must make some arrangement to take care of their low-level waste, either within their own borders or in neighboring states under regional agreements.

The record to date leads one to expect that the conflicts flowing out of all this will be bitter and protracted. Grass-roots citizen opposition will bring nuclear-waste referendums, recall petitions, and protective legislation in state legislatures and in Congress. Politicians at every level of government will be elected or turned out of office according to their responses. The issue will pit community against community, state against state, and people everywhere against the federal government. The early-warning signs are evident in South Dakota, Nevada, Washington, South Carolina, New York, and Massachusetts, among other states.

There was—and still could be—a better way. Much of the anxiety that nuclear waste now provokes would never have materialized if the federal government and the scientific community had been candid from the beginning. They were not. Both insisted that radioactive waste posed little or no hazard. Both insisted that the technology for dealing with it was proven. One glaring failure after another—from low-level burial grounds to reprocessing—proved the experts wrong and planted the seeds of public distrust.

To make matters worse, government, science, and industry, each for its own reasons, implemented programs that served special rather than national interests. The official definitions of waste are typical. Low-level waste now includes by-products from nuclear power plants that will remain hazardous for hundreds of years, as well as by-products from hospitals that will be harmless in days, weeks, or a few years. A rational system of waste categories would be a crucial first step toward the proper management of all waste, from the relatively harmless to the lethal.

The federal government has not taken the step, and there is little likelihood that it will. To revise federal regulations would be to suggest that a mistake had been made, a possibility that those in authority are unwilling to concede. Indeed, this refusal to admit mistakes, to acknowledge that some of the more serious questions about waste management remain unanswered, has brought the nation to its present predicament. It virtually guarantees future mistakes, only on a much larger scale because of the growing radioactivity in temporarily stored waste. It means that the safest waste-management systems will probably not be implemented. It also means that little effort will be made to consider alternatives.

For example, is the ferrying of intensely radioactive used fuel rods along the nation's highways, from scores of power plants to repositories, the most sensible way to deal with waste? Or would it be more prudent to store the rods permanently at power-plant sites? Is it wise to to put the largest concentration of waste ever manufactured in a hole in the ground, where it cannot be recovered and where no one is really certain what will happen to it? Or would it be more advisable to store it in a permanently retrievable fashion in the event the unexpected occurs? Does it make scientific sense—as opposed to political sense—to spread waste among the fifty states, including unsuitable areas? Or would it be more responsible to select a handful of the safest locations and place it there?

Given the current course of events, it is unlikely that most of these questions, and others of equal importance, will be properly addressed. Instead, it seems more probable that the experts will continue to pretend, as they have since the 1940s, that they have all the answers. Lest there is any doubt they do not, one need look no further than the experience of a group of Marshall Islands natives. That experience capsulizes man's past—and present—understanding of radioactive waste and how it behaves in the environment. More significant, it provides a chilling glimpse into the future, when the level of radioactivity that may work its way into the food chain and water supplies will be millions of times greater than it is now.

The natives were moved off the coral island of Bikini in 1946 to make way for United States hydrogen bomb tests. From 1946 to 1958, more than twenty bombs were exploded. The fallout contained the same radioactive materials found in commercial nuclear waste, and amounted to a mere fraction of the radioactivity now awaiting burial in the United States. A decade after the tests were completed, President Lyndon B. Johnson announced plans to permit the islanders to return. Johnson said that a committee of consultants, later described as a blue-ribbon panel, had advised the AEC that Bikini was "again safe for human habitation."

Over the next several years, federal cleanup crews stripped the atoll of vegetation contaminated with radioactive waste, put down a layer of fresh topsoil, and planted 100,000 coconut trees and other food crops. Houses and community facilities were built. The coconut trees were especially important. A Department of the Interior report pointed out that the coconut was "essential to life on a coral atoll, providing food, drink, building materials, and equally important, virtually the sole source of cash."

In deciding whether to permit the Bikini islanders to return home, President Johnson relied on radiological studies and recommendations by the AEC as well as on an analysis of those studies by the committee of blue-ribbon consultants. The panel of scientific experts, in a report stamped "Official Use Only" and treated as classified information, said that the Bikini islanders could resume their former life-style on the island and that they need avoid only one former food source—coconut crabs. The panel said it feared that the radioactivity in the crabs could rise above permitted levels because strontium 90 collected in their shells, which the crabs shed and ate. Otherwise, the scientists told the president, "there were no restrictions with respect to what [the islanders] were to eat."

The scientific panel also assured the president, "[T]he exposures to radiation that would result from repatriation of the Bikini people do not offer a significant threat to their health and safety." An EPA survey of soil, plants, and animals on the atoll in 1972 supported the committee's conclusions. With these promising reports in hand, the federal government allowed the Bikini islanders to go home in 1974.

The blue-ribbon panel of experts, the EPA, and other government health authorities turned out to be wrong. As the islanders began resettling, they drank coconut milk and well water and ate coconuts, breadfruit, papaya, sweet potatoes, pumpkins, arrowroot, and pandanus—all grown on the atoll— as well as fish. A Marshall Islands political leader told a House

Appropriations subcommittee in May 1978, "[W]e were assured all along, first by the Atomic Energy Commission, then [the] Energy Research and Development Administration, and now the Department of Energy, that there were no serious radiation problems on Bikini."

In truth, the freshly planted coconut trees and other food crops had absorbed the cesium 137 and strontium 90 wastes buried in the soil as a result of the nuclear tests. The fish were laced with cobalt 60. The well water was contaminated. Within four years, internal radiation levels among the islanders were ranging from 70 to 980 millirems annually.* The upper level represented a 342 percent increase since 1974. The growing radiation doses absorbed by the men, women, and children living on the island came from their eating food and drinking water spiked with radioactive waste.

Finally, in 1978, the islanders who had returned to Bikini just four years earlier, who had gone home to a place certified as more radiologically safe than Denver, Colorado, were evacuated once again. The food crops that the AEC and the panel of scientific experts once said could be eaten without fear were in fact inedible. Every single crop, a Department of the Interior official said later, "turned out to be contaminated when grown on Bikini." The Bikini islanders, resettled on another island now, have been told that they cannot go home until sometime well into the twenty-first century. In order to compensate the islanders, a 1983 agreement allocated $75 million to cover the "loss or damage to property and person."

Not only did the experts turn out to be wrong in their assessments of how radioactive materials would behave in the earth; they were also unable adequately to explain radiation's varying effects on the natives. During a hearing conducted by a House Appropriations subcommittee in May 1978, L. Joe Deal, then assistant director of the division of operational safety in the DOE, offered this explanation when asked why internal

---

*Present government standards in the United States recommend that each person in the population be exposed to no more than 170 millirems a year.

radiation levels of some Marshall Islanders were lower than others: "I am at a loss to answer that . . . unless the possibility [exists] that some of them didn't eat as many coconuts or drink as much coconut milk."

The response, typical of many replies to questions that the government really cannot answer, underscores the need for change. If America's sad experience with nuclear waste is ever to change for the better, the nation must abandon the way it has made waste-management decisions. It must more carefully study the alternatives and reexamine its approach to the problem of dealing with radioactive waste that will remain hazardous forevermore.

Supplementary Notes

Note for p. 100

*Construction of the Fermi plant was one of the earliest instances of the courts acting as arbiters of nuclear policies. When the AEC issued a construction permit, the United Auto Workers and other unions filed a lawsuit to block the project. They argued that the commission had failed to determine, as the law required, whether the plant could operate without undue risk to public health and safety. The AEC maintained that it did not have to make that decision until after the plant was built and it was time to issue an operating license. If it determined at that time that the plant could not be run safely, no license would be issued. In an internal memorandum kept secret, the AEC's own Advisory Committee on Reactor Safeguards disapproved the Fermi breeder, saying there "is insufficient information available at this time to give assurance the reactor can be operated at this site without public hazard." The unions charged that the AEC's issuance of a permit would "result in the construction of a nuclear reactor which, under present technological conditions, is inherently unsafe." They argued that after the plant was built at a cost of $45 million or so, the AEC would feel obligated to give it a license to operate, regardless of whether it represented a health and safety risk. The U.S. Circuit Court of Appeals in Washington, D.C., agreed with the unions. It blocked construction and sent the case back to the AEC. Warren E. Burger, now the chief justice, dissented. "I cannot join in the suggestion that members of the Atomic Energy Commission who have assumed obligations under oaths as binding as ours would permit an operation dangerous to the public because $40 or $50 million is invested in brick, mortar and steel. . . ." The government and Fermi's builders found a more receptive audience at the Supreme Court. By a seven-to-two vote, the high court overturned the appellate court decision and authorized Fermi's construction. In a dissenting opinion contrary to Burger's, Justice William O. Douglas rejected the suggestion that "safety findings can be made after construction is finished." He wrote that "when that point is reached, when millions have been invested, the momentum is on the side of the applicant, not on the side of the public. . . . No agency wants to be the architect of a 'white elephant.' " He called the AEC's decision and the court's majority opinion "a lighthearted approach to the most awesome, the most deadly, the most dangerous process that man has ever created."

Note for p. 198

*The long-term failure of the federal government's waste-management efforts is due in part to its inability to follow a consistent policy based on proven experience. Ocean dumping is part of that pattern. The government began discarding radioactive waste into the ocean without any notion of its consequenses. It ended the practice with the admission that the waste had not behaved as expected. Now it is gearing up to resume the practice with no better an understanding of what will happen than it had forty years ago. The campaign to revive ocean dumping was started by the navy, which has an aging fleet of atomic submarines and no place to put them. Over the next three decades, dozens of nuclear submarines, whose reactor equipment will remain radioactive for hundreds of years, must be disposed of. The navy has two options: sink the subs or cut up the reactor equipment and bury it at federal installations. The navy favors sea burial because it is cheaper. A suggestion in 1982 that the subs be scuttled in the Pacific Ocean off Cape Mendocino, California, or in the Atlantic Ocean off Cape Hatteras, North Carolina, not far from that state's prime tourist and fishing area on the Outer Banks, brought a quick response from Congress. Lawmakers tacked an amendment onto a federal gas tax bill that placed a two-year ban on the navy's ocean-dumping plans. As the moratorium neared an end, President Ronald Reagan's National Advisory Committee on Oceans and the Atmosphere recommended a resumption of ocean dumping in July 1984. The committee acknowledged that the "ecological effects of prolonged exposure to low-level radioactivity . . . are not well understood for either land or water ecosystems." Nonetheless, it said the "chances of radioactivity finding its way into the food we eat are minimal."

Note for p. 226

*The economic argument is a long-standing strategy of private companies and public officials to win civic support for nuclear-waste ventures. One of the first and most successful of the waste-for-jobs promoters was the late Nelson A. Rockefeller, former governor of New York. At groundbreaking ceremonies for the private reprocessing plant at West Valley in 1963, Rockefeller extolled the merits of the proposed plant: "Its greatest importance," he said, "is attracting new industry to this area. It places New York in the forefront of the atomic age now dawning [and] will make a major contribution toward transforming the economy of western New York and the entire state." Local newspapers picked up on the theme. The *Salamanca* (New York) *Republican-Press* said the plant would eventually make the village of West Valley, thirty miles south of Buffalo, an "urban area with a population of 24,000 . . . within 10 to 20 years." None of these predictions came true. Employment at the reprocessing plant peaked at 264 in 1968. In time, the number dwindled to 50. Plant expenditures topped out at $5.6 million in 1971. Total real-estate taxes paid by the plant operators to the town, county, and school district came to less than $1 million. From 1960 to 1980, the population of Cattaraugus County increased slightly, from 80,187 to 85,697. West Valley is still a village, with a population of about 400, unchanged since the early 1960s. Instead of serving as a magnet for economic growth, West Valley evolved into one of the costliest nuclear-waste blunders of the atomic age— a failure that may cost upward of $1 billion in federal money to clean up. For taxpayers nationwide, it would have been cheaper if the New York legislature and Congress, back in 1963, had just appropriated the $32 million it took to build the West Valley plant and given it to local residents to spend as they pleased. A similar tactic was used in Kentucky in 1962 when the state's residents were promised jobs and new industries if they would go along with a nuclear-waste dump in the state. After a private company proposed a low-level-waste burial ground at Maxey Flats, state officials endorsed the bid and stressed the economic advantages the dump would bring. "The biggest problem faced by the atomic industry is waste disposal," said James N. Neel, Jr., director of the Kentucky Atomic Energy Authority. "Therefore, this site is of basic importance to Kentucky. Its location here is expected to attract a number of atomic plants to this state." Maxey Flats operated for fourteen years, until 1977, when a state legislative report summed up the burial ground's record in attracting new industry to Kentucky in these terms: "Contrary to previously held hopes, the existence of Maxey Flats has not caused the location of a single nuclear industry in Kentucky. All the hopes and aspirations expressed for nuclear industry in the early sixties [have] come to nothing, and the Commonwealth has had to search elsewhere to expand its industrial base." Some of the more extravagant predictions of economic growth from nuclear waste have come from the federal government in its quest to find a site for an underground repository to bury used fuel rods from commercial power plants. In Texas, Utah, Mississippi, and Louisiana, where the Department of Energy has tested geological formations, the government has sought to downplay the hazards of a repository and emphasized the economic benefits such a facility would bring to an area. To make its case, the DOE prepared a sixty-seven-page booklet and distributed it to residents in areas being considered. "Preliminary estimates are that construction employment will peak at about 1,700 to 5,000 persons within about four years," the booklet stated. "Following construction . . . employment will subside to . . . 870 to 1,100 persons for thirty years. Direct purchases of goods and services are expected to create an additional 1,800 service jobs. New workers may increase the long-term population growth of the area. . . . Any large development such as a repository will bring new tax revenues into a community to help pay for the services and facilities needed." The emphasis on jobs and economic development had a strong appeal in two Texas counties, Swisher and Deaf Smith, near Amarillo, where the DOE has drilled test holes in an underground salt formation to determine whether used fuel rods could be buried there. Sparsely populated and rural, Swisher and Deaf Smith are among the poorest counties in Texas (19.3 percent of Swisher's families and 14.3 percent of Deaf Smith's are below the poverty level).

Note for p. 316

*Historically, the federal government has dragged its feet in acknowledging any connection between radiation exposure and human deaths. In many cases, the government neglected to inform employees of the potential risks of working in areas contaminated by radioactivity, and scores of workers who later developed cancer have sued the government. Although most say they were never told of the hazards they faced, some did at least know when they had been exposed to certain types of radioactivity. How did they know? The United States government held a beer party for them.

Beer was the standard medical treatment for employees who ingested certain radioactive materials in the 1960s at the Nevada Test Site, where nuclear warheads were detonated. It is the standard treatment in the 1980s at the federal Savannah River plant near Aiken, South Carolina, where nuclear-weapons materials are produced. During legal proceedings in 1980, Keith L. Prescott, a tenth-grade dropout from Park City, Utah, who went to work at the Nevada Test Site in 1961 at age thirty-five, recalled the beer-drinking sessions. Prescott, who was permanently disabled in 1969 and was diagnosed as suffering from multiple myeloma, is one of the former federal employees suing the government. In the early 1960s, he operated a mucking machine, scooping up debris in the underground tunnels carved out for bomb tests. He and others sometimes returned to the mines within twenty-four hours after a nuclear explosion. He maintains, as do others, that they were never told the amount of radiation they had received, only that it was harmless. But they were encouraged on occasion to drink beer.

"They'd have beer down at the change room," he said. "[Supervisors] told us they wanted us to go down and drink all the beer we could because it helped flush out [the radioactive] particles. . . ." Prescott then had this exchange with an attorney:

Attorney—"Do you remember who advised you to drink beer?"

Prescott—"Our supervisors was the ones that told us. . . . Just told us that there would be beer there and come and drink all we could."

Attorney—"How frequently was the beer furnished?"

Prescott—"Well, it was furnished quite often there for a time."

The government denies, as it usually does, that radiation had anything to do with the diseases suffered by Prescott and his colleagues. Sometimes, though, radiation wounds are so severe that the government has little choice but to acknowledge them. That was the case with Douglas Crofut of Henryretta, Oklahoma. On January 19, 1981, Crofut, a thirty-eight-year-old industrial radiographer with a record of at least sixteen arrests on charges of drunkenness, other alcohol-related offenses, and petty crimes, checked in to the Okmulgee, Oklahoma, hospital. He was suffering from radiation burns over his upper body and left arm. His left nipple was burned off. His bone marrow was destroyed. Physicians watched as the cells in his body degenerated "before [their] very eyes." As Crofut's attorney described the injury, "this thing was just a horrendous, large massive sore . . . kind of like a dinner plate above [his] breast and down through [his] chest area and it was even clear into the bone. You could look in there two or three inches."

Still, the NRC remained optimistic about Crofut's condition. Without identifying him by name, the commission stated in a report issued early in July 1981, "In late January, medical opinion was that the individual may have received a lethal dose of radiation. However, in May, the individual seemed to still be improving and his blood appeared to be nearly back to normal." Crofut died on July 27, 1981, just after the release of the optimistic NRC report. The cause of death listed on the death certificate: "Multiple complications from radiation burns accident." It was estimated that Crofut had been exposed to between 356 and 405 rems.

To this day, neither the NRC nor any other federal agency knows how, where, or under what circumstances Crofut received the lethal exposure. And for good reason. They never conducted a serious investigation. On the basis of a limited inquiry, the NRC announced that its investigators could find "no hard evidence to explain the injury." Instead, the commission contented itself with trying to link Crofut's exposure to the theft of a radiographic device from a truck owned by Bill Miller Inc. in Henryetta. Miller had informed the NRC on January 5, 1981, that the device, which contained thirty-three curies of iridium 192, turned up missing during a quarterly inventory conducted on January 2. The equipment was mysteriously and anonymously returned on January 5. No evidence tied Crofut to the theft, which remains unsolved. And there was no evidence to establish that he deliberately exposed himself to the radioactive material, as NRC probers hinted.

To support their theory, NRC investigators quoted an anonymous neighbor as saying that Crofut once "was observed trying to set fire to himself by dousing gasoline over his body with a rag and then making an unsuccessful attempt to ignite himself with a match." Another neighbor advised the NRC that Crofut had been seen "walking in the neighborhood at various hours of the day and night."

Crofut's attorney in Okmulgee, Richard D. Gibbon, is blunt about the radiographer's past. "He drank a lot, he had a lot of problems, and I think he had a bad reputation . . . as far as getting in trouble," Gibbon said. But he doubts that Crofut purposely exposed himself to radiation. Gibbon said that Crofut knew the NRC was "inferring that he had taken" the radiographic equipment, "but he denied it to me." Although Crofut met with his lawyer only a few times before his death, Gibbon said he had a feeling that Crofut was "the type [of] old boy that had enough sense, I think, to kind of shoot straight with his lawyer, because I think he had been around a lawyer enough." Gibbon said he could imagine Crofut telling him something like, " 'Yeah, I robbed a bank, but get me out of it.' But he never once gave any indication that he was involved to any extent, knew who stole [the radiographic device], or anything. I questioned him very thoroughly in that area and he denied all that."

Gibbon said that Crofut believed he had received the radiation injury while working on a pipeline in New Mexico in October 1980. Some radiographic tools contain nuclear materials capable of causing such wounds if protective shielding fails. Crofut told the same story to the NRC, saying that he noticed an irritation on his chest and arm in November 1980. Physicians interviewed by the NRC dismissed this account, saying that by the look of the injury, exposure should have occurred in late December 1980 or early January 1981, the period during which the radiographic device was reported missing. Whatever the truth, the NRC's attitude in such matters is best summed up in the conclusion of a report the commission issued just before Crofut's death: "The event [Crofut's radiation exposure] is not considered an abnormal occurrence at this time since it has not been established that the radiation exposure resulted from material subject to licensing by the Nuclear Regulatory Commission" or the states.

Perhaps the larger question left unanswered by Crofut's death is how someone with an admittedly serious alcohol problem, someone with a string of arrests—including one for a jailbreak—came to be licensed to handle radioactive material.

Note for p. 327

*The increased industrial use of measuring devices and other equipment containing nuclear materials has already led to a growing number of radiation-exposure accidents. The following random sampling of such incidents, compiled from NRC reports, offers some measure of the problem:

In Eveleth, Minnesota, several workers at the Eveleth Expansion Company were exposed to radiation from a control guage that contained ten curies of cesium 137. The guage was inside an iron ore pellet cooler. When a protective heat shield surrounding the cesium melted and no one noticed, workers received an estimated exposure of up to three rems.

In the Gulf of Mexico, near Intercoastal City, Louisiana, a radiographer for Analytic Inspection Inc. of Lafayette, Louisiana, and the captain of a barge received radiation doses estimated at ten to twenty-five rems. The captain's helper received two rems or less. The accident occurred when the barge tilted and a radiographic device containing eleven curies of cobalt 60 broke loose on the deck, rolled under a pump assembly, and was sheared open.

In Wauwatosa, Wisconsin, patients at Lakeview Hospital received excessive radiation doses of up to 840 millirems when they underwent diagnostic screenings. (The exposure from a chest X-ray is normally between 20 and 50 millirems.) This happened because hospital workers routinely injected patients with double the prescribed dose of technetium 99m, a radioactive agent used in scans of the brain, bone, liver, spleen, and lung. The workers did so to reduce the screening time and obtain brighter images; then they falsified hospital records to indicate that the correct dose had been given.

In Oklahoma City, an employee of the Mustang Services Company was removing a guage containing 1.5 curies of cesium 137 from a trailer that was being sold. During the process, the cesium fell out of the guage—a tool used to measure the thickness of pipe walls—and rolled unnoticed into a recess in the trailer floor. Several days later, an employee of the trailer's new owner began driving it to Houston. He stopped in Norman, Oklahoma, for engine repairs, and in Ardmore, Oklahoma, for fuel. The driver received a dose estimated at 1.4 rems before the cesium dropped through a hole in the trailer floor onto a bridge near Lewisville, Texas. It came to rest on the bridge's structural support, where it was later found with radiation-detection equipment.

In Corpus Christi, Texas, about two dozen employees of the Weatherby Engineering Company received radiation doses when they were unknowingly exposed to a radiographic device that contained seventy-two curies of iridium 192. Two nonradiographic employees had used the instrument and, instead of returning it to a sealed vault, had left it in the company darkroom. Another employee unwittingly sat next to the radioactive material for two hours, doing paperwork. That employee received a radiation dose estimated at 198 rems, enough to produce immediate physical symptoms—a melanoma in one eye, pain in the legs and buttocks, a reduced sperm count, and chromosomal changes. Another employee receive an estimated dose of 75 rems. Two dozen others received exposures ranging from 0.9 to 4 rems.

All these incidents were reported to the NRC. No one knows how many go unreported or unnoticed. But there seems little doubt that some companies are not eager to talk about their mistakes. In Phoenixville, Pennsylvania, an employee of Automation Industries Inc., a nuclear-material-handling subsidiary of GK Technologies Inc., discovered an abnormal growth under his right thumbnail in the summer of 1980. The condition worsened over the next several months, "with swelling, bleeding, sensitivity and cracking" of the thumbnail, according to an NRC report. About the same time, a second employee began to develop similar symptoms. The two men suspected that their job might be the cause. With their bare hands, they used pipe cleaners to remove radioactivity from contaminated industrial radiography sources. Responding to their questions, a plant manager conceded that the abnormal growths could be work related. Nonetheless, the company failed to acknowledge the need for medical attention. Instead, a third man was assigned to the radioactive cleanup work. After an NRC inspector visited the plant in January 1981, Automation Industries advised the commission that all three employees had received radiation doses far in excess of federal standards. The NRC subsequently estimated the cumulative doses to the fingers of the three men through 1980 at 25,000, 7,000, and 1,000 rems respectively. If those doses had been applied to the whole body rather than to the fingertips, all three men would have died. The NRC imposed no fines or penalties.

Sources

The records used in preparation of this book were drawn from local, state, and federal agencies and courts in more than two dozen states from New York to California, from Louisiana to Illinois. Wherever possible we have identified our sources in the text. What follows is not intended to be inclusive but rather an additional selective listing of these documents, which total some 125,000 pages.

Annual and Semiannual Reports to Congress. U.S. Atomic Energy Commission. 1945–1973.

"Handling Radioactive Wastes in the Atomic Energy Program." U.S. Atomic Energy Commission. October 1949.

"Atomic Power Development and Private Enterprise." U.S. Congress, Joint Committee on Atomic Energy, 83rd Cong., 1st sess., June 24, 25, and 29; July 1, 6, 9, 13, 15, 16, 20, 22, 23, 27, and 31, 1953.

"Development, Growth, and State of the Atomic Energy Industry." U.S. Congress, Joint Committee on Atomic Energy, 85th Cong., 1st sess., February 26, 27, 28, and March 5, 1957.

"Industrial Radioactive Waste Disposal." U.S. Congress, Joint Committee on Atomic Energy, 86th Cong., 1st sess., January 28, 29, and 30; February 2 and 3, 1959.

"The Nuclear Industry." 1965, 1969, and 1971. U.S. Atomic Energy Commission.

"Application Bureau County (Illinois) Building Permit." California Nuclear, Inc. Bureau County Zoning Board of Appeals, Princeton, Illinois. July 8, 1966.

"AEC Authorizing Legislation Fiscal Year 1968." U.S. Congress, Joint Committee on Atomic Energy, 90th Cong., 1st sess., January 25, February 7, 8, 9, and 28, 1967.

"Proposal to the State of South Carolina State Development Board to Build and Operate a Radioactive Waste Burial Facility." Intercontinental Nuclear, Inc. South Carolina State Development Board. November 4, 1968.

"Compensation for the People of Rongelap and Utirik." A report by The Special Joint Committee Concerning Rongelap and Utirik Atolls to the Fifth Congress of Micronesia. Second Regular Session, Saipan, Mariana Islands. February 28, 1974.

"To Provide Authorizations for the Trust Territory Government and for the People of Bikini Atoll." U.S. Congress, House, Committee on Interior and Insular Affairs, 94th Cong., 1st sess., March 24, 1975.

"Radioactive Waste Management." U.S. Congress, Joint Committee on Atomic Energy, 94th Cong., 2d sess., May 10, 11, and 12, 1976.

"NRC Task Force Report on Review of the Federal/State Program for Regulation of Commercial Low-Level Radioactive Waste Burial Grounds." Office of Nuclear Material Safety and Safeguards and Office of State Programs. U.S. Nuclear Regulatory Commission. March 1977.

"Decommissioning and Decontamination." U.S. Congress, House, Committee on Science and Technology, 95th Cong., 1st sess., June 15, 16, 1977.

"High-Level Nuclear Waste." U.S. Congress, House, Committee on Government Operations, 95th Cong., 1st sess., June 18, 1977.

"Nuclear Power Costs, Part 1." U.S. Congress, House, Committee on Government Operations, 95th Cong., 1st sess., September 12, 13, 14, and 19, 1977.

"Report of the Special Advisory Committee on Nuclear Waste Disposal." Research Report No. 142. Legislative Research Commission. Frankfort, Kentucky. October 1977.

"Radiation Exposures of Hanford Workers Dying from Cancer and Other Causes." Thomas F. Mancuso, Alice Stewart, and George Kneale. *Health Physics,* November 1977 (33): 369.

"Nuclear Waste Burial Grounds and Storage Sites in Illinois." U.S. Congress, House, Committee on Government Operations, 95th Cong., 1st sess., December 9, 1977, and February 23, 1978.

State of Illinois v. *Nuclear Engineering Company, Inc.* Circuit Court of Bureau County, Illinois. Civil Action 78-CH-2. March 10, 1978.

"Oversight. Nuclear Waste Management and Ionizing Radiation Research." U.S. Congress, House, Committee on Science and Technology, 95th Cong., 2d sess., June 7 and July 18, 1978.

"Oversight. Nuclear Waste Management." U.S. Congress, House, Committee on Science and Technology, 95th Cong., 2d sess., June 10, 13, 18 and August 1, 1978.

Nebraska Public Power District v. *General Electric Company.* U.S. District Court for the District of Nebraska. Civil Action 78-L-227. 1978.

"Geologic Disposal of High-Level Radioactive Wastes—Earth Science Perspectives." J. D. Bredehoeft et al. Geological Survey Circular 779. U.S. Geological Survey. 1978.

"Report to the President by the Interagency Review Group on Nuclear Waste Management." Washington, D.C. March 1979.

"Health Effects of Low-Level Radiation. Volume I." U.S. Congress, House, Committee on Interstate and Foreign Commerce, 96th Cong., 1st sess., April 19, 1979.

"Low-Level Radiation Effects on Health." U.S. Congress, House, Committee on Interstate and Foreign Commerce, 96th Cong., 1st sess., April 23, May 24, and August 1, 1979.

"Nuclear Waste Management." U.S. Congress, House, Committee on Interstate and Foreign Commerce, 96th Cong., 1st sess., May 15, 16, 17, 1979.

"Low-Level Ionizing Radiation." U.S. Congress, House, Committee on Interstate and Foreign Commerce, 96th Cong., 1st sess., June 13, 14, 15, 1979.

"Nuclear Waste Management Reorganization Act of 1979." U.S. Congress, Senate, Committee on Governmental Affairs, 96th Cong., 1st sess., July 5, 1979 (Chicago, Ill.), October 19, 1979, and February 13, 1980 (Washington, D.C.).

"Spent Fuel Management Study." Summary Report. Tennessee Valley Authority. September 1979.

"Low-Level Nuclear Waste Burial Grounds." U.S. Congress, House, Committee on Science and Technology, 96th Cong., 1st sess., November 7, 1979.

"NRC Regulation of Highly Enriched Uranium Operations at the Nuclear Fuel Services Facility, Erwin, Tennessee." SECY 79-650 and 79-650A. December 11, 1979, and January 2, 1980. Docket No. 70-143. U. S. Nuclear Regulatory Commission.

"Energy in Transition 1985–2010." Final Report of the Committee on Nuclear and Alternative Energy Systems. National Research Council. National Academy of Sciences. Washington, D.C., 1979.

"The State-by-State Assessment of Low-Level Radioactive Wastes Shipped to Commercial Disposal Sites." 1979, 1980, 1981, 1982. U.S. Department of Energy.

"Review of Medical Findings in a Marshallese Population Twenty-Six Years after Accidental Exposure to Radioactive Fallout." Robert A. Conrad, M.D., et al. Medical Department. Brookhaven National Laboratory. U.S. Department of Energy. January 1980.

"A Survey of the Commercial U.S. Nuclear Industry." Ohio Department of Energy. April 15, 1980.

"West Valley Demonstration Project Act." U.S. Congress, House, Committee on Interstate and Foreign Commerce, 96th Cong., 2d sess., July 28, 1980.

"The United States Nuclear Regulatory Commission and the Agreement States. Licensing Statistics and Other Data." Semiannual reports, 1980, 1981, 1982, and 1983. U.S. Nuclear Regulatory Commission.

"A Background Report for the Formerly Utilized Manhattan Engineer District/Atomic Energy Commission Sites Program." U.S. Department of Energy. September 1980.

"Report to Congress on Abnormal Occurrences." Quarterly, 1980, 1981, and 1982. U.S. Nuclear Regulatory Commission.

"Evaluation of Trench Subsidence and Stabilization at Sheffield Low-Level Radioactive Waste Disposal Facility." Sheffield, Illinois. Final Report. October 15, 1980–March 30, 1981. U.S. Nuclear Regulatory Commission.

"The Effects on Populations of Exposure to Low Levels of Ionizing Radiation: 1980." Advisory Committee on the Biological Effects of Ionizing Radiations. National Academy of Sciences–National Research Council. 1980.

"Spent Fuel and Waste Inventories and Projections." Annual reports, 1980, 1981, 1982, and 1983. Oak Ridge National Laboratory.

"1982 Department of Energy Authorization. Volume IV." U.S. Congress, House, Committee on Science and Technology, 97th Cong., 1st sess., February 25, 26 and March 3, 4, 5, 10, 16, 17, 18, 19, 20, 1981.

"State Planning Council on Radioactive Waste Management. Recommendations on National Radioactive Waste Management Policies. Report to the President." Washington, D. C. August 1, 1981.

"Landfilling of Special and Hazardous Waste in Illinois." A Report to the Illinois General Assembly by the Illinois Legislative Investigating Commission. Chicago, Illinois. August 1981.

"Semi-Annual Report on Strategic Nuclear Material Inventory Differences." U.S. Department of Energy. 1980, 1981, and 1982.

"Licensing Requirements for Land Disposal of Radioactive Waste." Draft Environmental Impact Statement on 10CFR Part 61. Four volumes. U.S. Nuclear Regulatory Commission. September 1981.

"Nuclear Waste Disposal." U.S. Congress, Senate, Committees on Energy and Natural Resources and on Environment and Public Works, 97th Cong., 1st sess., October 5 and 6, 1981.

"Low-Level Radioactive Waste Policy Act Report. Response to Public Law 96-573." U.S. Department of Energy. 1981.

State of Illinois v. General Electric Company and Southern California Edison Company. U.S. District Court for the Northern District of Illinois. Civil Action 81-2768.

David Bulloch et al. v. The United States of America. U.S. District Court for the District of Utah. Civil Action 81-0123C. 1981.

New York State Energy Research and Development Authority v. Nuclear Fuel Services, Inc., and Getty Oil Company. U.S. District Court for the Western District of New York. Civil Action 81-18E.

"Long-Term Management of Liquid High-Level Radioactive Wastes Stored at the Western New York Nuclear Service Center, West Valley. U.S. Department of Energy. June 1982.

"Status Report Low-Level Radioactive Waste Compacts." U.S. Department of Energy. July 1982.

"Financing Radioactive Waste Disposal." Congressional Budget Office. September 1982.

"Report of Working Group on Spent Fuel Management." (Castaing Report) Supreme Council for Nuclear Safety. Paris, December 1, 1982.

"Population Risks from Disposal of High-Level Radioactive Wastes in Geologic Repositories." Draft Report. U. S. Environmental Protection Agency. December 1982.

"Managing Commercial High-Level Radioactive Waste." U.S. Cong., Office of Technology Assessment. 1982.

"A Study of the Isolation System for Geologic Disposal of Radioactive Wastes." National Academy of Sciences–National Research Council. Washington, D. C. 1983.

"Mission Plan for the Civilian Radioactive Waste Management Program. Volumes I and II." U.S. Department of Energy. April 1984.

Memorandum Opinion. Irene Allen et al. v. The United States of America. U.S. District Court for the District of Utah. Central Division. Bruce S. Jenkins, Judge. May 10, 1984.

"Preliminary Notification of Event or Unusual Occurrence" (PNO reports). These reports, prepared as needed by the Nuclear Regulatory Commission, provide significant details on a variety of nuclear incidents, from the off-site seepage of radioactive waste at shallow-land burial grounds to lost radioactive materials and radiation exposure accidents. 1980–84.

Index